The Novels of G. K. Chesterton

The Novels of G. K. Chesterton

A Study in Art and Propaganda

IAN BOYD

BOOKS
10 East 53d St., New York 10022
(a division of Harper & Row Publishers, Inc.)

Published in the U.S.A. 1975 by
HARPER & ROW PUBLISHERS INC.,
BARNES & NOBLE IMPORT DIVISION

First published 1975 by Paul Elek Ltd., London

Copyright © 1975 by Ian Boyd

ISBN 0–06–490614–0

Printed in Great Britain

For my mother
and the memory
of my father

Contents

A*

Preface

The rather improbable hero of one of Chesterton's first novels is an old monk from Western Bulgaria. He had made himself happy, Chesterton explains, 'chiefly by writing the most crushing refutations and exposures of certain heresies, the last professors of which had been burnt (generally by each other) precisely 1,119 years previously'.[1] This single sentence sums up a good deal of what I want to say in this book. First of all, it illustrates the humour which irradiates all the novels and gives them much of their charm. Secondly, its light-hearted allusion to refuting and exposing heresies might be taken as a reminder of how much Chesterton's fiction is of a piece with the exuberant journalism with which he set out to change the political and social life of Edwardian England. Finally, the quotation and the wildly improbable situation which it implies are a reminder that the novels are always imaginative works. They blend humour with a social purpose which is essentially serious, but they are also the products of Chesterton's powerful allegorical imagination through which he sought to teach and to persuade by means of parable and allegory rather than by discursive reason.

These are some of the reasons why I believe Chesterton's fiction is a good starting-point for an evaluation of his achievement as a writer. I have limited my study of the fiction to the eleven novels which form the largest and most coherent part of it. The Father Brown stories, *The Club of Queer Trades*, and the other short stories have not been considered except incidentally. This is partly a matter of convenience. The Father Brown stories, for example, do not lend themselves to the kind of systematic and chronological analysis with which I have been able to study the novels. As Professor Robson points out, they were occasional work, ordered in batches by magazine editors, and hastily written by Chesterton to help finance his own newspaper.[2] The themes which are developed fully in the full-length novels and the novels which consist of linked short stories are only sketched in them. Consequently, there is no larger pattern to which they can be related.

I have also decided to say very little about any events in Chesterton's life except those that have immediate relevance to his novels. For that reason, his conversion to Catholicism in 1922 is scarcely mentioned. This conversion has, of course, been fully discussed both by his biographers and by himself in his other writings. It has, however, curiously little to do with his fiction. There is very little development in his religious thought. Between the publication of his first novel in 1904 and his death in 1936, he regarded himself as a Catholic. His conversion was the result of a personal decision that had more to do with a question of fact than a change in his religious convictions.

There is another reason why an emphasis on controversial biographical information would be out of place in a study of Chesterton's novels. His viewpoint was deeply Catholic and sacramental and this coloured everything he wrote. But his main concern in his fiction is with political and social views which he always distinguished very clearly from his personal religious viewpoint. In this regard he was merely following the practice he was later to establish in his own political movement which he insisted must always appeal to and include people from widely different religious backgrounds.

I must thank Miss Dorothy Collins, Chesterton's secretary and literary executrix, who has very generously allowed me to consult her rich collection of Chesterton material. I am also grateful for the advice of Mr John Sullivan and Dr Isobel Murray. I thank Messrs Paul Elek Ltd for permission to draw upon my contribution 'Philosophy in Fiction' in *G. K. Chesterton: A Centenary Appraisal* edited by John Sullivan (1974) which I have revised to form chapters 1 and 6 of this book, and the Editor of *New Blackfriars* for permission to quote five paragraphs from my article 'Chesterton and Distributism' which appeared in Vol. 55, No. 649 (June 1974). Finally, I thank the Canada Council for the grants which facilitated research that made this book possible.

Ian Boyd,
St Thomas More College,
November 1974   *University of Saskatchewan*

1 Introduction

It has been generally acknowledged that much of Chesterton's writing is frankly propagandistic both in its aims and in its methods. His reputation has always been that of a controversialist rather than a literary artist. At the same time, those who have studied his writing are aware of the obvious distinction between his directly controversial work and a considerable body of writing which might be called literature. The fact that the controversial works contain some of his best imaginative writing and the literary works some of his most significant political and literary commentary has of course made the division difficult to justify. But it would not be an unfair comment to describe most of the work in Chestertonian criticism as an effort to distinguish and perhaps to separate the art from the propaganda.

Among critics this division of Chesterton's work into art and propaganda becomes in practice a division between his mind and imagination. Those who prefer the imaginative writings are usually prepared to dismiss the propaganda as ephemeral journalism. Maisie Ward, for example, although she seems willing to defend any of the books which might be described as religious, suggests that politics distracted him from the literary career he was meant to follow.[1] And C. S. Lewis, in defending him from an attack by James Stephens in the *Listener*, distinguishes between the two senses in which an author belongs to his period: the first, the negative sense, in which he deals with things 'which are of no permanent interest but which only seemed to be of interest because of some temporary fashion'; the second, in which he expresses matter of permanent interest through forms 'which are those of a particular age':

The real question is in which sense Chesterton was of his period. Much of his work, admittedly, was ephemeral journalism: it is dated in the first sense. The little books of essays are mainly of historical interest. Their parallel in Mr Stephens's work is not his romances but his articles in the *Listener*. But Chesterton's imaginative works seem to me to be in quite a different position. They are, of course, richly redolent of the age in which they were composed. The anti-Germanicism in the *Ballad of the White Horse* belongs to a silly and transitory historical heresy of Mr Belloc's—always, on the intellectual side, a disastrous influence on Chesterton. And in the romances, the sword-sticks, the hansom cabs, the anarchists, all go back to a real London and to an imagined London (that of *The New Arabian Nights*) which have receded from us. But how is it possible not to see that what comes through all this is permanent and dateless?[2]

On the other hand, there is a large group of critics who are willing to jettison the more obviously literary works in order to preserve the more obviously controversial. Hugh Kenner, for example, defines the essential Chesterton as a metaphysician whose work is chiefly valuable for the insights it provides by way of aphorisms and analogies.[3] Similarly Etienne Gilson writes of his importance as a kind of philosopher.[4] And T. S. Eliot, although he admires some of the early literary work, particularly the Dickens criticism and what he calls the Stevensonian fantasies, argues that his importance is found in 'the place that he occupied, the position that he represented, during the better part of a generation'.[5] In fact he writes of him as if he were writing about the leader of a religious sect or a political party:

To judge Chesterton on his 'contributions to literature', then, would be to apply the wrong standards of measurement. It is in other matters that he was importantly and consistently on the side of the angels. Behind the Johnsonian fancy-dress, so reassuring to the British public, he concealed the most serious and revolutionary designs—concealing them by exposure, as his anarchist conspirators chose to hold their meetings on a balcony in Leicester Square. (The real Johnson, indeed, with his theology, politics and morals, would be quite as alien to the modern world of public opinion as Chesterton himself.) Even if Chesterton's social and economic ideas appear to be totally without effect, even if they should be demonstrated to be wrong—which would perhaps only mean that men have not the goodwill to carry them out—they were *the* ideas for his time that were fundamentally Christian and Catholic. He did more, I think, than any man of his time—and was able to do more than anyone else, because of his particular background, development and abilities as a public performer—to maintain the existence of the important minority in the modern world.[6]

But among critics whose interest in Chesterton is extra-literary, none perhaps have done more serious damage to his artistic reputation than the group which might be called the professional Catholics.[7] For them, he is an institution to be defended rather than an author to be discussed. A characteristic which defines their attitude is a defensiveness towards him, as a writer who needs their protection, combined with an astonishing ignorance and uncertainty about the writing they are trying to protect. Bernard Bergonzi, who betrays something of the same attitude himself in his somewhat exaggerated attempt to avoid it, seems to have them in mind when he comments on the way many of his co-religionists refuse to recognize, far less to discuss, the anti-Semitic element in his writing.[8] He might also have added that the refusal to evaluate him as a writer is frequently accompanied by a refusal to tolerate anyone else's criticism of him as a literary artist. At the first hint of criticism there is as it were an immediate closing of ranks, which is followed, as often as not, first by a perfunctory tribute to his personal qualities, and then by signs of an evident eagerness to change the subject. This attitude may be explained in terms of the altogether understandable gratitude which an embattled minority feels towards a writer whom they regard as their champion. But whatever its explanation as a cultural phenomenon, there is no doubt that those who share this view have helped to create an impression of him which they are the first to resent. Their preference for what appears to be his most controversial work and their refusal to discuss it in any detail has had the effect of fostering an antagonism towards him which is equally unbalanced and uncritical. It is significant, for example, that Orwell, who shows signs of knowing a surprising amount about his work, should nonetheless regard him as the leader of a group which in its discipline and like-mindedness corresponded in his view almost exactly to the Communist Party. His description of the later Chesterton as a violent propagandist is in fact merely a hostile version of the view popularized by the extremists among Chesterton's Catholic supporters:

Chesterton was a writer of considerable talent who chose to suppress both his sensibilities and his intellectual honesty in the cause of Roman Catholic propaganda. During the last twenty years or so of his life, his entire output was in reality an endless repetition of the same thing, under its laboured cleverness as simple and boring as 'Great is Diana of the Ephesians'. Every book that he wrote, every paragraph, every sentence, every incident in every story, every scrap of dialogue, had to demonstrate beyond possibility of mistake the superiority of the Catholic over the Protestant or the pagan. But Chesterton was not content to think of this superiority as merely intellectual or spiritual: it had to be translated into terms of national prestige and military power, which entailed an ignorant idealisation of the Latin countries, especially France.[9]

Even more curiously, however, the defence of Chesterton as a Catholic hero is frequently accompanied by an unmistakable note of patronage. Writers as different as Graham Greene and Evelyn Waugh, who agree in their preference for his controversial work, also agree in their somewhat equivocal praise for its 'simplicity'. Waugh confesses surprise at the number of critical studies his writing has provoked 'in all its ephemeral bulk', and he argues that in fact it scarcely needs an elucidation: he 'wrote especially for the common man, repeating in clear language his simple, valuable messages'.[10] His tribute to Chesterton's character amounts to a dismissal of his art:

He was a loveable and much loved man abounding in charity and humility. Humility is not a virtue propitious to the artist. It is often pride, emulation, avarice, malice—all the odious qualities—which drive a man to complete, elaborate, refine, destroy, renew, his work until he has made something that gratifies his pride and envy and greed. And in doing so he enriches the world more than the generous and good, though he may lose his own soul in the process. That is the paradox of artistic achievement.[11]

Greene's judgment is very similar. He argues that the simplicity which enabled him to write successful books of religious apologetics made it impossible for him to understand the squalid complexities of political life necessary to write successful novels:

For the same reason that he failed as a political writer he succeeded as a religious one, for religion is simple, dogma is simple. Much of the difficulty of theology arises from the efforts of men who are not primarily writers to distinguish a quite simple idea with the utmost accuracy. He restated the original thought with the freshness, simplicity, and excitement of discovery. In fact, it was discovery: he unearthed the defined from beneath the definitions, and the reader wondered why the definitions had ever been thought necessary. *Orthodoxy, The Thing,* and *The Everlasting Man* are among the great books of the age.[12]

The attempt to divide his work into art and propaganda ultimately fails both as a criticism of what he thought and as a description of what he wrote. One is asked to make a choice between books which are supposed to be art, but which on examination turn out to be a kind of propaganda, and books which are supposed to be admirable as propaganda, but which are acknowledged to be generally inartistic. Fortunately, however, this unnecessary dilemma can be resolved if one ignores the false assumptions on which it is based and examines the writing with some care. Among these writings, none offer a better starting-place for a revaluation of his achievement than do his novels. For of all his work, nothing is more difficult to fit into the familiar and misleading categories of art and journalism. They present special problems for those who would claim him as a purely literary artist because, although quite clearly imaginative works, they also quite clearly point to something which is generally considered as being outside the field of literature. If these books are novels, they are novels only in the loosest sense of the word. On the other hand, if they are propaganda, they scarcely conform to any popular notion of what propaganda is supposed to be. Occasionally, scattered passages repeat arguments which occur in the books of essays, but usually the arguments presented in them are presented in entirely imaginative terms. In fact they do not lend themselves to any easy description, for they are works which are a curious blend of literature and propaganda. Their meaning is certainly political and social, but it is usually expressed through the imaginative pattern which each of them reveals. And although they can be easily related to his social and political philosophy, very frequently they qualify it with unexpected and independent nuances of their own. Without fulfilling precisely the definitions of any of the terms, they may be described as political fables, parables, and allegories, or more simply and conveniently as novels. But whatever name one gives them,

they invite inquiry. For they stand in the strange and largely
unexplored borderline region of Chestertonian studies which
lies between art and propaganda, in which meaning is shaped
and expressed by imagination and in which fiction is used as a
means of accomplishing the twofold educational task which
Chesterton called 'training the minds of men to act upon the
community' and 'making the mind a source of creation and
critical action'.[13]

It is true that his own comments on the novels would seem to
discourage their serious consideration. Not only does he insist
that none of them are true novels, but he also claims that he
never attempted to be a novelist.[14] Speaking of the ideas he
wished to express through these books, he adds that the books
represent good ideas which have been spoiled.[15] There is of
course no need to accept an author's self-criticism as a necessarily
fair or final comment on his work. In one of the Dickens
prefaces, Chesterton himself anticipated a commonplace of
modern criticism by warning readers of the dangers of the
intentional fallacy in criticism.[16] Nonetheless his comments
must be taken into account. What is particularly interesting
about them is that in the very passage in which he deprecates
the value of the novels as works of literature he makes a claim
for their serious value as journalism. The fiction to which he
refuses the name of art is described as being part of a larger
effort in which writing is used as a means of bringing about
social change. The context of the passage is also significant. It
comes at the beginning of the large chapter in the autobiography in which he pays tribute to Belloc both as friend and
as a writer.[17] By identifying the aims of his own work with those
of Belloc, as he does at the conclusion of the passage, he is
perhaps allowing for the possibility that someone may make the
same claim for his work which he made for Belloc's but felt
unable to make for his own:

But it was not the superficial or silly or jolly part of me that made
me a journalist . . . In short, I could not be a novelist; because I
really like to see ideas or notions wrestling naked, as it were, and
not dressed up in a masquerade as men and women. But I could be
a journalist because I could not help being a controversialist. I do
not even know if this would be called mock modesty or vanity, in
the modern scale of values; but I do know that it is neither. It occurs
to me that the best and most wholesome test, for judging how far

mere incompetence or laziness, and how far a legitimate liking for direct democratic appeal has prevented me from being a real literary man, might be found in a study of the man of letters I happen to know best; who had the same motives for producing journalism, and yet has produced nothing but literature.[18]

There are two important elements in this statement which provide valuable insights into the kind of fiction he wrote. The first is his insistence that his imaginative work is like his other writing in its concern with the conflict of ideas. In novels written according to this plan one would expect to find what one does in fact find, characters who are primarily types representing conflicting political and social points of view. Secondly the passage also suggests that the novels can be directly related to the political and social preoccupations of their author. The 'direct democratic appeal' of which he speaks suggests that the fiction is an extension of the journalism which he wrote in order to bring about the political and social changes which he thought necessary and that the novels are in fact political allegories written as a kind of political propaganda. In an essay published in *G.K.'s Weekly,* in discussing his general aims as a writer, he writes of his desire to 'awaken the imagination':

. . . and especially that extreme and almost extravagant form of imagination that can really imagine reality. The true aim of art is to awaken wonder, whether the wonder takes the form of admiration or anger. It is natural for us to say in the ordinary way of speech, that monopoly is monstrous; but a certain mystical clarity of light is needed in which to see it actually as a monster . . . we can hardly avoid having, in propaganda like this, a considerable element of fable and fantasy and all that the serious may call nonsense. Believe me, it is not half so nonsensical as what they call sense. If we have included a great many burlesques and travesties along the same lines of satire, it is for the perfectly practical reason mentioned above. It is that men must be made to realize, if only by reiteration, how utterly unreal is the real state of things.[19]

What Chesterton meant by this kind of writing is never clearly expressed in any of his books, but there is some evidence that he associated it with the kind of allegory which is an expression of an almost Platonic view of life. Abrams's definition of allegory as the simple conversion of a doctrine or thesis into a narrative 'in which the agents and sometimes the setting as well, represent general concepts, moral qualities, or other abstractions' describes only a part of what he meant by the term.[20] Similarly the definition of a parable as a short narrative 'presented so as to bring out the analogy, or parallel, between its elements and a lesson that the speaker is trying to bring home to us' is also unsatisfactory as a complete description of what he meant.[21] For one thing, there is no evidence that he made any distinction between allegory and parable. When he uses these terms, he uses them as though they were interchangeable. In his study of William Blake, he provides his own definition of the ordinary meaning of allegory ('taking something that does not exist as a symbol of something that does exist'),[22] and he then goes on to say that this definition must be reversed if one is to understand Blake's poetry. Writing of the lamb as a symbol of innocence, he comments, 'he meant that there really is behind the universe an eternal image called the Lamb, of which all living lambs are merely the copies or the approximation. He held that eternal innocence to be an actual and even an awful thing.'[23] It is this view of allegory which Chesterton makes his own:

> But the main point here is simpler. It is merely that Blake did not mean that meekness was true and the lamb only a pretty fable. If anything he meant that meekness was a mere shadow of the everlasting lamb. The distinction is essential to anyone at all concerned for this rooted spirituality which is the only enduring sanity of mankind. The personal is not a mere figure for the impersonal; rather the impersonal is a clumsy term for something more personal than common personality. God is not a symbol of goodness. Goodness is a symbol of God.[24]

The implication of this view is that the whole of human life is made up of an unending series of hieroglyphs which it is the business of the allegorist to select and interpret. There is no question of a thesis which can be presented alternatively as a symbolic narrative or as a discursive argument. A parallel argument can indeed be constructed which expresses partly at least the truth which is expressed imaginatively by the allegory, but the allegory is never a mere translation of a discursive argument into symbolic terms. There is a sense in which the meaning does not exist apart from the allegory which reveals it. This may be why Chesterton speaks of the artistic mind that 'sees things as they are in a picture'.[25] And finally this may be why, in one of the later novels, the central character makes a claim for an entirely symbolic view of life: 'I doubt,' Gabriel Gale says, 'whether any of our action is really anything but an allegory. I doubt whether any truth can be told except in parable.'[26]

This notion of allegory helps to clarify what he meant by fiction as a kind of propaganda. The novels are political in the general sense that they are directed towards the illumination of the political and social questions which he believed to be of essential importance. Occasionally, too, one is able to recognize what seem to be topical political issues in the background of the novels, whether it is the Boer War in *The Napoleon of Notting Hill* or the General Strike in *The Return of Don Quixote*. But although the novels sometimes have their beginnings in particular political or social problems, their allegorical form gives these incidents a more general significance. Adam Wayne and Juan del Fuego are far more important as types of the small nation's doomed heroism than they are as representatives of the Boer resistance which gave Chesterton the idea for their creation. And Michael Herne and Douglas Murrell have clearly more to do with the dangers of a particular kind of political detachment than they have to do with the incipient Fascism and ironic Conservatism which they also represent.

The direct democratic appeal of which Chesterton speaks has little resemblance to the kind of political fiction which, for example, H. G. Wells may have taught us to expect by that phrase. In Wells's case, the novels which he began to write after 1910 were characterized by endless discussions about the social questions of the day and the increasing dependence on characters as commentators. Chesterton very seldom expresses his social philosophy in fiction of this kind. There are occasional passages of topical satire in the novels but their allegorical quality always remains sufficiently strong to prevent any of them becoming political dialogues cast in the form of fiction. What one actually finds is the kind of literature which John Holloway examines in *The Victorian Sage*. It is fiction used as a way of mediating imaginatively a particular political view of life. As Holloway remarks, this prophetic and seer-like quality cannot be explained entirely by rhetoric, since it can be achieved at least as successfully in the form of a novel as it can in the form of a discursive essay. Indeed his description of what the sage sets out to do in his writing might be applied equally well to what Chesterton sets out to do in his fiction:

. . . the sage has a special problem in expounding or in proving what he wants to say. He does not and probably cannot rely on logical and formal argument alone or even much at all. His main task is to quicken his reader's perceptiveness; and he does this by making a far wider appeal than the exclusively rational appeal. He draws upon resources cognate, at least, with those of the artist in words. He gives expression to his outlook imaginatively. What he has to say is not a matter of 'content' or narrow paraphraseable meaning, but is transfused by the whole texture of his writing as it constitutes an experience for the reader.[27]

In this book I consider the way in which Chesterton's novels mediate a distinctive political and social view of life. And although I shall attempt to identify the political and social themes which are common to the fiction and the other writing, I shall not be primarily concerned with the fiction as a source for his thought. The qualifications and special nuances which his views acquire when they appear in fictional form will of course be noted and commented upon, but the central aim of the book will be an evaluation of the novels themselves. In a word, the main effort will be directed towards examining the way in which they work. And although this study may contribute towards an evaluation of his impact as the propagandist of a particular political 'myth' and of his place in English literature today, it will attempt to do so by recording a series of careful and chronological readings of eleven novels.

2 The Early Novels

The chief interest of Chesterton's first two novels is the way in which they define a political view which is characteristic of the entire body of his fiction. *The Napoleon of Notting Hill* and *The Ball and the Cross* are in fact the most representative of all the novels. This is true not only of the themes which they present but also of the way in which they present them. Most of the themes on which the later novels turn are at least sketched, from the theme of the meaning of madness and sanity in a world in which the terms are sometimes confused, to the theme of wonder and its power of transforming a commonplace environment by making it romantic. Other recurrent themes, which are more lightly sketched, are the distrust of the state, the primacy of private over public life, and the insistence on the impossibility of politics providing an ultimate remedy for man's unhappiness.

The way in which these themes are developed is also characteristic of the method used in the subsequent fiction. This is of course particularly true of the much criticized and frequently misunderstood use of allegory. Chesterton's characterization is in terms of the typical rather than the individual, so that what one encounters in his fiction is not a series of fully rounded characters, but a series of political and social types. The importance of each character is in what he represents and in what he tells one about a particular Chestertonian point of view rather than in what he is. In *The Napoleon of Notting Hill*, for example, a character such as Buck is important because he presents Chesterton's view of the quintessential business man, and James Barker, although insignificant as an individual, is important as the very ideal of the Chestertonian politician. Even more important, however, than the introduction of the familiar Chestertonian types, is the introduction of two of them to provide the central conflict and the central theme in each of the novels. Adam Wayne and Auberon Quin in the first instance and Evan MacIan and James Turnbull in the second are the first of the opposed but complementary heroes whose conflict and eventual reconciliation provide the form and the chief political meaning of many of the later novels.

It must, however, be emphasized that the representative character of the early fiction becomes fully apparent only when one studies the first two novels together. It is true that *The Napoleon of Notting Hill* is itself the most directly political of all the novels, but its treatment of politics is not altogether characteristic. For although it provides an imaginative statement of many of the political themes, it does not include an imaginative statement of the most significant of them. The argument of the novel involves the general question of the relationship of irony to political earnestness and the more particular question of the meaning and value of nationalism in relation to Imperialism. And although the novel ends with the apotheosis of the common man, it says nothing about the relationship of politics to religion.

For a consideration of this theme, which is central to Chesterton's fiction, one must turn to the main argument of *The Ball and the Cross*. Admittedly there is a sense in which the situation described in this novel is even more explicitly political than the comic misunderstanding between the provost of Notting Hill and the artist king. For although the Atheist bookseller and the Catholic gentleman quarrel ostensibly about religion, they also represent political positions, which are classically leftist and rightist. But if one wishes to study the way in which the whole of Chesterton's fiction is represented in the earliest part of it, the importance of *The Ball and the Cross* must be located in its religious theme. By relating politics to an order of supernatural values which transcends politics, the novel gives a meaning to nationalism which is not found in *The Napoleon of Notting Hill*, but is present in the later fiction.

If the study of the representative character of the early fiction requires that one study both novels, it is also true that the novels must be studied as the separate works of fiction which they are. This is particularly true of *The Napoleon of Notting Hill*, which requires some understanding not only of the particular background against which it was written, but also of the particular political point of view which it was meant to express.

The Napoleon of Notting Hill was published in 1904, but it had its beginning in two events which occurred some years earlier. The first of these was a plan which Chesterton had worked out as a child for the possible defence of a street in his home district of North Kensington. The childish fancy involved the capture of a water tower and the threat to flood the valley in which an enemy was camped. In the dedicatory poem Chesterton explains to Belloc and to the reader the way in which the novel grew out of this curious daydream:

> This legend of an epic hour
> A child I dreamed, and dream it still,
> Under the great grey water-tower
> That strikes the stars on Campden Hill.[1]

The second event was the Jameson Raid of 1895 and the outbreak of the South African War a few years later. For Chesterton the raid and the war which eventually followed it were two aspects of a single event which provided him with a kind of political illumination. In his autobiography, in commenting on the genesis of his early political views, he describes the way in which he was torn between the claims of Socialism and Imperialism on the one hand and an inner instinct for a political system on the smallest possible scale on the other. The war was important not because it added significantly to his political knowledge, but because it provided him with a way of resolving the conflict. In the approval which the Imperialists and Socialists seemed to give to the policy of unification and centralization, he saw the proof that the two movements were equally abhorrent and essentially the same. And in the Boers' apparently hopeless resistance to this policy, he saw the heroic embodiment of his own instinctive political dream. It was an event which taught him the first principle of his political beliefs: he must always be on the side of the small nation. In his own words, it was an event which 'not only woke me from my dreams like a thunder-clap, but like a lightning-flash revealed me to myself'.[2]

But it was only as the war continued and the British armies began to encounter unexpected difficulties that his early memory of the defence of a London street and his new sympathies for the Boers began to coalesce in the shape of an idea for his novel:

. . . the note struck from the first was the note of the inevitable; a thing abhorrent to Christians and to lovers of liberty. The blows struck by the Boer nation at bay, the dash and dazzling evasions of De Wet, the capture of a British general at the very end of the campaign, sounded again and again the opposite note of defiance; of those who, as I wrote later in one of the my first articles, 'disregard the omens and disdain the stars'. And all this swelled up within me into vague images of a modern resurrection of Marathon or Thermopylae; and I saw again my recurring dream of the unscalable tower and the besieging citizens; and began to draw out the rude outlines of my little romance of London.[3]

It would be a mistake, however, to limit the significance of the novel's origin to what might seem to be a matter of private feelings, without considering the more general values which these feelings imply. The defence of Notting Hill against the outer world has little interest either as an illustration of generous, though perhaps somewhat muddled sympathy for the underdog, or as an indication of a precocious bent for military tactics. Whatever psychological light the fantasy throws on his temperament and whatever the historical rights and wrongs of the Boer War, the inward instinct of which Chesterton writes and which he tried to express in his novel is chiefly important because of its more general significance. This significance is indeed somewhat difficult to define. It seems to be connected with his admiration for something which he calls 'the poetry of limits'.[4] In later writings, he refers to this feeling for strict limits and the most local of patriotisms in his criticism of those who attempt to rebuke spirit with mere matter, citing as examples of this error men as dissimilar as H. G. Wells, who mistakenly believes in a cosmos which dooms,[5] and Herbert Spencer, who is 'an imperialist of the lowest type', because of his 'contemptible notion'[6] that the size of the solar system ought to overawe the spiritual dogma of man.

But the feeling is never in fact translated into a clear statement. Perhaps the closest Chesterton comes to this is in another passage in *Orthodoxy*, where, in explaining how each of his ultimate attitudes towards life corresponds to a Christian belief ('instinct after instinct was answered by doctrine after doctrine'),[7] he says that his subconscious conviction of a small cosmos had a fulfilled significance in the Christian notion of creation; 'for anything that is a work of art must be small in the sight of the artist'.[8] The same thought is expressed in 'Lepanto':

> The Pope was in his chapel before day or battle broke,
> *(Don John of Austria is hidden in the smoke)*
> The hidden room in man's house where God sits all
>   the year,
> The secret window whence the world looks small
>   and very dear.[9]

And so, in his view, the universe itself became a kind of small nation for which he could feel affection and address by diminutives. Finally, and even more clearly, in a passage towards the conclusion of one of his last books, he underlines the connection between his early intuition and his mature political and religious views:

> It was my instinct to defend liberty in small nations and poor families; that is, to defend the rights of man as including the rights of property; especially the property of the poor. I did not really understand what I meant by Liberty, until I heard it called by the new name of Human Dignity. It was a new name to me; though it was part of a creed nearly two thousand years old.[10]

Thus, in spite of the obvious parallels with the Boer War, the novel is in no way a true historical allegory. An outline of the plot makes it immediately clear that the point by point equivalents of the traditional allegory are entirely absent. It begins with the choice of Auberon Quin as king and the implementation of his madcap scheme for restoring medieval pageantry to this England of the future. And it continues in the central part of the novel with the revolution of Notting Hill. Adam Wayne, the provost of the district, refuses to permit the destruction of Pump Street for the sake of a city-wide plan of industrial development, and when his appeal to the King's Charter of the Cities is rejected, he and some of the inhabitants of the street wage a successful war against the armies of the entire city. In the final part of the novel, Notting Hill itself becomes the centre of an empire. Auberon is still king and, to his bewilderment and amusement, he discovers that the neo-medievalism which he began as a private joke is now accepted as a wise social arrangement. But at the same time the nationalism of Notting Hill spreads to the districts which it has conquered, and the novel ends with a final battle in which Adam Wayne's army is annihilated.

The anti-Imperialist and anti-Socialist meaning of the novel is quite plain. A public house, a church, and a few shops, huddled together on a single street, are immeasurably more important and worth defending than the empire of the Imperialists or the World-State of the Fabians. Whether the Boers are more truly represented in the hopeless plight of Nicaragua, the last small nation to resist annexation at the beginning of the novel, or in the unexpected victories of Wayne's armies in the central part of the book, which correspond in a way to the early Boer victories that had delighted Chesterton, or in the heroism with which Wayne fights his final battle at the novel's conclusion, does not really matter. For what the novel celebrates is the superiority of the human spirit to mere force and numbers. What is hateful to Wayne is the same thing which made the Boer War hateful to Chesterton; it is something he called the 'vile assurance' of those who regard victory as 'an almost automatic process like the operation of a natural law'.[11]

In view of Chesterton's well known concern for social justice, the complete absence of social conflict in the novel is at first puzzling. It might seem to suggest an inability to deal with social problems, or worse still, an insensitivity to their seriousness. The anti-progressive note, which is struck somewhat defiantly in the prologue, in a sentence which may have given Orwell the title for *Nineteen Eighty-four*, would seem to support this reading: 'When the curtain goes up on this story, eighty years after the present date, London is almost exactly like what it is now.'[12] Not only is the resemblance between the England of 1904 and the England of 1984 complete to details such as Hansom cabs and top hats but, by a predictable paradox, the new society which Auberon introduces is in fact medieval. Gradually, however, one learns that a great deal has happened in a world that has remained materially unaltered. Among other things, it becomes apparent that the England in which nothing is supposed to have happened has become part of a cosmopolitan world state which denies the existence of separate nationalities. More than that, the England which is presented in the novel shows no signs of suffering from the Edwardian problems of hunger and poverty. Indeed one would seem to be in a post-Marxist period, in which a Fabian bureaucracy lingers on, long after the social evils that preoccupied the Fabians have disappeared. But whether the social problems have in fact been solved in the best Fabian manner or whether they have been simply ignored, the problem which does confront the England of the future is quite different from the problems which had exercised the early Socialists. This problem might be called the problem of the grey monotony of life.[13] It is the question Chesterton believed the Fabians had never considered, although he thought that they had done much to aggravate it. 'You have left certain human needs out of your books,' he wrote to H. G. Wells, 'you may leave them out of your Republic.'[14]

It is part of Chesterton's same indirect method that the ironic defects of his own Utopia are implied without ever being stated. Nothing is what it appears to be. Thus the system of government by lot at first suggests the perfection of democracy, since it seems to imply an absolute trust in the ordinary citizen's ability to rule. In fact it is an index of a total lack of interest in politics. The king is chosen 'like a jury man upon an official rotation list',[15] partly because of the apathy of the citizens, and partly because the position carries no real power with it. Auberon quickly discovers that his liberty to do anything he pleases does not include the liberty to do anything that seriously displeases the businessmen who are the real rulers of the empire. In a moment of crisis, the theoretically absolute ruler learns the limits of his authority and the reader learns that the bureaucratic Utopia is also a plutocracy. So, too, with the claim that the empire includes all the talents of the peoples it absorbs. In fact, as the experience of Juan del Fuego, the last President of Nicaragua, suggests, nothing distinctive from the conquered nation is preserved except the bitterness of its patriots. Indeed Chesterton's England of 1984 bears a strong resemblance to Conrad's republic in *Nostromo*. Like Sulaco, the ideal society of the future is materially comfortable and spiritually bankrupt.

A list of the negative qualities of the Utopia does not, however, exhaust the novel's meaning. There is a positive meaning, too, which is revealed by a series of ironic reversals and by a series of symbolic effects. The choice of Auberon as king, for example, does vindicate the cynical political system which enables the choice to be made.[16] Nor is the popular basis of the system nearly as large as James Barker suggests when he speaks of an enduring democracy founded on the stupidity of all men. In fact the choice is made from only a very small part of the total population:

> Democracy was dead; for no-one minded the governing class governing. England was now practically a despotism, but not an hereditary one. Someone in the official class was made King. No one cared how: no one cared who. He was merely a universal secretary.[17]

As a man who cares only for a joke, he exploits the comic possibilities of his authority to the full, and in doing so sets in motion forces which destroy the system which brought him to power. But he is as much a victim of the situation he creates as the men who enabled him to do so. The artistic side of his temperament is satisfied by the Charter of the Cities, which makes his artistic dreams come to life and provides him with the delightful spectacle of self-conscious businessmen in heraldic costumes. But the irresponsible humorist is also a dangerous man. By converting Adam Wayne to a political philosophy which he does not believe himself, he discovers to his surprise that his joke has changed first into something like an epic and ultimately into something like a tragedy.

Adam Wayne's failure to understand Auberon provides the chief conflict in the novel. The Notting Hill war in which Wayne's tiny army wins victory after impossible victory does possess a kind of romantic grandeur, but this is being constantly undercut by the reader's awareness that Auberon laughs at the things which he taught Wayne to admire. When Auberon appoints himself war correspondent, Wayne's epic is in the gravest danger of becoming a farce.[18] What one discovers in fact is that the real conflict is not between the empire and the absurdly small nation that rebels against it, but between the frivolous satirist and the humourless fanatic. Even the victory of Notting Hill does nothing to resolve this unconscious antagonism. Success corrupts the suburb, and it becomes the centre of a new kind of Imperialism and the focus for the envy and the hatred of all the patriots which its tyranny creates. But for Auberon it remains ridiculous. One can argue, as Wayne does, that the destruction of Notting Hill by the bureaucrats and businessmen marks its ultimate victory, because its enemies are now inspired by the very patriotism they had previously ridiculed.[19]

> Do you not see that it is the glory of our achievement that we have infected the other cities with the idealism of Notting Hill? It is we who have created not only our own side, but both sides of this controversy. O too humble fools—why should you wish to destroy your enemies? You have done something more to them. You have created your enemies.[20]

By the end of the novel their contempt has given way to hatred, and in fighting Notting Hill they have come to accept Notting Hill's view of itself. But Auberon's judgment still throws Wayne's achievement into doubt. Only in the strange confrontation after the last battle is this conflict finally resolved.

The meaning of this concluding episode is difficult to assess unless one makes an effort to understand Chesterton's use of symbols throughout the novel. One thinks for example of the emphasis on the heraldic colours of Notting Hill. In the final battle, Wayne tears a yellow shred from the banner of the victors: ' "Here is one colour! . . . and here!" he cried, pointing to his own blood, "here is the other." '[21] The incident derives its meaning from the fact that the president of Nicaragua makes an identical gesture with the same colours at the beginning of the novel. In his lament for the last of the small nations and in his somewhat theatrical rhetoric about 'the sanctity of colours', he provides the symbolic explanation for the later event:

> . . . Señor, you asked me why, in my desire to see the colours of my country, I snatched at paper and blood. Can you not understand the ancient sanctity of colours? The Church has her symbolic colours. And think of what colours mean to us—think of the position of one like myself, who can see nothing but those two colours, nothing but the red and the yellow. To me all shapes are equal, all common and noble things are in a democracy of combination. Wherever there is a field of marigolds and the red cloak of an old woman, there is Nicaragua. Wherever there is a field of poppies and a yellow patch of sand, there is Nicaragua. Wherever there is a lemon and a red sunset there is my country.[22]

The implication is that Notting Hill has by its choice of the Nicaragua colours continued the life of the tiny republic destroyed by the Imperialists and that the idea of Notting Hill may similarly survive the destruction of its army.

Another and more important example of symbolic writing is the use of symbolic types as characters. In fact the characters must be identified as types if the novel is to be understood. This is particularly true of the two main characters, who become, in the words of the final chapter, little more than voices. Wayne is easily recognized as the ideal of idealists, and the symbolic overtones of the name 'Adam' give an added meaning both to his attempt to create a new world and to his defeat under the great tree in Kensington Gardens.[23] Auberon Quin is much more difficult to identify as a type, perhaps because he is based on the character of Max Beerbohm and has something of the complexity of his original.[24] In fact Auberon's many-sidedness explains part of the difficulty one has in understanding the concluding incident in the novel. He has become so much an individual that it is a shock to discover that he is meant primarily as a type. For the ultimate confrontation between Wayne and Quin is not a confrontation between individuals, but a confrontation between earnestness and humour. What the novel finally implies is that this conflict, which is the source of the entire action of the novel, can only be resolved by the common man who possesses the balance which both Quin and Wayne lack. Modern society has polarized the comic and the serious spirits, whereas their opposition is unnecessary and tragic. 'Mr McCabe thinks that I am not serious,' Chesterton writes in *Heretics*, 'but only funny, because Mr McCabe thinks that funny is the opposite of serious. Funny is the opposite of not funny, and of nothing else.'[25] What the novel suggests is that this division will be remedied only when political power is given to the ordinary citizen who sees 'no real antagonism between laughter and respect'.[26] So, in a novel in which there is no representative of the working classes, an ultimate equilibrium is achieved symbolically when Auberon Quin and Adam Wayne leave to wander the world together. For they are finally identified as 'the two lobes of the brain of a ploughman'.[27]

Thus the allegorical element which becomes clear only towards the conclusion of *The Napoleon of Notting Hill* is present in *The Ball and the Cross* from the beginning. A summary of the novel's action makes this clear. The story begins with the capture of a monk by Professor Lucifer, and the remainder of the novel is concerned with the attempt of a Catholic High-lander called MacIan and an atheist Lowlander called Turnbull to fight a duel about their religious differences. The duel is constantly interrupted until the two characters are imprisoned in the same mad-house where the professor has imprisoned the monk. The world seems to be in the hands of Lucifer's friends, but the novel ends with the burning of the asylum and the mass escape of all the characters who have been prisoners. Because of the Stevensonian exuberance with which the first novel is narrated, a careless and slightly imperceptive reader might miss its meaning as a political parable. There is much less danger of this happening in *The Ball and the Cross*. It would require an imperceptive reader indeed who could read a novel which begins with a conflict between a Bulgarian monk named Michael and a mad scientist named Lucifer without suspecting some allegorical intent. And in fact the reader would soon discover that there are very few realistic scenes and very little realistic detail of any kind in the novel. Even the 'ball' and the 'cross' of the title, which refer literally to the ball and the cross of St Paul's Cathedral, are obviously far more important as references to the relationship between the world and the church, which is the main theme of the novel, than they are as rather obvious descriptive features of a London landmark. Similarly, when the flying ship hovers somewhat awkwardly above the dome of the cathedral, it is clear that this happens not in order to enable Chesterton to describe an aeronautic marvel of the future in the manner of Jules Verne or H. G. Wells, but in order for him to continue his account of the leisurely debate between the scientist and the monk.

The same is true of the main section of the novel. Little attempt is made to give an air of plausibility to the endless series of interruptions which prevent MacIan and Turnbull from fighting their duel. Clearly the interruptions are more important than the duel they interrupt. The sentimental pornographer, the Tolstoyan pacifist and the Nietzschean decadent, who interfere with the quarrel between science and religion, are introduced not as individual characters but as individual features of the Edwardian age which Chesterton wishes to satirize. Moreover the unreal intrusion of their follies into the story of the duel also draws attention to how much the duellists have in common and how essentially unreal is their quarrel. The conclusion of the novel is a still more obvious example of the same indifference to realism. What is

B

important about the improbable imprisonment of all the
characters in the lunatic asylum and their still more improbable
escape is not its interest as a curious adventure, but the way in
which it presents a disturbing image of society as a universal
madhouse from which one can only escape by revolution.

In spite of the more overtly symbolic quality of *The Ball and
the Cross*, its themes and preoccupations relate it directly to *The
Napoleon of Notting Hill*. The points of similarity between the
two novels make the two works companion pieces which throw
considerable light on each other. And although each novel is
complete in its own right, there is a sense in which the conflict
between MacIan and Turnbull continues the conflict between
Wayne and Quin. MacIan's religious idealism is substituted
for Wayne's political fanaticism, and Turnbull's disbelief is
substituted for Quin's ironic detachment. The English draper's
assistant and the artistic dilettante reappear in the characters
of a Highland gentleman and a Lowland bookseller.

Wayne and Quin are finally identified as the complementary sides of life which are required for political balance. The
conflict between MacIan and Turnbull has a very similar
meaning. Although at first reading the novel might seem to
suggest that the religious values of MacIan are affirmed in
total and unqualified opposition to the rationalistic values of
Turnbull, this is not really the case. Turnbull's eventual
conversion does imply that the closed world of the rationalist
should be open to the supernatural values of the Christian.
But what is equally true yet far easier to overlook is the
significance of the change which MacIan also undergoes. One
misreads the novel if one fails to see that his romantic other-
worldliness is finally transformed and humanized by the values
of intellectual honesty and social awareness which Turnbull
expresses through his atheism. In the first novel, Chesterton
underlines the political danger of the separation of earnestness
and humour; in the second novel, he underlines the danger of
the separation of religion and rationalism.

But the main interest of *The Ball and the Cross* is not that it
substitutes religious conflict for political conflict, but that it
interprets religious conflict in terms of a political difference. It is
not merely that Turnbull is a revolutionary as well as an atheist
and MacIan a Jacobite as well as a Catholic, but that their
political views are so closely connected with their religious

beliefs that they become in a way an exact expression of them. In this sense, the novel studies a curious interaction between religion and politics, in which the implications and the peculiar dangers of the one are reflected and clarified by the other.

This can perhaps be most clearly seen in the two dream sequences. As the projections of the political and social aspirations of a romantic Catholic and a revolutionary Socialist, the dreams indicate flaws which are at once political and religious. What they actually present are the alternative and contrasting Utopias of the reactionary and the Socialist; but what gives them their particular interest is their presentation of each Utopia at the moment at which it goes wrong and the way in which they suggest that each Utopia goes wrong along precisely the same lines.

The main outline of MacIan's dream presents few surprises. As one might expect, the Utopia it describes is a theocratic monarchy. And the setting helps to set the mood for a fantasy which is from the first as predictable as it is romantic. Appropriately enough, the dream takes place on one of the moonlight nights, which, we are told, are particularly dear to MacIan: 'He was out in the garden on one such luminous and ghostly night, when the steady moonshine toned down all the colours of the garden until almost the strongest tints to be seen were the strong soft blue of the sky and the large lemon moon.'[28]

In fact the moon contributes a great deal to the atmosphere of romantic illusion which is characteristic of the entire dream. The flying ship which brings the summons to MacIan looks at first 'like a bright chip knocked off the moon',[29] and it is the gleam of moonlight on its white steel which makes it gleam, 'like the armour of Sir Galahad'.[30] The messenger himself is described as a 'tall marble figure that might have been made out of solid moonlight',[31] and the theatrical lighting of the moon adds a specious air of mysticism to the pose which he adopts: 'Evan saw that the only figure in it was robed in white from head to foot and crowned with snow-white hair, on which the moonshine lay like a benediction'.[32]

With this kind of *mise en scène*, one is not really surprised to learn that MacIan is summoned to a war that will vindicate every romantic lost cause. At first the appeal is a general one to the Tory's respect for what are called 'the thrones of authority' and 'all ancient loyalty to law',[33] but the rhetoric of the messenger also exploits the Tory's traditional respect for an authority which is both paternal and impersonal. Thus, we are told that he speaks 'with the simple authority of some forgotten father revisiting his children',[34] and when MacIan asks him directly who he is, he identifies himself as the personification of law, 'I must not say who I am until the end of the world; but I may say what I am. I am the law.'[35] And in answer to a question about his message, the floodgates of romantic make-believe are opened, and he answers in a passage which becomes almost a parody of the confusion and touching absurdity of the romantic imagination. Not only has 'the king'[36] returned, but 'our kings have come back to us',[37] and with their return, every romantic lost cause has been restored:

'. . . that which has returned is Stuart and yet older than Stuart. It is Capet and Plantagenet and Pendragon. It is all that good old time of which proverbs tell, that golden reign of Saturn against which gods and men were rebels. It is all that was ever lost by insolence and overwhelmed in rebellion. It is your own forefather, MacIan with the broken sword, bleeding without hope at Culloden. It is Charles refusing to answer the questions of the rebel court. It is Mary of the magic face confronting the gloomy and grasping peers and the boorish moralities of Knox. It is Richard, the last Plantagenet, giving his crown to Bolingbroke as to a common brigand. It is Arthur, overwhelmed in Lyonesse by heathen armies and dying in the mist, doubtful if ever he shall return.'

'But now—' said Evan, in a low voice.

'But now!' said the old man; 'he has returned.'[38]

As the dream continues, none of the naive romanticism disappears, but it is gradually undercut by an increasing emphasis on order, which gives it a new and vaguely sinister meaning. The view of the stars from the flying ship, for example, becomes part of the argument for a hierarchical and anti-egalitarian society which is dominated by a superior ruling class:

'There is an answer to all the folly talked about equality. Some stars are big and some small; some stand still and some circle round them as they stand. They can be orderly, but they cannot be equal.'

'They are all very beautiful,' said Evan, as if in doubt.

'They are all beautiful,' answered the other, 'because each is in his place and owns his superior. And now England will be beautiful after the same fashion.'[39]

In England the war waged to restore this authoritarian rule has in fact been already won. Consequently MacIan is able to see the actual realization of his hopes. What he sees in the panoramic view of Ludgate Hill reveals an odd and disturbing mixture of medieval pageantry and the methods of the modern police state. There are knights, 'with spurs and plume' and 'splendid armour',[40] but they are patrolling the streets as mounted policemen, and the workers whom they are directing, although 'quietly but picturesquely clad',[41] are somewhat listless: 'All the old black-coated bustle with its cockney vivacity and vulgarity had disappeared.'[42] The social order which this scene suggests is not immediately repellent to MacIan. One of the more subtle ways in which the dream indicates the curious egoism of the romantic temperament is MacIan's assurance that his place in the new society will be with the rulers rather than with the ruled. The flattering suggestion is that he is one of those whom the guide calls 'the superior type',[43] for whom one must allow 'a certain high spirit and haughtiness'.[44]

It is significant, too, that the Utopia is described in the language of art and that its appeal is as much aesthetic as religious and political. It even has its own kind of architecture, which might be called totalitarian Gothic, since it is designed to bring back the past in its most authoritarian form. The perfection of the new style of art is presented in the view of the redecorated St Paul's, where three circles of silver-armoured knights form a guard of chivalry around the cross standing on a globe which is now draped or destroyed. In what may be one of Chesterton's rare Anglo-Catholic jibes at the triumphal mentality of MacIan and contemporary Catholics, the dome forms what might be regarded as a papal tiara:

> MacIan drew in his breath, as children do at anything they think utterly beautiful. For he could imagine nothing that so echoed his own visions of pontifical or chivalric art as this white dome sitting like a vast tiara over London, ringed with a triple crown of swords.[45]

What finally betrays the Utopia as a parody of MacIan's hopes is its ruthless subordination of the individual to what is supposed to be the common good. The crisis comes in a scene in which MacIan, looking down at the corner of Bouverie Street, sees one of the policemen on horseback striking 'one old grumbling man'[46] and, at the same time, notices the guide's look of approval: 'I saw on your mouth the twitch of your infernal sophistry.'[47] To his protest that discipline is not so important as justice, the guide answers: 'Discipline for the whole society is surely more important than justice to an individual.'[48] In a moment of insight, MacIan suddenly understands that there is something wrong about his dream of a theocratic state. What the single picture of injustice teaches him is the meaning of what has been called the mysterious cleavage indicated by the words right and left: '. . . the pure man of the right detests justice and charity, always preferring, in principle, in the words of Goethe (himself an enigma who masked his right with his left), injustice to disorder.'[49] At the moment when the good reactionary's dream comes true, he discovers that he is no longer a reactionary. And so his final protest is the protest of a disillusioned romantic: 'Something is wrong; everything is wrong. You are not an angel. That is not a church. It is not the rightful king who has come home.'[50]

But what makes the dream of MacIan particularly interesting to a student of Chesterton's fiction is the way in which it presents a criticism of the political position which is generally regarded as distinctively Chestertonian. Imaginatively it answers the political argument which is popularly supposed to be that of Chesterton himself. The restoration of a medieval society, the romantic nationalism, the incipient Fascism, and the theocratic hopes, are all elements which many critics have detected in Chesterton's own thought.[51] In the dream they are all given concrete and vivid expression, and are all rejected.

The difference between the kind of political sensibility which Chesterton really possesses and the kind of political sensibility his critics have attributed to him becomes clearer when one compares the Catholic Utopia described in MacIan's dream with the very similar Catholic Utopia described in R. H. Benson's *The Dawn of All*.[52] It is not only that Benson's novel provides a grotesque and detailed elaboration of the theocratic ideal which is merely outlined in the dream, but that the ideal which is accepted uncritically in the one novel is dismissed decisively in the other. Moreover it is dismissed by Chesterton for the same reason for which it is accepted by Benson.[53] It might of course be argued that Chesterton is concerned with pointing out the dangers of something which in theory he might still regard as very good indeed. The corruption of the romantic medievalism of Notting Hill does not necessarily call into question the ideal which has been corrupted. So, too, the transformation of MacIan's dream of chivalry into an authoritarian nightmare does not necessarily call into question the dream which has been transformed. But the astonishing fact remains that in *The Ball and the Cross*, as in *The Napoleon of Notting Hill*, a social order for which the Conservative imagination is supposed to pine—and there is a great deal of the Conservative in Chesterton as well as in Adam Wayne and Evan MacIan—is by an effort of the imagination anticipated and rejected.

Turnbull's dream provides both a contrast and a complement to the dream of MacIan. The setting indicates at once the similarity and the difference. The garden of the asylum once again provides the starting-point, and the time is once again night. But the moonlight appropriate to MacIan's romantic illusions is replaced by the twilight and the red sunset which is in keeping with Turnbull's revolutionary mood and creed. The careful and rather stage-like setting is completed by the violent wind storm which also reflects Turnbull's longing for violent social change:

Long strips and swirls of tattered and tawny cloud were dragged downward to the west exactly as torn red raiment would be dragged. And so strong and pitiless was the wind that it whipped away fragments of red-flowering bushes or of copper beech, and drove them also across the garden, a drift of red leaves, like the leaves of autumn, as in parody of the red and driven rags of cloud.

There was a sense in earth and heaven as of everything breaking up, and all the revolutionist in Turnbull rejoiced that it was breaking up.[54]

Step by step Turnbull's dream repeats the stages of MacIan's dream, but it repeats them in an appropriately revolutionary key. The guide is dressed in the casual style of a popular leader, but his white hair and cleft chin easily identify him as the same messenger who came for MacIan. The flying ship is also, one presumes, the same, but it brings Turnbull not towards a distant war of restoration but to a revolutionary war which is still raging in London and which is meant to introduce the new progressive era. The view of St Paul's and Ludgate Hill once again provides the central focus of the dream, but now it is the ball which is standing and the cross which is stricken and fallen sideways.[55]

The argument which proceeds during the dream presents a simple reversal of MacIan's religious and political ideals. Instead of the restoration of papal authority and kingship, the guide speaks of the destruction of the pope and all the kings.[56] And the setting, which is again used as a kind of cosmic basis for the political argument, is no longer the fixed and hierarchical universe of the Conservative, but the giddy falling universe of the sceptic and revolutionary. Instead of MacIan's stars, we have the lights of the asylum, which, when seen from the flying ship, become 'the fallen stars of servitude'.[57] Even the motion of the flight contributes to this view of an unstable universe in which the shifting sunset clouds become 'the leaping flags of liberty':[58]

'. . . You have only to climb far enough towards the morning star to feel that you are coming down to it. You have only to dive deep enough into the abyss to feel that you are rising. That is the only glory of this universe—it is a giddy universe. . . . The heavens are full of revolution—of the real sort of revolution. All the high things sinking low and all the big things looking small. All the people who think they are aspiring find they are falling head foremost. And all the people who think they are condescending find they are climbing up a precipice. That is the intoxication of space. That is the only joy of eternity—doubt.'[59]

There are other ways in which the second dream repeats the first. Thus the language of art is used in a similar way and the guide makes essentially the same claim for the post-revolutionary society that he made for the traditionalist one. Once again beauty and art are supposed to be substituted for poverty and squalor:

'On that very place where now there sprawls one drunken wastrel of a pavement artist more or less wishing he were dead—on that very spot there shall in the future be living pictures; there shall be golden girls and boys leaping in the sun.'[60]

Similarly the same kind of egoism which one noted in the first dream is more apparent in the second. Like MacIan, Turnbull assumes that the success of the war somehow depends on his participation in it. And the guide once again encourages the assumption. 'We counted on you,'[61] he tells him, and he leaves no doubt about the position which Turnbull is meant to occupy: 'I am taking you to the front of the revolutionary war, where you will be one of the first revolutionary leaders.'[62]

The description of the bombardment of London does introduce a distinctively new element to Turnbull's dream. It is reminiscent of the kind of scene H. G. Wells described in scientific romances such as *The War in the Air* and *When the Sleeper Wakes*.[63] And the exultation at the prospect of violence anticipates the attitude of Chesterton's own Anarchist Council in *The Man Who Was Thursday*. What the messenger promises Turnbull in fact is a kind of secular Armageddon:

'I have brought you here,' he answered, 'to take part in the last war of the world.'

'The last war!' repeated Turnbull, even in his dazed state a little touchy about such a dogma; 'How do you know it will be the last?' . . .

'It is the last war, because if it does not cure the world forever, it will destroy it.'[64]

But the event which causes Turnbull to disavow his Utopia is connected with the very violence he looked forward to. His revulsion with the revolution is the result of seeing what an actual revolution looks like. What he quickly discovers is that the 'rather elaborate' programme of Dr Hertz[65] is in fact a programme for the systematic extermination of an entire social class. At first his longing for revolution was unqualified: 'The Revolution—yes, that is what I want right enough—anything, so long as it is a revolution.'[66] Now he discovers that the revolution destroys the very people it claims to help. 'The hopeless slave population',[67] which is 'too tired and weak even to join the social war',[68] turns out to be the poor. MacIan found himself unable to approve a single act of injustice towards a single poor man; Turnbull finds himself unable to approve a single and much more terrible act of injustice towards a single section of the poor:

'Are all the poor people with the Revolution?' he asked.

The other shrugged his shoulders. 'All the instructed and class-conscious part of them without exception,' he replied. 'There were certainly a few districts; in fact, we are passing over them just now—'

Turnbull looked down and saw that the polished car was literally lit up from underneath by the far-flung fires from below. Underneath whole squares and solid districts were in flames, like prairies or forests on fire.[69]

What the cumulative effect of this series of similarities between the two dreams suggests is an identification between the two Utopias in which they occur. What seems to be implied is that there is a point at which the terms right and left become interchangeable. There is no real moral difference between the neo-medieval theocracy and the progressive classless society. The well drilled and soberly clothed workers whom MacIan sees are no different from the laughing, well-clothed workers who are supposed to inherit Turnbull's Socialist Utopia. Each group seems to consist of the survivors of a campaign of terror and repression; they might very well be the same people. Indeed the only significant difference between the two Utopias is the rhetoric with which the guide defends them. The social order dominated by religion, cut off from the world, and the social order dominated by secularism, cut off from religion, are indistinguishable. In the end, those who use religion as a substitute for politics and those who use politics as a substitute for religion build the same unhappy kind of society.

The identification of Utopias in the dream sequence does not however present a solution to the political problem which it suggests. As in *The Napoleon of Notting Hill*, the point at issue is not really a question of social reform, but a problem that remains after the work of social reform has been completed. The difficulty which is signified by the corruption of the Utopias is in fact never given a precise name in either of the novels, but it seems clear that it is the same difficulty which Chesterton refers to in his other writings as original sin. Perhaps the closest analogy to his treatment of this question is found in C. S. Lewis's science-fiction trilogy. In novels such as *Out of the Silent Planet* and *That Hideous Strength*, there is the same emphasis on the reality of the fall of man—our 'bent' condition, in Lewis's terminology—and the same difficulty in determining whether an anti-Utopia is more accurately labelled leftist or rightist. In the latter novel, it is true, the small group of conspirators who gather around Ransom form a kind of political and moral alternative to the scientific conspiracy which they are trying to combat, but there is no suggestion that this organization might itself, in Chestertonian fashion, become corrupt. Nonetheless, Lewis's scientific directors speak in the very accents of Chesterton's Professor Lucifer. Indeed the theme of both *That Hideous Strength* and *The Abolition of Man* is perfectly summed up in the answer the guide makes to Turnbull's affirmation that people have rights: 'Yes, indeed! Life is sacred—but lives are not sacred. We are improving Life by removing lives.'[70]

Another and more contemporary parallel to Chesterton's identification of Utopias can be found in John Buchan's *A Lodge in the Wilderness*.[71] Published in the aftermath of the Conservative electoral defeat of 1906, the book sets out by means of a political dialogue to examine the theory and implications of Imperialism. The comparison is made more interesting because of the brief and somewhat patronizing allusion to Chesterton which Buchan includes in his book.[72] 'Mr Chatterton' is one of the anti-Imperialist writers who fail to understand the need for quantity in transforming the quality of a people. Alan Sandison is surely correct in locating the central argument of the book and the central political statement of the early Buchan in the passages towards the end of the novel in which Lord Appin identifies the empire with the church: 'I maintain that our view of empire gives that empire something of the character of a church . . . our empire will be another, and more truly Catholic, church.' And later: ' "It is a religion," he said, "to me, and I think to others." '[73] As Dr Sandison comments, it is at this point that 'political and religious institutions merge and the ideal of social organization is complete.'[74] He might also have referred to the passage in which Hugh Somerville quotes a certain Père Antoine ('a man who all his life has preached a mystical religion'),[75] who makes the same point with equal force: 'The State is taking the place of the old Church, and politics are acquiring a new meaning.'[76] Indeed the identification between religion and politics is also implied by the frequent and rather tasteless use of scripture to describe the imperial dream.[77] The church of empire is in fact very similar to MacIan's theocratic state and Turnbull's secular church. In both cases, it is difficult to decide whether politics have been exalted to a kind of religion or religion degraded to a kind of politics. The practical result of this confusion is also curiously similar. For there is a passage in Buchan's book in which a gentle and quiet-spoken woman outlines a solution to the problem of poverty in Edwardian England which requires the destruction of a social class she calls the irredeemables.[78] The coincidence between her views and the views of MacIan's and Turnbull's guide is remarkable. In fact her plan for slum clearance might have been based on the same principles which the guide explains to Turnbull:

'Dr Hertz has convinced everybody,' said Turnbull's cicerone in a smooth voice, 'that nothing can really be done with the real slums. His celebrated maxim has been quite adopted. I mean the three celebrated sentences: "No man should be unemployed. Employ the employables. Destroy the unemployables." '[79]

In Buchan's book, the programme of class liquidation is allowed to stand almost without comment or protest; in Chesterton's novel it is received with immediate moral revulsion.

The central focus of *The Ball and the Cross* is, however, provided not so much by the dreams, but by the events which make up the conclusion of the novel. It is at this point that all the characters that one meets throughout the story are again gathered together in the garden of the lunatic asylum. And although there is also a dream-like quality to these final incidents, the precise character of the conclusion is best described not as a dream but as an apocalypse. In fact it is this distinction which MacIan elaborates in one of his final conversations with Turnbull:

'There are two states where one meets so many old friends,' said MacIan; 'One is a dream, the other is the end of the world.'
'And you say—'
'I say this is not a dream,' said Evan in a ringing voice.
'You really mean to suggest—' began Turnbull.
'Be silent! Or I shall say it all wrong,' said MacIan, breathing hard. 'It's hard to explain, anyhow. An apocalypse is the opposite of a dream. A dream is falser than the outer life. But the end of the world is more actual than the world it ends. I don't say this is really the end of the world, but it's something like that—it's the end of something. All the people are crowding into one corner. Everything is coming to a point.'[80]

The point to which everything is coming would seem to be the meaning of the allegory. But one shares something of MacIan's difficulty in expressing what it is, because although the novel points towards this meaning, it never clearly expresses what it is. But at least part of the meaning is suggested by an action which precedes the dreams. In the last of the many attempts to fight the duel, the two duellists, who are officially regarded as madmen, find themselves with genuine lunatics as seconds: a man who claims to be God and a man who claims to be Edward VII. The obvious appropriateness of the situation to the allegorical meaning of the novel is underlined by the questions which Turnbull and MacIan ask their new friends. Turnbull begins by asking the pathetic impostor questions which echo the unanswerable questions which God asks in the Book of Job: 'Why does a rose have thorns? Why do rhinoceroses have horns?'[81] and he continues in language which now echoes the argument from apparent waste in Butler's *Analogy*: 'You make a hundred seeds and only one bears fruit. You make a million worlds and only one seems inhabited. What do you mean by it, eh? What do you mean by it?'[82]

MacIan, on the other hand, questions his second with the severity which a Jacobite reserves for a usurper:

'What right had you stunted German squires,' he cried, 'to inter-fere in a quarrel between Scotch and English and Irish gentlemen? Who made you, whose fathers could not splutter English while they walked in Whitehall, who made you the judge between the republic of Sidney and the monarchy of Montrose? . . .

'What good have you ever done to us?' he continued in harsher and harsher accents, forcing the other back towards the flower-beds. 'What good have you ever done, you race of German sausages? Yards of barbarian etiquette, to throttle the freedom of aristocracy! Gas of northern metaphysics to blow up Broad Church bishops like balloons. Bad pictures and bad manners and pantheism and the Albert Memorial. Go back to Hanover, you humbug. Go to—.'[83]

Apart from its somewhat ponderous wit, this episode provides another interesting illustration of what Turnbull and MacIan stand for. Turnbull's reference to the biblical theme of the suffering of the innocent suggests once again what the novel has already implied, that there is a religious quality to the disbelief of a man who is preoccupied with the God he denies.[84] In contrast, MacIan's religiosity is again revealed as secular. Not only is it significant that it is Turnbull and not he who carries on the dialogue with the pseudo-deity, but the unreal quality of the theatrical loyalty to the Stuarts which he expresses in his conversation with the pseudo-Edward VII recalls the similarly unreal quality of much of his religious conversation.

The decision which they make to abandon the duel makes the same point much more clearly. There is a sense in which it amounts to a confession of the way each of them has distorted the reality he claimed to represent and defend. MacIan finally sees himself not as the church, but as a parody of the church: 'I am the massacre of St Bartholomew. I am the Inquisition of Spain.'[85] And Turnbull sees himself not as the proof of the sufficiency of reason, but as the proof that the reason which refuses to admit the possibility of the supernatural is ultimately irrational. What both of them come to understand is that the distortion of the ball and the cross in each of their dreams corresponds to a distortion in each of their ideologies and temperaments. MacIan's dream of a romantic Christianity which seeks to ignore the world is like the cross without the world which Christ comes to save; Turnbull's dream of a scientific rationalism which destroys the cross is like a world unable to remain itself without divine intervention:

'If the world has some healthy balance other than God, let the world find it. Does the world find it? Cut the world loose,' he cried with a savage gesture. 'Does the world stand on its own end? Does it stand, or does it stagger?'

Turnbull remained silent, and MacIan said to him, looking once more at the earth: 'It staggers, Turnbull. It cannot stand by itself; you know it cannot. It has been the sorrow of your life. Turnbull, this garden is not a dream, but an apocalyptic fulfilment. This garden is the world gone mad.'[86]

But it is not after all the argument which brings the quarrel to a conclusion. What resolves the conflict is partly the insight provided by the two dreams and partly the religious and moral reality represented by the imprisoned monk. Moreover the dreams are able to have their effect only because Father Michael lies buried in Lucifer's prison cell. He is a witness to the higher supernatural reality which transcends and resolves their particular quarrel. It is true that the duel ends at the moment when the duellists recognize Professor Lucifer as the guide of their dreams and as their common enemy. But this discovery also involves the recognition that the monk is the one person whom the Professor genuinely dreads.[87] The larger and more cosmic struggle between Michael and Lucifer, with which the novel begins and ends, is the real means of bringing their smaller and more personal quarrel to an end. When MacIan and Turnbull see the monk for the first time they find themselves in the presence of a religious force which has no political bias and in whose presence the futility of the duel becomes evident. Once again, it is MacIan who interprets the meaning of the event:

'I can't see it—and yet I will try to describe it. Turnbull, three days ago I saw quite suddenly that our duel was not right after all.'
'Three days ago!' repeated Turnbull. 'When and why did this illumination occur?'
'I knew I was not quite right,' answered Evan, 'the moment I saw the round eyes of that old man in the cell.'[88]

But any discussion of the meaning of this fictional apocalypse must also take into account the peculiar atmosphere of the prison asylum in which it takes place. In view of George Orwell's dislike for Chesterton's social and political views, it is ironical that there is a certain resemblance between the world he describes in *Nineteen Eighty-four* and the world-prison Chesterton describes in *The Ball and the Cross*. The details, of course, are very different. Orwell's thought-police and surveillance by television are not easily mistaken for the prison life which Chesterton describes with its labyrinth of sealed cells and its curiously modern system of hygiene. And in fact much of what Chesterton describes, from the patient smiles of the prison doctors to the big bowl of cocoa the prisoners are forced to drink, can be explained by his distrust of science and his fondness for satirizing it. But the resemblance between the atmospheres of the two novels remains. Chesterton's futuristic England, like Orwell's, is nominally a Socialist democracy, but actually an oligarchical tyranny. There is also an Orwellian note in the contradiction between the apparent freedom of the prisoners and the real helplessness of their situation. Even the escape, which they think they have achieved by themselves, turns out to be something which has been carefully arranged for them. And the liberty they seem to achieve is only apparent, since during their imprisonment the whole of England has become a prison in which those unable to produce a certificate of sanity can be arrested in any village at the will of their jailers. A more interesting and even closer parallel is the way in which the masters of the two worlds manipulate the past. Those engaged in the unending task of rewriting history in Orwell's novel might have taken their cue from the methods used by the rulers of Chesterton's asylum. At the conclusion of the novel, the characters are told that their cure will consist in being made to understand that the events they took part in never happened:

'But the popular excitement about the alleged duel continued, and we had to fall back on our old historical method. We investigated, on scientific principles, the story of MacIan's challenge, and we are happy to be able to inform you that the whole of the story of the attempted duel is a fable. There never was any challenge. There never was any man named MacIan.'[89]

But *The Ball and the Cross* does not end on the pessimistic Orwellian note of the triumph of tyranny. A revolution takes place in the madhouse, and Durand, the bourgeois inn-keeper, lights a fire which burns down the prison. As the guards and functionaries escape, Professor Lucifer and his medical and sociological experts fly away in the same machine in which Lucifer appeared at the beginning of the story. The climax of both the revolution and the novel occurs at the moment when the imprisoned monk, in answer to MacIan's strange appeal to 'save us all',[90] walks through the centre of the fire, singing a canticle like one of the children in the fiery furnace:

As the echoes of Evan's last appeal rang and died in the universal uproar, the fiery vault over his head opened down the middle, and, reeling back in two great golden billows, hung on each side as huge and harmless as two sloping hills lie on each side of a valley. Down the centre of this trough, or chasm, a little path ran, cleared of all but ashes, and down this little path was walking a little old man singing as if he were alone in a wood in spring.[91]

Even at this point optimism is not exhausted. There is a hint that Turnbull and MacIan will marry the women they love. And the fact that Turnbull makes a gesture in acknowledgement of the monk's miracle means presumably that the religious harmony achieved in the novel will also be reflected in each of their marriages.[92] Even Lucifer's deputies, the odious Quayle and Hutton, are included in the happy ending. The imagery of soteriology which is used in the description of their deaths suggests that the fire into which they are thrown is a metaphor for purification rather than destruction: 'No, they are not lost. They are saved. He has taken away no souls with him, after all.'[93]

There is little doubt that the fire Durand lights represents partly at least the revolution which is meant to refashion society. Indeed Durand is a figure who recurs frequently in Chesterton's fiction; he is a type of the French middle class, whose stolid practicality is supposed to have brought about the limited revolution which Chesterton admired and wished to see emulated. There is also a sense in which his role in the novel demonstrates another favourite Chestertonian principle, according to which a revolution, like any important political event, must occur first in the world of thought before it can occur in the world of actuality. This may explain why Durand, before lighting the fire, takes time to explain his own version of Rousseau's Social Contract. He is as it were laying the theoretical basis for his practical action. And his long catalogue of personal complaints ends with these words:

'It is useless to tell me that you do all this by law. Law rests upon the social contract. If the citizen finds himself despoiled of such pleasures and powers as he would have had even in a savage state, the social contract is annulled.
. . . 'I only ask you to admit that if such things fall below the comfort of barbarism, the social contract is annulled. It is a pretty little point of theory.'[94]

With this information, one scarcely needs Turnbull's help in interpreting the meaning of the fire. To Quayle's question, 'How can it have happened?' he answers, 'How did the French Revolution happen? . . . It happened because some people fancied that a French grocer was as respectable as he looked.'[95]

But although the historical analogue for the fire is sufficiently clear, the significance of the fire in its relation to the rest of the novel presents certain difficulties. One might argue, for example, that a revolution is at once too simple and too destructive a solution to the problem which the novel has presented. It has at least the appearance of being contrived. And certainly there is little in the novel which prepares for an event whose chief value would seem to be the ease with which it solves a problem which has seemed to be insoluble. By linking

the fire with the French Revolution Chesterton may indeed
have meant to suggest that the revolution in the future, if it is
to succeed, must be based on the pattern of a revolution which
has been tried and proved successful in the past. But in the
crisis as serious as the one which confronts the characters of the
novel, with the whole of England in the hands of powerful
conspirators, it is rather difficult to believe in a solution which
consists in a can of petrol and a match.

A more serious objection to the revolutionary allegory is that
it is out of harmony with the thematic logic of the novel. If a
revolution were to come at all, it should surely have been the
work of Turnbull and MacIan, who would then have had an
opportunity to correct in practice the egoism which marred the
revolution of their dreams. Moreover, the imagery of the final
portion of the novel suggests a religious not a secular apocalypse. The final chapter, with its title 'Dies Irae', prepares the
reader not for an implausible bourgeois revolution, but for an
incident which will express the conclusion of the debate about
religion and politics which has been going on throughout the
story. What the novel seems to imply is the importance of
striking a balance between the supernatural and the natural
values represented by the two central characters. The duel, the
dream sequence, and the final reconciliation which Father
Michael brings about, are all concerned with a question which
has little apparent connection with the fire which Durand
lights.

What one would have liked to see and what the novel fails
sufficiently to express is the precise nature of the new relationship between the values of MacIan and Turnbull which is
established at the end of the novel. It is clear that although
Turnbull's rationalism is finally subordinated to the supernaturalism of MacIan, the supernaturalism is not affirmed
without qualifications. Nature needs grace in a way that grace
cannot be said to need nature, but the two principles are
complementary and not contradictory. And if the novel
emphasizes nature's need for grace, it also implies that grace
finds its meaning in the nature which it completes and perfects.
In a word, the novel moves towards a definition of the relationship of politics to religion and the statement of something like a
theology of grace. And it is the failure of the conclusion of the
novel to provide a satisfactory expression of this harmony which

is the real reason for one's disappointment. What one hoped for was something equivalent to the song which Alfred sings to Guthrum in *The Ballad of the White Horse*:

'Therefore your end is on you,
Is on you and your kings,
Not for a fire in Ely Fen,
Not that your Gods are nine or ten,
But because it is only Christian men
Guard even heathen things.

For our God hath blessed creation,
Calling it good. I know
What spirit with whom you blindly band
Hath blessed destruction with his hand;
Yet by God's death the stars shall stand
And the small apples grow.'[96]

3 The Pre-War Novels

It is difficult to find any obvious common characteristic in the novels which Chesterton published between 1908 and 1914. They mark a distinctive period in his literary development and accurately reflect his political thinking in the pre-War years, but more than any other group of novels they create the impression of being heterogeneous in character. The themes found in each of them suggest his preoccupations in a particular period, but they are themes which link them not so much to each other, but to the earlier and later groups of novels. The curious double allegory of *The Man Who Was Thursday* has only a slight connection with the themes developed in the other pre-War novels, but its dramatization of a purely personal mood and its treatment of anarchy and order anticipates some of the themes dealt with in the later fiction, particularly in *The Poet and the Lunatics* and *The Paradoxes of Mr Pond*. *Manalive* has the same curious air of being isolated from the other novels in the pre-War group, but its treatment of the theme of wonder recalls *The Napoleon of Notting Hill* and the part played by Innocent Smith recalls the role of Father Michael in *The Ball and the Cross*. *The Flying Inn* is equally distinctive, although its use of type characters associates it with the early romances and its somewhat negative political satire and apocalyptic tone link it to the Distributist novels which follow it.

The peculiar allegorical quality of *The Man Who Was Thursday* presents at once its most original feature and its chief difficulty in interpretation. For there is a sense in which the one novel contains two distinctive allegories, which are indeed related, but never completely integrated into a coherent whole. The first, which might be called the personal or private allegory, presents the story of Chesterton's reaction to what he regarded as the pessimism of the nineties. The second, which might be called the public or the political allegory, is concerned with the story of an individual's conflict with an international conspiracy which in fact never exists. The relationship between the two allegories is of course obvious. The terrors of the young policeman who discovers that his enemies are secret friends are as unnecessary as the terrors of the young Chesterton who discovers that he is living in an essentially friendly universe. The private allegory is the story of a man whose enemies turn out to be friends, and the political allegory is an elaboration of his misunderstanding. The interest and the poetic power of the novel comes from the way in which the political story, which is meant to illustrate the private allegory, gradually takes on an independent life and meaning of its own. The situation which haunts the imagination long after the fears of Chesterton's alter-ego have been explained away presents a doomed hero fighting a hopeless battle against a world-wide conspiracy of wealthy and powerful men.

Chesterton's own comments on the novel illuminate only the personal allegory. On the two occasions on which he discussed the novel, he was content to emphasize the way in which it allegorized a mood he experienced in the nineties against which he finally reacted. 'It was intended', he writes, 'to describe the world of wild doubt and despair which the pessimists were generally describing at that date, with just a gleam of hope in some double meaning of the doubt, which even the pessimists felt in some fitful fashion.'[1] On another occasion, however, he denied that the novel had anything to say about an ultimate kind of optimism: 'I was not then considering whether anything is really evil, but whether everything is really evil.'[2] In fact Chesterton's explanation adds little to what the dedicatory poem to E. C. Bentley already made sufficiently clear. Indeed it is the poem rather than the explanation which draws attention to the way in which the novel expresses both the almost incommunicable sense of loneliness in a bewildering moral struggle and the sense that the adolescent difficulties were no less terrifying for being largely imaginary. At the same time the poem suggests the new psychological and moral poise which the novel also represents:

> This is a tale of those old fears,
>   Even of those empty hells,
> And none but you shall understand
>   The true thing that it tells—

Of what colossal gods of shame
  Could cow men and yet crash,
Of what huge devils hid the stars,
  Yet fell at a pistol flash.
The doubts that were so plain to chase,
  So dreadful to withstand—
Oh, who shall understand but you;
  Yea, who shall understand?

· · ·

Between us, by the peace of God,
  Such truth can now be told;
Yea, there is strength in striking root,
  And good in growing old.
We have found common things at last,
  And marriage and a creed,
And I may safely write it now,
  And you may safely read.[3]

Perhaps the most useful function of both Chesterton's comments and his dedicatory poem is the way in which they draw attention to the frame-story which encloses the central action of the novel. The fears of which he speaks in both instances are, as the sub-title reminds us, only a nightmare, but the nightmare takes place in the comfortable suburb which is described at the beginning and the end of the novel. The story of Gabriel Syme as a member of the Brotherhood of Anarchists must be related to the frame in which the story is placed. And the very details of the adventure in Saffron Park are important to an understanding of the dream-adventure which follows it. In the dream, the debate with Lucian Gregory is presented in another form, but it is essentially the same debate which begins in the park. A conflict in ideas is translated into the conflict of a Stevensonian romance. Even the smaller details of the frame-story throw light on the central action of the novel. The sound of a barrel-organ which Syme hears as he talks to Rosamund provides him with the courage he needs when he hears it again during his dream-meeting with the Anarchists. In the park, the music is a reminder of his love: 'His heroic words were moving to a tiny tune from under or beyond the world':[4] in the dream, the music is a reminder of his role as a representative of the common people:

He found himself filled with a supernatural courage that came from nowhere. The jingling music seemed full of the vivacity, the vulgarity, and the irrational valour of the poor, who in all those unclean streets were all clinging to the decencies and the charities of Christendom.[5]

Similarly, Syme's courtship of Rosamund not only provides what may be a graceful allusion to Chesterton's own courtship of Frances in the somewhat similar artistic colony of Bedford Park, but also prepares the way for Syme's meeting with Rosamund at the end of the novel and for the part she is supposed to play in inspiring the central action of the story: '. . . in some indescribable way, she kept recurring like a motive in music through all his mad adventures afterwards, and the glory of her strange hair ran like a red thread through those dark and ill-drawn tapestries of the night.'[6]

The meaning of the personal allegory is also suggested by the purely descriptive passages which one finds in the frame-story. This is particularly true of the description of the sunset with which the novel begins and the description of the sunrise with which it concludes. At first these passages might seem to be examples of what Ronald Knox has called Chesterton's weakness for mere scene-painting and brilliant word-pictures,[7] but on closer examination it becomes clear that far from being irrelevant digressions, they have an obvious relation to the main action and present important emblems of what the action means. Thus the most significant and obvious thing about the Saffron Park sunset is that it is a sunset. It expresses symbolically the *fin de siècle* mood of pessimism which is the central theme of this novel. On the other hand, the quiet and remarkably effective description of the sunrise at the end of the novel expresses perfectly the way in which Syme's fears are finally transformed into a new mood of hope:

Dawn was breaking over everything in colours at once clear and timid; as if Nature made a first attempt at yellow and a first attempt at rose. A breeze blew so clean and sweet, that one could not think that it blew from the sky; it blew rather through some hole in the sky.[8]

The contrast suggested by the two descriptions is however more than a simple contrast between despair and hope. The particular quality of the despair is also suggested, and suggested in a way which anticipates both the dream which follows and the cautious optimism which eventually follows the dream.

Thus the sunset is described in explicitly apocalyptic language: 'This particular evening, if it is remembered for nothing else, will be remembered in that place for its strange sunset. It looked like the end of the world.'[9] The weird imagery of colours as feathers which seem to brush the earth suggests a suffocating evil and malice, and foreshadows the story of the conspiracy: 'The whole was so close about the earth, as to express nothing but a violent secrecy. The very empyrean seemed to be a secret.'[10] And yet, at the same time, the description also suggests an opposite mood. The 'red-hot plumes' which cover up the sun are hiding 'something too good to be seen',[11] and the enclosed sky which seems to oppress is also emblematic of something which is called at the end of the novel 'some impossible good news, which made every other thing a triviality, but an adorable triviality'.[12] The sky, we are told, 'expressed that splendid smallness which is the soul of local patriotism. The very sky seemed small'.[13]

The movement from pessimism to a qualified optimism which is expressed in the frame-story's contrasting descriptions of sunset and sunrise is also represented in the dream itself. The unmasking of successive enemies who turn out to be friends has the authentic quality of the transformation of despair into something like optimism. Similarly the pursuit of Sunday by the Six Days and the investiture of the Six in their symbolic garb also suggests the discovery of an ultimate hope which lies behind the terror. In fact the entire dream can be interpreted in terms of Chesterton's sacramental view of life, according to which nature both conceals and leads to the divine. What the dream finally presents is a kind of Meredithian argument for nature's essential goodness as an ally which ultimately comes to the rescue. Thus, in one of Syme's final speeches, he interprets his adventures in language which might have been inspired by Butler's *Analogy*:

'Listen to me,' cried Syme with extraordinary emphasis. 'Shall I tell you the secret of the whole world? It is that we have only known the back of the world. We see everything from behind, and it looks brutal. That is not a tree, but the back of a tree. That is not a cloud, but the back of a cloud. Cannot you see that everything is stooping and hiding a face? If we could only get round in front—'[14]

The chief imagery used in the personal allegory to present

this philosophy of optimism is the imagery of masks. From one point of view, the masks represent what Chesterton regarded as the scepticism of the nineties, which had such an obsessive influence on him during his Slade school days. Thus Syme, while fleeing through the Normandy woods, sees the forest as a symbol of the scepticism represented by Impressionistic art:

The inside of the wood was full of shattered sunlight and shaken shadows. They made a sort of shuddering veil, almost recalling the dizziness of a cinematograph. Even the solid figures walking with him Syme could hardly see for the patterns of sun and shade that danced upon them. Now a man's head was lit as with a light of Rembrandt, leaving all else obliterated; now again he had strong and staring white hands with the face of a negro. . . . Was he wearing a mask? Was anyone wearing a mask? Was anyone anything? This wood of witchery, in which men's faces turned black and white by turns, in which their figures first swelled into sunlight and then faded into formless night, this mere chaos of chiaroscuro (after the clear daylight outside) seemed to Syme a perfect symbol of the world in which he had been moving for three days, this world where men took off their beards and their spectacles and their noses, and turned into other people. . . . Was not everything, after all, like this bewildering woodland, this dance of dark and light? Everything only a glimpse, the glimpse always unforeseen and always forgotten. For Gabriel Syme had found in the heart of that sun-splashed wood what many modern painters had found there. He had found the thing which the modern people call Impressionism, which is another name for that final scepticism which can find no floor to the universe.[15]

But from another point of view, the masks represent not the 'mere chaos of chiaroscuro', but the sense that the frightening appearances of things hide an encouraging secret. The president of the Anarchist conspiracy who is seen only in daylight turns out to be the leader of the anti-Anarchist conspiracy who sits in the dark room and is never seen. The deadliest enemies are all of them secret friends. As C. S. Lewis remarks, the pattern of the story suggests a comparison with Kafka:

. . . read again *The Man Who Was Thursday*. Compare it with another good writer, Kafka. Is the difference simply that the one is 'dated' and the other contemporary? Or is it rather that while both give a powerful picture of the loneliness and bewilderment which each one of us encounters in his (apparently) single-handed struggle with the universe, Chesterton, attributing to the universe a more complicated disguise, and admitting the exhilaration as well as the terror of the struggle, has got in rather more; is more balanced: in that sense, more classical, more permanent?[16]

The apparently unnecessary terror which the masks create is also given a meaning. For it is through this seemingly gratuitous suffering that Syme gains his new hope. He had after all joined the anti-Anarchist police force because of his exasperation with the apparent smugness of the forces of order: '. . . I could forgive you even your cruelty if it were not for your calm.'[17] At the end of the novel, he is identified with the forces of order he had previously reviled, and it is Gregory, the one real Anarchist, who repeats his protest: 'Oh, I could forgive you everything, you that rule all mankind, if I could feel for once that you had suffered for one hour a real agony such as I—'[18] It is precisely the suffering that Syme has undergone in the time which has intervened between the two complaints which enables him to understand the difficulty which was once his own:

'I see everything,' he cried, 'everything that there is. Why does each thing on the earth war against each other thing? Why does each small thing in the world have to fight against the world itself? . . . For the same reason that I had to be alone in the dreadful Council of the Days. So that each thing that obeys law may have the glory and isolation of the anarchist. So that each man fighting for order may be as brave and good a man as the dynamiter. So that the real lie of Satan may be flung back in the face of this blasphemer, so that by tears and torture we may earn the right to say to this man, "You lie!" No agonies can be too great to buy the right to say to this accuser, "We also have suffered." '[19]

And when the dream ends with Syme asking Sunday the same question and hearing the distant voice reply, 'Can ye drink of the cup that I drink of?', the echoes from the Book of Job acquire a more particular and more religious significance.[20] For the story of the optimism which comes through suffering is now associated with the mystery of the Incarnation and the suffering of God.

The novel does therefore work to a remarkable extent in the way in which Chesterton said it was intended to work. It can be read as a convincing allegory of the solution to a personal problem, in which fear and scepticism are transformed into a real although cautious optimism, just as the apocalyptic sunset of Saffron Park is transformed into the new dawn of romantic hope. But the personal allegory does not exhaust the novel's meaning. In dramatizing his rejection of the supposed *Zeitgeist* of the nineties, Chesterton also presents an allegory of a political problem which remains after the private problem has been solved. The nightmare has a political meaning which to a degree undercuts and reverses the personal meaning which is meant to explain the nightmare away.

The political meaning is first suggested by the nature of the philosophical police force which is supposed to combat Anarchy. This curious organization remains interesting even though the conspiracy it fights exists only in the minds of the policemen, and the conspirators and policemen alike exist only in the mind of Syme. It is interesting not only because it might provide a plot for a kind of John Buchan adventure story, but because it is very much in keeping with Chesterton's own political and social thought. What the policeman on the Thames embankment invites Symes to take part in is in fact an elaborate though secret heresy hunt. The implication, which is entirely Chestertonian in spirit, is that the educated are the real criminal class:

'You have evidently not heard of the latest development in our police system,' replied the other. 'I am not surprised at it. We are keeping it rather dark from the educated class, because that class contains most of our enemies. . . . The head of one of our departments, one of the most celebrated detectives in Europe, has long been of [the] opinion that a purely intellectual conspiracy would soon threaten the very existence of civilization. He is certain that the scientific and artistic worlds are silently bound in a crusade against the Family and the State.'[21]

The nature of the supposed Anarchist movement which the policemen combat is also in line with Chesterton's misgivings about the defects of Edwardian society. His conviction that great wealth carries with it great danger both to the person who possesses it and to the society in which he lives is given vivid imaginative expression in the picture of an Anarchist movement which is controlled by an immensely wealthy group of conspirators. Sunday himself is described as a mad Edwardian financier with cosmopolitan connections and right-hand men who are South African and American millionaires.[22] Like John Buchan's criminal millionaires, Sunday and his henchmen combine enormous wealth with nihilistic principles. And there

is a similarly Buchanian flavour to the contrast between
Sunday's real and apparent position. Like Lumley and Medina,
he is equally capable of directing a world-wide conspiracy or
taking the chair at a humanitarian meeting. It is easy to
imagine Ratcliffe's description of what Sunday has done as part
of the plot of Buchan's *The Powerhouse* or *The Courts of the
Morning*:

> Can you think of anything more like Sunday than this, that he
> should put all his powerful enemies on the Supreme Council, and
> then take care that it was not supreme? I tell you he has bought
> every trust, he has captured every cable, he has control of every
> railway line. . . . The whole movement was controlled by him; half
> the world was ready to rise for him.[23]

But there are important differences in the way in which
Chesterton and Buchan treat this similar theme. Buchan's
criminal millionaires are often defeated by the good millionaires
who are their counterparts. There is little moral difference
between the millionaire hero and the millionaire villain except
that one tries to preserve the system which the other tries to
destroy. And indeed, in one instance, the hero and the villain are
the same person. For Castor is both the sinister cosmopolitan
who creates a secret empire based on drugs and slave labour and
the kindly philanthropist who destroys his own creation.[24]

From Chesterton's point of view, Buchan's heroes and villains
are interchangeable. His own thinking on this question is
summed up in Colonel Ducroix's casual comment on the
wealthy of a small French town: ' "Four out of the five rich men
in this town", he said, "are common swindlers. I suppose the
proportion is pretty equal all over the world. The fifth is a
friend of mine, and a very fine fellow." '[25] Even the exception to
this rule is a somewhat doubtful case, and Syme has no difficulty
in believing that he, too, is treacherous: 'I suspected him from
the first. He's rationalistic, and what's worse, he's rich. When
duty and religion are really destroyed, it will be by the rich.'[26]
In Buchan's novels, the criminal behaviour of the wealthy never
ceases to be a surprise: it has the special note of something
monstrous, since it is the betrayal of society by those who are
assumed to be its best and wisest guardians. In Chesterton's
novels, the wickedness of the wealthy is more or less taken for
granted: it is their occasional decency which surprises. The

picture which is presented in *The Man Who Was Thursday* and which recurs throughout Chesterton's fiction is that of the wealthy as the permanent enemies of the social order and the poor as its permanent defenders:

'The poor have been rebels, but they have never been anarchists: they have more interest than anyone else in there being some decent government. The poor man really has a stake in the country. The rich man hasn't; he can go away to New Guinea in a yacht. The poor have sometimes objected to being governed badly; the rich have always objected to being governed at all. Aristocrats were always anarchists, as you can see from the barons' wars.'[27]

Another expression of the same attitude is reflected in what is supposed to be the very organization of the Anarchist society. The inner and outer circles of the movement correspond approximately to the social division between the rich and the poor. The rank and file of the movement are for the most part simple people with genuine grievances who seek social improvement and the punishment of tyranny. Even the rhetoric which appeals to them suggests their naïvety. What they like best are the clichés of romantic revolutionaries:

'I do not go to the Council to rebut that slander that calls us murderers; I go to earn it.' (Loud and prolonged cheering.) 'To the priest who says these men are the enemies of religion, to the judge who says these men are the enemies of law, to the fat parliamentarian who says these men are the enemies of order and public decency, to all these I will reply, "You are false kings, but you are true prophets. I am come to destroy you, and to fulfil your prophecies." '[28]

The serious danger is presented by the inner ring of Anarchy. This is the group which is described as a kind of church. Whereas the outer ring who repeat Anarchist jargon unthinkingly form the laity of the movement, the inner ring who are completely cynical about official Anarchist beliefs form a sort of revolutionary priesthood. The two rings represent at once the division between the rich and the poor and the moral division between what the policeman calls 'the innocent section' and 'the supremely guilty section'.[29] The members of the inner ring do not desire social reform or improvement of any kind or even complete freedom from restraint. Indeed they possess something of Chesterton's own scepticism about the possibility of progress and something of his conviction about the reality of original

sin. They are inspired by a spirit which has been described as
the psychic undercurrent of revolutionary politics which, in
Buddhist fashion, teaches two things only—sorrow and the
ending of sorrow.[30] Behind the slogans of this 'rich and powerful
and fanatical church', one can detect a longing for death:

'They also speak to applauding crowds of the happiness of the
future, and of mankind freed at last. But in their mouths . . . these
happy phrases have a horrible meaning. They are under no illusions;
they are too intellectual to think that man upon this earth can ever
be quite free of original sin and the struggle. And they mean death.
When they say that mankind shall be free at last, they mean that
mankind shall commit suicide. When they talk of a paradise without
right or wrong, they mean the grave. They have but two objects, to
destroy first humanity and then themselves.'[31]

The complete meaning of this theory is never developed in
the novel, but even in its incomplete form the description of the
Anarchist conspiracy presents a suggestive critique of the
revolutionary spirit. In *The Napoleon of Notting Hill* Chesterton
argues the case for a balance between political idealism and
irony. In *The Ball and the Cross* he suggests the need for a
balance between secular and transcendental values. And in
both these novels, the impossibility of social happiness resulting
from mere material improvement is more or less taken for
granted. But in *The Man Who Was Thursday*, he carries the
argument one stage further. What he suggests is that there is an
undercurrent in the desire for social reform which may eventually be turned against society itself, so that the reformers who
have despaired of reform may seek a kind of Nirvana instead.[32]
In the first of the pre-War novels, Chesterton has translated his
hatred of Edwardian plutocracy into a fantasy in which the
revolutionary reformers and the rich coalesce for the purpose of
pure nihilism, and a small band of common people make a vain
attempt to rally the populace for a last desperate stand against
their masters.

This is the meaning of the novel at the level of imagination.
Superimposed on this political parable is the private parable
about Chesterton's years of depression between 1891 and 1896.
However effective and interesting the personal allegory may be,
it weakens and contradicts the equally interesting and effective
political allegory which is subordinated to it. The terrifying
figure of Sunday becomes the somewhat unconvincing figure of

the good policeman. And the story of the Anarchist Brotherhood and the ineffectual attempts to thwart it becomes first an
extraordinarily detailed account of a misunderstanding and
finally the inconsequential material of a nightmare. *The Man
Who Was Thursday* is therefore a curiously ambivalent book. It
may be read in the light of the dedicatory poem as a kind of
extended commentary on the Book of Job, recounting the story
of the new hope which is achieved through the anguish of doubt
and isolation. At the same time it may also be read as a powerful
though incomplete allegory on the social dangers of wealth and
the meaning of the extreme revolutionary spirit. A personal
comment on the ethos of the nineties ends as a serious political
comment on a perennial political problem.

It is not surprising to learn that there are four years between
the publication of *The Man Who Was Thursday* in 1908 and the
publication of *Manalive* in 1912. There is little to suggest that
the one novel follows the other, and indeed the two works have
so little in common that it is difficult to compare them. Instead
of an obvious and even heavy-handed allegory, one has a novel
which reads like a realistic drawing-room comedy. The complicated plot of a Stevensonian romance is replaced by an
action which is almost entirely verbal. The somewhat rambling
episodic structure of an adventure story which carries one to
France and back and forth through London is replaced by the
neat two-part structure of a story which presents its problem
and solution in a suburban boarding-house, which one never
really leaves from the moment the hero clambers over its
garden-wall until the moment when he and his wife take their
sudden and unobtrusive departure at the end of the novel. The
puzzling and incompletely integrated philosophical and political allegories of the one novel are followed by the symbolism
of a novel whose quality of almost instant communicability
associates it with drama rather than allegorical romance.

The apparent simplicity and directness which seems to
distinguish *Manalive* from *The Man Who Was Thursday* is also
characteristic of the novel's meaning and purpose. What the
novel teaches is less a political or philosophical theory than an
attitude towards life. The story is concerned mainly with the
effect which Innocent Smith has on a few lodgers in a suburban
boarding-house. Ronald Knox has compared the role of Smith
in transforming the lives of the lodgers with that of the mys-

terious stranger in Jerome K. Jerome's *Passing of the Third Floor Back* in transforming the lives of a similar group of lodgers:

> [Smith] represents the innocence and the fresh eyes of childhood investing with excitement and colour the drab surroundings—or so they have seemed hitherto—of half a dozen unsuccessful and disillusioned people. . . . In fact he is a spirit—the spirit of youth reborn.[33]

Knox also suggests the further and more obvious parallel between the simplicity of what Smith teaches the guests and the simple theme of wonder which Chesterton teaches his readers throughout much of his writing. The effect Smith has on the boarding-house guests is the effect Chesterton wished to have on the pre-War reading public. In both cases the simple lesson to be taught is essentially that 'life was after all worth living if only we would see its values from a new angle'.[34]

Although there is much in what Knox says, the emphasis on the simplicity of the novel is somewhat misleading. Smith is certainly a kind of Dr Fell figure, and he may be regarded, like Sunday, as another of Chesterton's unconscious portraits of himself. And many of the literary devices used to tell the story are certainly more simple than subtle. The symbolic meaning which seems to be attached to the initials on Innocent Smith's trunk possesses the same kind of naïvety which seems to belong to his character and there is no difficulty in understanding what it means. There is a similar directness to Smith's allegorical actions and his strange broken way of speaking, which are his simple way of drawing attention to the obvious facts of everyday life that are frequently taken for granted.[35] But when one examines the novel more closely, it becomes clear that its air of complete ingenuousness is more apparent than real. In fact there are two important features of the novel which are surprisingly complex. The first has to do with the function of the private court, and the second with the method of narration.

The High Court of Beacon provides a large part of the novel with the form of a court case. From one point of view this might be regarded as the *reductio ad absurdum* of the self-governing principle of *The Napoleon of Notting Hill*, since it extends the self-government of a single suburb to the self-government of a single house. But from another point of view this emphasis on the importance of the family unit does suggest a sort of programme of political reform: 'You believe in Home Rule for Ireland,' Smith remarks to Michael Moon. 'I believe in Home Rule for homes.'[36] And Smith's description of political rebellion spreading from city to city as thousands of houses light fires to signal their new independence has something of the same appeal which one finds in Adam Wayne's Charter of the Cities:

'Let this be really Beacon House. Let's light a bonfire of independence on the roof, and see house after house answering it across the valley of the Thames! Let us begin the League of the Free Families! Away with Local Government! A fig for Local Patriotism! Let every house be a sovereign state as this is, and judge its own children by its own law, as we do by the Court of Beacon.'[37]

The merely romantic appeal of the idea is also supported by a kind of political argument. The realistic Michael Moon finds Chestertonian reasons for implementing the apparently absurd scheme. He argues that many problems which are insoluble by the official methods of the state are able to be solved by the more informal methods of the household. Moreover official methods of administration are largely corrupt, so that any kind of private justice is preferable to any available kind of public justice. The attitude towards official English Courts which this argument implies expresses Chesterton's view of the English judicial system as a method of class repression:

'It is really true that human beings might often get some sort of domestic justice where just now they can only get legal injustice . . . It is true that there's too much official and indirect power. Often and often the thing a whole nation can't settle is just the thing a family could settle.'[38]

It is also true that the Court of the Beacon does work surprisingly well. Whereas official methods would likely result in the confinement of Smith in a prison or a madhouse at least until his confusing story could be translated into the language of a police court, a more sensible conclusion is reached with much less fuss by means of an afternoon's discussion in the boarding-house court. More than that, the national types represented on the court give it an unusually wide range of qualities to draw on. The prosecution consists of Dr Pyne and Moses Gould, who represent a combination of American idealism and something which Chesterton regarded as Jewish

c

practicality. The defence consists of Arthur Inglewood and
Michael Moon, who represent a blend of English civility and
Irish realism.[39] The trial is in fact an illustration of what a new
and better kind of justice might be like. Inglewood, for example,
is persuaded to take part in it, because, as the embodiment of a
spirit which is absent from English law but very much present
in the English character, he prefers private discretion to public
officiousness: '[He] would often endure wrongs rather than
right them by scenes and serious rhetoric.'[40] Even Mrs Duke,
who is the comic parody of the judiciary, makes her kind of
ineffectualness seem endearing. Although she never understands what the trial she presides over is about, her very failure
to do anything contributes to the solution of the problem: 'Her
only idea is to hush things up or to let things slide. That just
suits her.'[41] It is significant, too, that Dr Pyne has no difficulty
in believing that the court is a venerable institution which
serves a valuable social purpose; for him, it is 'part of the
mediaeval mummeries of the Old Land'.[42]

The chief importance of the High Court of Beacon, however,
is its connection with the narrative method which is used in the
novel. For it is the evidence presented to the court which
enables the book to acquire the form of an epistolary novel.
Instead of letters written by the hero himself, the court deals
with letters written about the hero by hostile acquaintances and
understanding friends. In this alternating way, the succession of
improbable accusations of murder, burglary, desertion, and
bigamy, are introduced and answered. And the simple rhythm
of the story is established, whereby each eye-witness account of
an apparent crime is answered by an eye-witness explanation
of the crime's real meaning.

It might seem that this indirect method of narration does
little more than give an essentially simple story an element of
suspense which it would otherwise lack. But in fact the narrative
method creates little suspense. It is clear from the first that
Smith is never in any real danger of being convicted by the
family court. And it is also clear in each instance, even before
the case for the defence is presented, that he is guilty of no real
crime. The reader is able to guess that the attempted murder of
the Warden of Braikespear College is merely a drastic method
of compelling a theoretical pessimist to admit that he is glad to
be alive. And one does not really need the help of the two

clergymen who follow Smith over the rooftops of a London terrace to guess that the house he eventually breaks into is his own. Nor is one surprised to learn that Smith's desertion of his family and his journey round the world ends with the return to his own house, and that the woman he courts and marries several times is his own wife. One is also able to guess that the moral meaning of the crimes is concerned with an attempt to recover the lost sense of the wonder and glamour of everyday life.

The narrative method must be seen not as a gratuitous complication of what would otherwise be a simple story, but as an essential means of conveying the novel's meaning. In fact it is impossible to separate the narrative method from the story it is used to narrate. The indirect method of narration is as important to *Manalive* as it is to the meaning of *Heart of Darkness*. Indeed there are illuminating parallels which might be drawn between the techniques used in the two novels. The lawyer, accountant, director of companies, and the unidentified narrator in Conrad's story serve a similar function to the chance guests of Beacon House who conduct Innocent Smith's trial. Marlow repeatedly interrupts his own story to ask his listeners if they understand what it means. And although it is difficult to evaluate the effect the story has on his audience, it is clear that at least one listener has caught the significance of what he has heard. For the very fact that the first narrator retells the story is a sign that he has understood its significance. Marlow tells the story to his tiny audience in the belief that literature can illuminate in the same way as experience, and one is meant to suppose that the first narrator repeats the story for the same reason to the larger audience which reads the book.

Chesterton's narrative method has a similar aim. What the epistolary form suggests is not only that Smith is never in any serious danger, but that in a sense he is never really being judged. It is not he, but the people who are judging him who are on trial. And although the four sets of letters display a technical complexity which is unusual in Chesterton's fiction, they are chiefly important for their effect in converting the judges to Smith's point of view. The narrative method in fact represents a kind of moral and political education. Smith's judges are in the same position as Marlow's audience: they are supposed to be taught by what they hear. That they are largely unaware of this aim until it is actually accomplished is an additional irony. And the further purpose of the letters is also the same as that of the Conrad narrative. By appealing to the small audience of lodgers who hear them read, they also appeal to the larger audience of the Edwardian public who read the book. It is in this sense that the parallel between Innocent Smith's effect on Beacon House and Chesterton's effect on Edwardian England takes on its fullest meaning. What happens to the jaded and disillusioned boarding-house guests is a metaphor of what Chesterton wishes to see happen to the equally jaded and disillusioned people of his age. What both Chesterton and Conrad have done by their choice of narrative methods is to make an implicit claim for literature as a moral force.

But although the private court of Beacon House and the letters which are presented to it as evidence provide the form of the novel, it is also worth considering in some detail the meaning of the story which emerges in this oblique way. The four incidents which the letters narrate fall into two groups: the attempted murder of the warden and the burglary charge on the one hand, and the desertion and bigamy charges on the other. In each group of incidents, there is one incident which is chiefly significant for its political and social meaning and one incident which possesses a more personal and philosophical meaning. Thus the story of the attempted murder of Dr Eames deals with the more or less private theme of Chesterton's reaction to the mood of the nineties which he had already presented in *The Man Who Was Thursday*. And the brief account of the bigamy story dramatizes the familiar Chestertonian philosophy of the romance of everyday life which he had already developed in *The Napoleon of Notting Hill*. But in the two remaining incidents, political and social questions provide the major themes. In the Hawkins-Percy letters, Chesterton examines the question of property in a Capitalist society from the Christian Socialist point of view, and in the letters from four nations, which describe Smith's journey round the world, he examines the question of the political and social meaning of the family. All the letters are meant to transform the attitudes of the boarding-house court and the readers, but only in these two groups of letters does Chesterton seek a kind of political and social transformation.

The Hawkins-Percy letters not only provide a consecutive account of an adventure, but they also constitute a kind of debate between a political reactionary and a political progressive. Canon Hawkins's letter does not require careful study or close reading. It is interesting as an example of one of the rare occasions on which Chesterton uses the devices of a naïve narrator for the purposes of satire. But Canon Hawkins is perhaps too much the stage parson of Victorian farce, and the humour with which he is presented is too heavy-handed to be really amusing. As a type character, he represents the section of the clergy who are isolated from the industrial poor they are supposed to serve. Like the earnest Imperialist who narrates Belloc's *Emmanuel Burden*, the Canon unconsciously creates a prejudice in favour of the things which he criticizes. Thus the Christian Socialists never appear in a more favourable light than they do in the canon's attack on them. But although the letter presents a vivid picture of its author's political stupidity, the canon, like all the characters in the novel, is eventually judged by his reaction to Smith and the most damaging comment on him which the letter reveals is his failure to respond to this influence.

Raymond Percy's letter, on the other hand, indicates that Smith's influence is decisive. It is of course true that the moral turning-point in Percy's life has taken place long before he meets Smith and that his original conversion is a conversion from a merely aesthetic Christianity to the socially relevant Christianity represented by Christian Socialism. His early beliefs are largely a matter of artistic taste, but in meeting the real poor in his Hoxton parish, he learns to identify Christianity with a sort of revolutionary political programme. As a character, he combines the Anglo-Catholic ritualism of Percy Dearmer and the Socialist convictions of Conrad Noel. And his account of the genesis of his political awareness echoes Chesterton's account of his early association with the Christian Social Union:

. . . I had treated the Church Militant as if it were the Church Pageant. Hoxton cures that. Then I realised that for eighteen hundred years the Church Militant had been not a pageant, but a riot—and a suppressed riot. There, still living patiently in Hoxton, were the people to whom the tremendous promises had been made. In the face of that I had to become revolutionary if I was to continue to be religious. In Hoxton one cannot be a conservative without being also an atheist—and a pessimist. Nobody but the devil could want to conserve Hoxton.[43]

Although the meeting with Smith does not weaken this revolutionary spirit, it gives it a somewhat different meaning. What the meeting teaches him is a paradoxical respect for property which is based on a kind of contemptuous pity for property owners. The suggestion is that the reform which requires the redistribution of property also requires a sense of compassion for those to whom property is everything. Nothing is said about the stability and virtues of the property classes whose absurdity and venality are more or less taken for granted. Even theft itself is at first made to seem reasonable:

The law-breaking of my companion seemed not only seriously excusable, but even comically excusable. Who were all these pompous preposterous people with their footmen and their foot-scrapers, their chimney-pots and their chimney-pot hats, that they should prevent a poor clown from getting sausages if he wanted them? One would suppose that property was a serious thing.[44]

In fact what Smith finally teaches him is that property must be respected not because of its value, but because of its worthlessness. By taking part in Smith's unreal burglary of his own house, Percy acts out a kind of moral pantomime which reveals the true meaning of possessions and the true pathos of the worldly:

'. . . all stealing is toy-stealing. That's why it's really wrong. The goods of the unhappy children of men should be respected because of their worthlessness. . . . That is why I could not take them away. I did not mind so much, as long as I thought of men's things as their valuables, but I dare not put a hand upon their vanities.'[45]

At the conclusion of the episode, Percy is completely converted to Smith's point of view and the letter becomes a sermon. What Percy stresses in his summing-up is the prophetic meaning of Smith's character. He sees his eccentricities as a sign of a faith which is 'mystical, and even child-like and Christian', and he sees his optimism as a way of recovering a sense of wonder, '[lashing] his soul with laughter to prevent it falling asleep'.[46] What Percy has learned from this Christian optimism is an attitude towards property which goes beyond the demand for social justice which is characteristic of Christian Socialism.

The remedy for the very real social injustices which preoccupy the Christian Socialists must somehow include the gratitude for simple things and limited private possessions which the Christian Socialists have tended to ignore.

The way in which the letters provide a political and social education is even more clearly illustrated in the letters from four nations which recount Smith's journey round the world in search of his own home. Julius West criticizes the lack of realism implied by the very existence of these letters,[47] and Garry Wills in answer provides the obvious explanation of how they come to be available.[48] But both the criticism and the explanation are rather beside the point. What is important about the letters is their meaning and the way in which they work. The pattern followed in each of them is much the same. One begins with an account of a chance meeting with Smith which is followed in the rest of the letter by an account of a discussion about the meaning of the family in political and social life. And in each of the letters the narrator is a clearly defined national type who is the embodiment of a particular political or social tradition. Jules Durobin in his sea-front café, like Monsieur Durand of *The Ball and the Cross*, is another version of the French middle-class tradition; Paul Nickolaio-vitch, the station-master from the central plains of Russia, is a spokesman for Russian Liberalism; Wong-Hi, the Chinese temple-dweller, is a representative of what passed as the wisdom of the East in Edwardian drawing rooms; and Louis Hara, the tavern-keeper in the Californian Sierras, is the spokesman for the national tradition of a country which is supposed to lack a national identity.

At first it might seem that the letters are simply essays cast in dialogue form, in which distinctively national social views are argued by distinctively national social types. This is in a sense true. But the letters are also dramatic, since the conversa-tions recounted in them have an effect both on Smith and on the people who write them. For the narrators, the meeting they describe is also an occasion for questioning and sometimes modifying their own views. For Smith, the effect of the four conversations is cumulative, so that although he argues with each narrator in turn, the view he expresses to his opponent in one conversation is usually the view expressed by his opponent in the previous conversation. What he learns in one meeting becomes the starting-point for the next. Thus the letters become the record of a kind of political education, in which each narrator contributes something to the total social philosophy which is found in the letters considered as a group.

The dialogue between Durobin and Smith is chiefly interesting for its outline of a curious theory of the national basis of political thought. Durobin's formula for happiness is an example of what Chesterton regarded as a typically French pragmatic wisdom. He stresses the need for an awareness of human limitations: '. . . reason tells a man from the first to adapt his desires to the probable supply of life.'[49] And with this stolid practicality, he can see little value in Smith's poetic view of life: 'I am elderly, and the *fumisteries* of the young men are beyond me. I go by common sense, or, at the largest, by that extension of applied common sense called science.'[50] What Smith sees as the great achievement of this sort of French realism is the French Revolution which he believes protected a national tradition by achieving limited goals:

'Yes, your damned smug, settled, sensible sort made the French Revolution. Oh! I know some say it was no good, and you're just back where you were before. Why, blast it all, that's just where we all want to be—back where we were before! That is revolution— going right round. Every revolution, like every repentance, is a return.'[51]

But although an Englishman can learn from the French experience, social theories are indigenous to the country in which they are developed and without serious alterations cannot be applied to the social problems of another nation. Differences in national temperaments are an expression of differences in national culture which make the politics of one country unsuitable for another. The implications of this theory of separate political forms for separate nations receive their fullest development in Chesterton's fiction in *Tales of the Long Bow*, where the differences between nations are seen as the justification for a policy of almost total insularity. In *Manalive*, however, the reference to the French Revolution does little more than provide the suggestion that Smith's journey is a sort of metaphor for an English equivalent of the same thing. The English lack the French ability to combine for a revolutionary purpose, so that their revolution, when it comes, will

be an individualistic effort directed mainly towards the restoration of the family unit and their highly individualistic culture.
Thus the conversation with Durobin not only marks a stage in
the development of Chesterton's theory of nationalism, but
also anticipates the outline of the typical Distributist revolution
described in subsequent novels, in which an army of the common people marches into the countryside to fight the
apocalyptic battle which introduces the new social order based
on the supremacy of domestic life:

'I am going to have a revolution, not a French Revolution, but
an English Revolution. God has given to each tribe its own type of
mutiny. The Frenchmen march against the citadel of the city
together; the Englishman marches to the outskirts of the city, and
alone.'[52]

The dialogue with Paul Nickolaiovitch recounted in the
second letter presents a critique of a more dangerous and more
modern form of the revolutionary spirit. Instead of the limited
but sensible Liberalism of the French bourgeoisie Nickolaiovitch represents a class of people almost entirely isolated from
the nation in which they live. The rootlessness of this kind of
Liberalism is suggested partly by the Russian's fondness for
quotations from Shaw and Ibsen and partly by his embarrass-
ment at Smith's quotations from the Russian folk tales which
he has not heard since his childhood and which move him in
spite of himself. The alienation from folk literature is presented
as an analogy to the alienation from the permanent ideals of
the people which led to the failure of the Russian Revolution
of 1905.[53] By their loss of permanent values to which to return,
the Liberals have become incapable of leading a successful
revolution:

'. . . don't you see that all these real leaps and destructions and
escapes are only attempts to get back to Eden—to something we
have had, to something at least we have heard of? Don't you see one
only breaks the fence or shoots the moon in order to get *home*?'[54]

The dialogue by the Chinese temple moves the argument
one stage further, from the criticism of sceptical Liberalism to
the criticism of sceptical Conservatism. Wong-Hi believes in
the permanence of something he calls 'the Celestial Principles',[55]
and in following an elaborate and unchanging ritual which
keeps him in harmony with the rhythm of the material world

C*

he leaves the existence of a transcendent order of being an open question: 'So long as men offer rice at the right season, and kindle lanterns at the right hour, it matters little whether there be gods or no. For these things are not to appease gods, but to appease men.'[56] Smith recognizes the value of this life as 'old and wise and satisfying',[57] but he is convinced that the scepticism which lies behind it makes reform and revolution impossible. What is most significant about his argument is not the way in which he presents what is almost a defence of Western Imperialism ('We are so vulgar and violent, we have done you so many iniquities—it is a shame that we should be right after all'),[58] but the way in which he becomes a spokesman for a West which includes the revolutionary tradition of the Russians and the French as well as the English. In spite of the wide variety of political and religious beliefs in Europe, Europeans never doubt their right to carry out reform or bring about revolution. In this sense, even Nickolaiovitch's confused and ineffectual Liberalism is partially vindicated, because it assumes the subordination of political systems to the individual rather than the individual to the political system: 'We are right because we doubt and destroy laws and customs—but we do not doubt our own right to destroy them. For you live by customs, but we by creeds.'[59]

The conversation with Louis Hara in the Californian mountains provides the subject for the fourth letter and brings the political argument to its conclusion. The French bourgeois teaches Smith the need for a distinctively English revolution, and the Russian Liberal teaches him the need for maintaining a fixed ideal against which a political theory can be measured and judged. And the unchanging Conservatism of China teaches him the dangers of a fundamental scepticism. What his American conversation teaches him is more difficult to explain, but it might be described as a Christian version of the Chinese philosopher's argument about the need for special places. The inhuman grandeur of the Californian mountains, which seems to reduce all human endeavour to a triviality, becomes part of an argument for local loyalties and for a particular national identity which can save one from the moral vertigo which afflicts Hara. As in *The Ball and the Cross*, the argument ultimately depends on a belief that the order of nature is completed and perfected by the order of grace. The piety to one's own land and people, which was represented by the Chinese temple-dweller's loyalty to his unending routine, finds its completion in the Christian doctrine of beatitude, which is the final element in Smith's political and social philosophy:

'I mean that God bade me love one spot and serve it, and do all things however wild in praise of it, so that this one spot might be a witness against all infinities and the sophistries, that Paradise is somewhere and not anywhere, is something and not anything.'[60]

There are also some indications that Smith's journey is as important a means of political education to the four narrators as it is to him. By moving from country to country, and by carrying the truths he learns from one conversation to another, he influences the lives of the people he meets. This influence is implied rather than stated. Thus the very fact that the letters are written is an indication of what he has accomplished. But there are other indications of the kind of change he has brought about. The prosaic Durobin who prides himself on his common-sense implies that Smith makes him feel like a poet;[61] Nickolaiovitch, in spite of his insistence on the falseness of Smith's views, admits that he has been moved by what he said and ends his letter with characteristic naïvety by asking if Smith has produced any 'literary works'[62]—an ironic touch, since Nickolaiovitch's own letter forms part of the only book for which Smith can be said to be responsible; and Wong-Hi's unnecessarily emphatic affirmation of his belief in the celestial principles suggests that his self-assurance has been somewhat shaken.[63] But the final letter provides the clearest and most interesting example of Smith's influence on the letter-writers. In the vaguely Yeatsian passage with which this letter ends, there is a suggestion that Smith's visit has made Hara conscious of his own unhappiness and conscious too of his own country's lack of an identity: 'But since he went a fever of homelessness will often shake me. I am troubled by rainy meadows and mud cabins I have never seen; and I wonder whether America will endure.'[64]

What makes these indications of Smith's influence on these letter-writers most significant is the way in which they relate the letters directly to the main theme of the novel in which they appear. The influence of Smith moves from those who meet him in different countries to those in Beacon House who read the accounts of the different meetings. Thus the story of Smith's initial effect on the four lodgers is repeated and reinforced by the story of his effect on the political and social thought of the four strangers whose letters are read by the lodgers. The situation described at Beacon House is presented in miniature and an apparent digression becomes representative of the central theme.

The reconciliations between Michael Moon and Rosamund Hunt and Arthur Inglewood and Diana Duke bring the novel to the conventional conclusion of a social comedy. But the allegorical links with the earlier fiction remain more striking than the atmosphere of a drawing-room drama. What seems to be an Edwardian farce is in the words of the novel itself 'an apocalypse in a private garden'.[65] The predicament of the boarding-house lodgers is after all very similar to the predicament of the citizens of England in *The Napoleon of Notting Hill*, and the achievement of Innocent Smith in rescuing a group of people who have been 'unconsciously imprisoned in the commonplace'[66] is very similar to the achievement of Auberon Quin and Adam Wayne. The contrast in both instances is the contrast between the prosaic appearance of London life and the romance which this prosaic appearance disguises. The differences are of course obvious, but they can be explained in terms of the development of Chesterton's political thought and they are largely differences in emphasis. The change in setting from the London street to the London suburban house is in keeping with Chesterton's change from the politics of the small nation to a more Distributist emphasis on the political meaning of the home as the basic social unit.

The essentially allegorical character of *Manalive* also becomes evident when one compares the role of Smith with the role of Father Michael in *The Ball and the Cross*. Both are examples of the Chestertonian character which might be called the Fool.[67] And although the monk exists primarily as a symbol, whereas Smith is much more nearly a fully-rounded character, in both cases the emphasis on the moral power of character as a transforming force is the same. And in fact in both instances, there is the same kind of identity between character and intelligence. The goodness of Innocent Smith, like the goodness of Father Michael, is a way of knowing,[68] since it provides a sort of moral illumination which turns even a casual meeting into a moment of judgment in which those who find themselves in the presence of goodness are revealed for what they are and become much better or much worse as a result of the meeting. Smith scarcely speaks or acts, and yet he has a decisive influence on the life of Beacon House; and Father Michael, who remains silent and inactive in his prison cell, resolves the conflict between Turnbull and MacIan. The wisdom and importance of both men is dependent not on what they do but on what they are.

It is a commonplace of Chestertonian criticism that the period immediately prior to the First World War marks the climax of Chesterton's disillusionment with English parliamentary politics. This was the time of his final break with the *Daily News* and his brief association with the *Daily Herald*, when he called openly for a revolutionary alliance to destroy the parliamentary system which he declared to be irreformable. And although none of the views he expressed during this time were entirely new, the uncharacteristically bitter tone with which he expressed them does mark a sharp and significant change. There is no need to attempt a complete explanation for this new mood of bitterness, which is sufficiently explained partly by his brother's recent conviction for criminal libel, and partly by the growing rancour and confusion of parliamentary life itself, and partly, too, by the approach of the crippling physical and emotional illness which threatened Chesterton's own life late in 1914. But it is necessary to take this new mood into account for an understanding of the last of the pre-War novels, because it forms part of the background against which *The Flying Inn* was published early in 1914.

It is true that *The Flying Inn* is in many ways a jovial and light-hearted book. Like some of the Distributist novels, which it foreshadows in this as in many other respects, it ends with a triumphant march and an apparently effortless victory against a vaguely cosmopolitan enemy. And if the social revolution which is achieved is largely negative in inspiration, there is a suggestion that it has at least inaugurated a new age of social justice. Even the theme of romantic love which threatens to become tragic ends happily with the hint that Dalroy and Joan Brett will eventually marry. Nor does Lord Ivywood's madness do much to mar the general mood of happiness. Indeed it removes the last obstacle to the marriage, and in any case, it is prepared for so elaborately from the beginning of the book that at the end it is as much a relief to the reader as it is a convenience to the heroine.

And there is further evidence of what might be described as almost exuberant and irrepressible hilarity. Humphrey Pump would seem to be a purely comic creation of Dickensian dimensions, and the drinking songs, for which the novel is best remembered, can scarcely be described as melancholy. Nonetheless the cheerfulness is at odds with the deeper implications of the novel. As with much of Belloc's verse, the high spirits and loud fun may be interpreted as attempts partly to overcome and partly to disguise something which might be described as political despair.

The first indication of this can be seen in the picture of society which the novel presents. It is a picture which is chiefly revealed by the absurd career of Misysra Ammon, whose progress from the sea-side resort to the Ivywood drawing-room marks the stages of a social indictment. His success increases as he mounts the social ladder, and it is his audiences which are satirized as much as he. The social success is in fact a comment on the people who lionize him. Among the poor, his mad lecture attracts first an indifferent crowd of working people and then only a flock of sea-gulls. At the next stage of his advance, among the middle classes, he lectures to a foolishly attentive group of people who call themselves the Society of Simple Souls. And among the representatives of the aristocratic and financial worlds who gather in the Ivywood drawing room, he delivers his teetotal lecture to an audience which is stupefied with the drink they have forbidden the common people. There is no suggestion that the Prophet of the Moon is much affected by his social success; his fanaticism protects him from the snobbery and insincerity which characterize his followers. Nonetheless the movement from what is supposed to be low society to what is supposed to be high society represents a movement of moral decline.

The hostility towards the English middle and upper classes extends towards many of the English social and political institutions, which are also savagely satirized. Thus the chapter devoted to higher-criticism and the career of Mr Hibbs However is really a sustained passage of invective against the kind of scholarship which isolates its practitioners from

commonsense and the kind of journalism which enables a
writer to excuse or disguise the unpleasant truths which he is
supposed to expose and condemn. A good deal of social
commentary and, one suspects, a good deal of Chesterton's
personal experience as a journalist, is occasionally compressed
into a single sentence: '. . . evening papers are often more
honest than morning papers, because they are written by ill-
paid and hard-worked underlings in a great hurry; and there
is no time for more timid people to correct them.'[69] But in
spite of its topicality, the satire moves from the particular
to the general. As C. S. Lewis points out, Hibbs However is
the embodiment of perennially bad journalism.[70] And the
sketch of his career makes it plain, if his very name has not
already done so, that Chesterton is again describing a type
rather than an individual. His history represents the story of
the decline of journalism, rather than the story of an individual
journalist's decline.

The central situation of the novel is also far removed from the
contemporary fashions which are the ostensible targets of
Chesterton's criticisms. The formation of the Anglo-Turkish
empire and the invasion of England first by Turkish customs
and finally by a Turkish army are events which are far-fetched
even by the casual standards of verisimilitude Chesterton
usually maintains in his novels. One is far closer to the
futuristic England of Notting Hill than one is to the England of
1914. It is true that there are some signs that the story is set in
vaguely Edwardian times, and it is possible that the description
of the war, which provides the starting-point for the adventures,
might have some relation to the Balkan wars which took place
during the pre-War years: 'There had just come to an end the
long agony of one of the many unsuccessful efforts to break the
strength of Turkey and save the small Christian tribes.'[71]
But the real parallels to the situation described in the novel are
found in the world of Adam Wayne and Auberon Quin. As in
the earlier novel, the initial defeat of a distant and tiny nation
by a world empire is eventually followed by the equivocal
victory in England of a popular force against the same enemy.
And in both novels, the early defeat and the final victory turn
on essentially similar issues. The annexation of Nicaragua by
the Americans anticipates the unjust peace which is imposed
on the people of Ithaca by the powers of Europe, for in both

novels the victories which are won are the victories of amateur
soldiers against professional armies and what is exalted is the
heroic spirit which enables men to fight against impossible odds.

At the same time, the particular themes which are developed
in *The Flying Inn* are very different from the themes of
medievalism and neo-Imperialism which one finds in *The
Napoleon of Notting Hill*. These themes are presented with
surprising economy in the account of the peace conference,
where almost every statement on the agenda prepares the way
for a separate strand of the story. Thus the Turkish insistence
on the destruction of the Greek vineyards foreshadows Lord
Ivywood's attempt to destroy the English Inns and the attempt
by Captain Dalroy and Humphrey Pump to save them. And
the reference to the legalized abduction of Christian women
prepares the way for the story of Joan Brett's courtship and her
eventual discovery that the eminently respectable atmosphere
of Ivywood Hall stinks of polygamy. Even the apparently
irrelevant part played by Gluck ('the German Minister with the
far from German face') later enables Chesterton to express his
dual obsession with Prussian militarism and cosmopolitan
Jewish finance. Only the curious item about the importation
of Chinese miners to Greece is totally irrelevant to the story
which follows, except perhaps as a reminder of how much the
wild fantasy of a futuristic England derives its inspiration from
the particular political issues of Edwardian politics which
exercised Chesterton and his circle of friends.[72]

These few political and social themes are as it were the
threads on which are strung the seemingly random collection
of incidents and anecdotes and songs which make up the main
action of the novel. But although the novel has little plot in the
ordinary sense of the word, the underlying presence of these
themes does give it a curious kind of unity. In the end, everything is related to the few concerns which are outlined at the
peace conference of Ithaca. An example of the way in which
even the digressions contribute to the novel's unity can be seen
in the story of Dorian Wimple. At first the story of the aesthetic
poet seems to be a particularly outrageous example of the
kind of leisurely digression to which Chesterton sacrifices the
unity of a novel. One suspects that the Poet of the Birds is
brought into the book simply to provide Chesterton with an
excuse for writing some rather heavy-handed satire on a kind of

poetry which he seems neither to have liked nor to have under-stood. In fact, however, Wimple's story becomes the means of sharpening the focus of the novel. Like the account of Smith's travels in *Manalive*, the digression eventually reinforces a central theme. For the story of Wimple is after all the story of the way the most unlikely person can become a revolutionary. Moreover the change he undergoes is the result of his applying the same principles which enabled him to write his preposterous poetry to another and more obvious side of life. His injunction that there is 'no earthly creature that a poet should forget'[73] had previously taught him to sympathize with people such as his own chauffeur whose feelings he had previously ignored. The movement from revolutionary poetry to revolutionary action is completed by an incident which relates his story directly to what might be called the moral turning-point of the novel. In the scene which takes place in the smoking-room in the House of Commons, Wimple tells Lord Ivywood his views about the new drinking laws and the speech which he plans to make against them. In this passage, which expressed Chesterton's growing contempt for what he regarded as the decadence of parliament, Wimple speaks of the danger that the parliament which has become a club for the rich may acquire the reputation of an evil tavern:

'Indeed, indeed, Philip, you are in deeper waters than you know. *You* will abolish ale! *You* will make Kent forget hop-poles and Devonshire forget cider! The fate of the Inn is to be settled in that hot little room upstairs! Take care its fate and yours are not settled in the Inn. Take care Englishmen don't sit in judgment on you as they do on many another corpse at an inquest—at a common public-house! Take care that the one tavern that is really neglected and shut up and passed like a house of pestilence, is not the tavern in which I drink to-night; and that merely because it is the worst tavern on the king's highway. Take care this place where we sit does not get a name like any pub where sailors are hocussed or girls debauched.'[74]

This passage marks not only the moment at which the careers of the two men intersect, but also the moral crisis in each of their lives. It represents the beginning of Wimple's complete awakening and Ivywood's complete fanaticism. The upward movement of one line of action in the story is crossed by the downward movement of another. Wimple's decision to help the common people whom he has just discovered leads to Ivywood's decision to betray his friend:

Then he and his crutch trailed out of the long room, leaving the sleeping man behind. Nor was that the only thing that he left behind. He also left behind an unlighted cigarette and his honour and all the England of his fathers—everything that could really distinguish that high house beside the river from any tavern for the hocussing of sailors. He went upstairs and did his business in twenty minutes in the only speech he had ever delivered without any trace of eloquence. And from that hour forth he was the naked fanatic; and could feed on nothing but the future.[75]

The use of political typology in the novel also contributes to its unity. And the part played by Lord Ivywood is perhaps the most obvious example of the way in which this is done. Considered as an individual, he is a mere villain of melodrama, whose main purpose is to attempt to foil the adventures of the owners of the flying inn. What rescues him from absurdity and what gives the rather futile action in which he is involved a serious political meaning is the sense he conveys of being something more than a mad squire. The preposterous individual is also an interesting political type. Perhaps the most effective way in which Ivywood achieves typical significance is through the imagery which is used to describe him. Almost every detail makes its own point and contributes to a single and unified impression of the doctrinaire politician.[76] The continual emphasis on his social position and his family connections might suggest that he is simply a representative of the English aristocracy. But the comparison which is made between him and the equally aristocratic Joan Brett indicates that he represents a particular kind of aristocrat:

It was the whole of her type and a great deal of her tragedy that all that was natural in her was still alive under all that was artificial . . . Like most aristocrats, she would carry cynicism almost to the suburbs of the city of Satan; she was quite as irreligious as Lord Ivywood, or rather more. . . . But the difference remained in spite of her sophistries and ambitions; that her elemental communications were not cut, and his were.[77]

This breaking of communications with the order of nature is the defining characteristic of the Ivywood type. He is in fact the archetypal progressive who is alienated from the complexities of the real world which cannot be brought into the over-simplified and limited political theory which he has developed. The peculiar oriental architecture of his new country house is an early indication of his separation from the culture of the nation which he wishes to lead. Indeed the very setting of Ivywood Hall, with its path to the woods and the sea carefully boarded up, suggests an attempt to exclude the English countryside from the artificial inner world which Ivywood has created in contradiction to it. And his final madness can be interpreted as the breaking of the last link with the outer world which refuses to conform to the inner pattern of his thought. His madness, like the madness which Chesterton later describes in *The Poet and the Lunatics*, involves the denial of human limitations. Unwilling to accept the variety and complexities of real life, he eventually makes the blasphemous claim to the divine right of refashioning the world according to his conception of it:

'Do you think you made the world, that you should make it over again so easily?'

'The world was made badly,' said Philip, with a terrible note in his voice, 'and I *will* make it over again.'[78]

The danger which Ivywood represents has little to do with the particular issues which preoccupy him. The Turkish alliance and the teetotal laws are merely the form which his fanaticism takes. Chesterton's own fear that the ruling class would make use of Socialism as another way of oppressing the poor may have given him the idea for the career of Ivywood as a progressive politician.[79] And Chesterton's opposition to the Licensing Bill of 1908 may have suggested the progressive reform which Ivywood tries to introduce.[80] But the perennial and terrifying political danger which Ivywood represents is something which exists quite independently of the theories and topical events which may have suggested his creation. As C. S. Lewis remarks, it is as a type that Ivywood achieves a permanent interest:

Is Lord Ivywood obsolete? The doctrinaire politician, aristocratic yet revolutionary, inhuman, courageous, eloquent, turning the vilest treacheries and the most abominable oppressions into periods that echo with lofty magnanimity—is this out of date?[81]

The comic songs and verse also contribute occasionally to the unity of the novel. Curiously enough, the satiric verse has the least direct connection with the story it is supposed to illuminate. The drinking songs are perhaps appropriate to one of the main themes of the story, but they do little to clarify it. Thus the vegetarian song has little significance, except perhaps as an illustration of the crude and almost schoolboy quality of much of Chesterton's anti-Semitism.[82] And the main story would lose nothing by the excision of the song of the bad grocer, except a rather weak attack on the commercial spirit.[83] Among the songs and doggerel verse, the Ivywood song comes closest to being a successful commentary on the main theme of the novel. In it, the relationship of the governing class to the nation which it governs is represented by the image of the ivy and the oak. What is suggested once again is the essential opposition between the rooted agrarian tradition and the parasitic and rootless progressive tradition which threatens to destroy it:

> But though they cut the throats of men
> They cut not down the tree,
> And from the blood the saplings sprang
> Of oak-woods yet to be.
> > But Ivywood, Lord Ivywood
> > He rots the tree as ivy would,
> > He clings and crawls as ivy would
> > About the sacred tree.[84]

Occasionally, however, the verse is even more directly related to the novel and helps to further the main action. Perhaps the best example of verse which both illuminates the story and leads to political action is the song of revolution. The plaintive and military beat of its strange dactyls is entirely in harmony with the mood of the novel, and its words sum up much of what the novel has to say about the decadence of parliament and the need for revolution. Moreover the poem itself plays an important part in furthering the central action. Wimple associates the phrase 'Who goes home?' with a time of political and moral crisis, 'the night he was betrayed by sleep and by a friend'.[85] And he explains to Dalroy that the cry is part of an old custom going back to the days when members of parliament were liable to be attacked in the streets. It is this phrase which provides Dalroy both with the inspiration for his anti-parliamentary song and with the refrain which goes with it. The song, which is sung at the beginning of the revolution during the march on parliament and later during the march on Ivywood Hall, derives its dramatic effectiveness from the way it repeats and underlines the political meaning of the novel.

It is a call to revolution. What it expresses in fact is the despair with party politics and the belief in the impossibility of parliamentary reform. Parliament, it suggests, is in the hands of a clique; 'They cry in their parliament "Who goes home?" ' A favourite Distributist contrast between the essentially healthy nation and its corrupt capital city is implied by the images of death and decay which are used to describe London, 'the city set upon slime and loam' and 'the city of graves'.[86] And although the revolution which is prophesied and invoked will destroy all those associated with the evil system, the very completeness of the catastrophe will create a kind of understanding in the class which the revolution destroys:

> 'Yet these shall perish and understand
> For God has pity on this great land.'[87]

The note of exultation with which the song concludes is perhaps the simplest and most moving expression of Chesterton's revolutionary mood in the pre-War years:

> 'Men that are men again; who goes home?
> Tocsin and trumpeter! Who goes home?
> For there's blood on the field and blood on the foam
> And blood on the body when Man goes home.
> And a voice valedictory. . . . Who is for Victory?
> Who is for Liberty? Who goes home?'[88]

The verse of Humphrey Pump is an even more integral part of the novel. Pump himself is important, because he is an embodiment of the Common Man whom Chesterton eulogizes in all his writing and now at last introduces as a central character in his fiction. The *Times Literary Supplement* sees Pump simply as a comic character, 'one of the few characters in English fiction who could stray into the Pickwick Club and never be detected as an intruder.'[89] His real importance in the novel, however, is as a representative of the inarticulate ordinary citizens whom Chesterton calls the secret people.[90] He is the one character in the novel who is supposed to understand the local traditions of England which are endangered by Ivywood's reforms and presumably rescued by the revolution. That is why the political implications of his songs are worth considering. Not unexpectedly they are songs of someone who is politically uncommitted. They suggest an attitude of amused tolerance towards the fads of the aristocracy and the middle classes. If there is any political label which might be applied to them, it would be Tory. Deference to an eccentric squire is clearly an accepted and unquestioned part of Pump's simple code of behaviour. And his interminable musical history of an English road is as exhaustive as it is apolitical:

> . . .
> Then left, a long way round, to skirt
> The good land, where old Doggy Burt
> Was owner of the 'Crown and Cup',
> And would not give his freehold up;
> Right, missing the old river-bed,
> They tried to make him take instead
> Right, since they say Sir Gregory
> Went mad and left the Gipsies be,
> And so they have their camp secure:
> And though not honest, they are poor.[91]

But Humphrey Pump's elliptical conversation also achieves on occasions the quality of verse. And it is in one of these passages of poetic prose that Chesterton presents his best picture of the Tory common man who is about to become a revolutionary. Indeed one might argue that the revolution begins not when the revolutionary army is finally formed, but in the scene in which Humphrey Pump makes his protest from the abandoned cave in the Ivywood garden. This is one of the few occasions when Ivywood is described as an aesthetic poet, and there is a suggestion that his failure to understand Humphrey's protest is really a failure to understand the sort of poetry which is native to the English people:[92]

'My lord, I would like a word. I learned my catechism; and never was with the Radicals. I want you to look at what you've done to me. You've stolen a house that was mine, as that one's yours. You've made me a dirty tramp, that was a man respected in church and market. . . . Do you think because you go up to London and settle it with Lords in Parliament, and bring back a lot of papers and long words, that makes any difference to the man you do it to? By what

I can see, you're just a bad and cruel master, like those God punished in the olden days . . .'[93]

But if Humphrey's speech and the shooting of Lord Ivywood which follows it are meant to mark the symbolic beginning of the revolt of the common people, it can scarcely be described as an impressive beginning. The incident is in fact somewhat ambiguous. Significantly Ivywood is wounded and not killed. And Humphrey remains as passive after the incident as he was before it happened. When the revolution takes place, he plays no important part in it. Indeed the difficulty one has in evaluating this inconclusive event reflects the difficulty one has in evaluating the similarly inconclusive conclusion of the novel. For it is impossible to say what the revolution actually accomplishes apart from the defeat of the Turkish army. No clue is provided to what the shape of the post-revolutionary society will be. In a curious way, political questions are muffled and the novel ends with such purely domestic matters as the engagement of Patrick Dalroy and Joan Brett and the confinement of Lord Ivywood in a private asylum.

It is tempting to explain the inconclusiveness of the last of the pre-War novels in terms of the inconclusiveness of Chesterton's own political position in the late pre-War years. And indeed his *Daily Herald* articles seem to share many of the same qualities and defects which one finds in *The Flying Inn*. They are written in the same uncharacteristically bitter tone and express the same collection of apparently random antipathies ranging from attacks on Fabian Socialism and industrial Capitalism on the one hand to parliamentary government and the English aristocracy on the other.[94] And like the novel, the articles also fail to present any clear outline of the political alternative with which Chesterton wished to replace the existing political system. Julius West, writing from what seems to be the viewpoint of a Fabian Socialist, has described the years 1913 and 1914 as a period of Chesterton's political decadence in which the extremes meet and Chesterton produced both his best and his worst work:

It was not a technical decline, but the period of a certain intellectual weariness, when Chesterton's mental resilience failed him for a time, and he welcomed with too much enthusiasm the nasty ideas from which no man is wholly free.[95]

What West has particularly in mind is the anti-Semitism which he discovers both in *The Flying Inn* and in the *Daily Herald* articles. His analysis might very well be right. What is certainly true is that the later pre-War years mark a period of political transition for Chesterton. The brief connection with the *Daily Herald* ended abruptly at the beginning of the War. And the long and severe illness, which happened shortly afterwards with equal abruptness, seemed to end his writing career for an indefinite period of time. The novels which he published after the War seem to have been written in a different spirit and with a different purpose. Many of the qualities which one notes in *The Flying Inn* and the other pre-War novels remain, but the movement in the post-War fiction is towards a greater and greater emphasis on the positive side of his political beliefs. Thus *The Flying Inn* may be described as a novel of transition, since it can be described with equal accuracy as the last and most idiosyncratic of the pre-War romances or as the first and most imperfect of what might be called the Distributist novels.

4 The Distributist Novels

Chesterton never gave a systematic account of what he meant by Distributism anywhere in his writing, but the outline of this socio-political philosophy is clear to anyone who is familiar with his work and that of the circle of writers to which he belonged. As the name implies, Distributism meant first of all that property should be distributed in the widest possible way. Belloc stated the case for this policy in *The Servile State*, which he published in 1912 and which became the text-book of the movement. He argued that Socialism and State Capitalism were helping to create the same kind of society in which power would be concentrated in the hands of a small ruling class and security would be given to a permanent proletariat whose economic position would be fixed by law. The only alternative to the 'slave' state was the Distributist state of small peasant ownership and workers' guilds. The nearest approximation to this simple society was found in medieval times. Consequently Distributists must be prepared to repudiate modern industrialism in its present form and work for a return to the medieval past. The way in which this theory was interpreted among Belloc's followers is best illustrated by a quotation from A. J. Penty's Distributist manifesto published twenty-five years later:

Distributists agree with Socialists in their condemnation of the present system of society, but they think the evil is far more deeply rooted than socialists suppose . . . Distributists propose to go back to fundamentals, and to rebuild society from its basis in agriculture, instead of accepting the industrial system and changing the ownership, which is all that Socialists propose. Apart from their conviction that industrialism is essentially unstable and cannot last, Distributists refuse to accept it as a foundation upon which to build, because they believe that large scale industry may be as great a tyranny under public as under private ownership. They therefore seek to get the smallholder back into industry as they seek to get him back on to the land; and they accept all the implications which such a revolutionary proposal involves.

Chesterton's own interpretation of this theory is more difficult to determine. Involvement in what might be called Distributist politics dominated the latter part of his life, but it is doubtful whether the gradual change in political emphasis which this involvement represents can be called a conversion to Distributism. As a schoolboy he regarded himself as a Socialist. His connection with the movement that was later to become Distributism began in 1916 when he took his brother Cecil's place as editor of the *New Witness*.

In 1911, during a railway strike, he wrote 'The Song of the Wheels'. This poem provides an interesting example of the way in which his early political verse anticipates the Distributist protest about the mechanization of life in a Capitalist society:

Call upon the wheels, master, call upon the wheels;
We are taking rest, master, finding how it feels,
Strict the law of thine and mine: theft we ever shun—
All the wheels are thine, master—tell the wheels to run!
Yea, the wheels are mighty gods—set them going then!
We are only men, master, have you heard of men?
. . .

King Dives he was walking in his garden in the sun,
He shook his hand at heaven, and he called the wheels to run,

Sitting in the Gate of Treason, in the gate of broken seals,
'Bend and bind them, bend and bind them, bend and bind them
    into wheels,
Then once more in all my garden there may swing and sound and
    sweep—
The noise of all the sleepless things that sing the soul to sleep'.

The official existence of Distributism as a political movement began only with the publication of *G.K.'s Weekly* in March 1925, or more accurately perhaps with the founding of the Distributist League in September 1926. But Chesterton's own version of the Distributist philosophy had been formulated more or less completely many years before. What seems to have happened in the post-World War One years is that the emphasis in his political thought gradually shifted from an attack on what he called the corruptions and hypocrisies of modern political life to an increasingly positive argument in favour of the Distributist programme of land distribution and worker control.

The Man Who Knew Too Much is the first of a group of post-War novels which might be called the Distributist novels. Although the political meaning of these novels is quite distinct, each of them emphasizes a particular aspect of Distributism. *The Man Who Knew Too Much*, which describes the political adventures of Horne Fisher and the political education of Harold March, represents the *New-Witness* stage of Distributism during which Chesterton was primarily concerned with the exposure of what he believed to be the corruption of English government.[1] *Tales of the Long Bow* and *The Return of Don Quixote* on the other hand correspond to the stage of Chesterton's political writing during which he began publishing *G.K.'s Weekly* and became president of the Distributist League,[2] and was chiefly concerned with presenting Distributism as a practical alternative to both Capitalism and Socialism. The movement from the sustained attack on the English political system in *The Man Who Knew Too Much* to the detailed history of the agrarian revolution in *Tales of the Long Bow* and the history of an attempt to remedy industrial problems in *The Return of Don Quixote* does constitute a progression from the negative to the positive side of Distributist politics.

The difference between the first novel and the two novels that follow it should not however be exaggerated. It is true that *The Man Who Knew Too Much* remains closer in spirit and method to the polemical journalism of Belloc and Cecil Chesterton than it is to the more mellow and literary tone of *G.K.'s Weekly*. The focus of the novel is narrowly and exclusively political, and little attempt is made to relate political to social reform in the manner of the later novels. Nonetheless Horne Fisher's story presents in an episodic and unsystematic way the essentials of Distributism. The revolution which it describes does after all look forward to the Distributist revolution described in *Tales of the Long Bow*, and its brief examination of the implications of a medieval pageant antici-pates in a striking way the study of medieval politics in *The Return of Don Quixote*.

If *The Man Who Knew Too Much* anticipates features of the Distributist novels which it introduces, it also recalls features

of the pre-War novels which it succeeds. The careful balance
between the beginning and the end of the novel recalls *The
Man Who Was Thursday*; and the emphasis on literature as a
kind of moral illumination recalls *Manalive*, just as its satire
and loosely episodic structure recall *The Flying Inn*. It resembles
the earlier novels, too, in its use of allegory. What sets *The Man
Who Knew Too Much* most sharply apart from the earlier
fiction is the realistic presentation of the character of Horne
Fisher. In even the latest of the early novels, one is always aware
of the typical significance of the characters. Innocent Smith,
in spite of his individual foibles and eccentricities, has an
obvious symbolic meaning. And the characters of *The Flying
Inn* from Ivywood, the doctrinaire politician, to Gluck, the
Jewish financier, and Pump, the Chestertonian common man
are all of them recognizable types. But it is much more
difficult to discover the typical significance of Horne Fisher.
Unlike the usual Chestertonian hero, he seems to represent
nothing but himself. This is true even of the peculiarities of his
social position, which are idiosyncratic rather than typical. The
new realism can of course be partly explained by the way in
which the central action depends on the strange complexity of
Fisher's character: the success of the novel requires a
convincing portrait of a man of action who is unable to act.
But whatever the reason it is clear that Chesterton has taken
unusual pains to give Fisher the complexity of a fully-rounded
character.

A further explanation for the realistic presentation of Horne
Fisher, which goes a long way towards explaining the particular
and specifying details of his character and situation, is found in
Maisie Ward's suggestion that he may have been based on the
similarly complex character of Maurice Baring.[3] What makes
Mrs Ward's comment particularly interesting is the way in
which her own description of Maurice Baring borrows
unconsciously from Chesterton's description of Horne Fisher.
It is not merely that much of what she says about Baring
applies equally well to Fisher, but that it applies to him more
accurately. Her description of the importance of Baring's
social connections ('related to most of the aristocracy and
intimate with most of the rest')[4] is in fact somewhat
exaggerated, but it does describe perfectly the social position
of Fisher, whose cousins and connections, we are told, 'rami-

fied like a labyrinth all over the governing class of Great Britain.'[5] When one recalls that Maisie Ward seems to have known Baring, her very inaccuracies take on a new significance, as though the distinction between an acquaintance and a fictional character has been blurred and confused in her mind.

It is also significant that the comparison occurs in an attempt to describe an interior and elusive quality in Baring's character which she can only define by referring to the character of Horne Fisher. It is the similarity of temperament and attitude which she calls 'a sort of detachment, a slight irony about a world that he has not cared to conquer'.[6] Nature it seems has indeed imitated art. Horne Fisher does not remind her of Baring; Baring reminds her of Horne Fisher. There are other trivial but interesting points of resemblance which might also be noted without difficulty. Both Baring and Fisher are bachelors; both belong to wealthy Whig families; both have relatives involved in politics.[7] The vague reference to Ashton Fisher's position, 'rather more tremendous than the Viceroy' suggests the position of Baring's Uncle Cromer in Egypt and in India, and if one is willing to extend the comparison to Baring's semi-autobiographical novel *C*, one may also note the coincidence that both men have a brother called Harry. And then, too, there is the obvious similarity in physical appearance. The description of the young Fisher with his bald head and drooping moustache recalls Ethel Smyth's picture of the young Baring in Copenhagen; while the picture of the older Fisher on the dust-jacket of the Darwen Finlayson edition of the novel looks very much like the portrait of the middle-aged Baring in James Gunn's 'Conversation Piece'.[8]

None of this of course enables one to say simply that Horne Fisher is Maurice Baring. Such a judgment would be foolish as well as misleading. As Maisie Ward remarks, 'such a suggestion from life is never more than a hint for creative art'.[9] And Chesterton has himself commented on the fallacies involved in identifying a fictional character with a person in real life. In his introduction to *Little Dorrit*, he considers the possible connection between Dorrit and Dickens's father and points out that figures in literature can be copied from anyone or anything and that often a writer gathers hints for a character from many people.[10] However, he also concedes that occasionally a single person provides the artist with the

main idea for a single fictional person.[11] But Chesterton implies
that the origin of a character is only significant for what it tells
one about the novel in which the character exists. A knowledge
of the failure of Dickens's father can therefore be relevant to
an understanding of a novel whose theme Chesterton sees as
'the victory of circumstances over a soul'.[12] The relevance of
Chesterton's comments to *The Man Who Knew Too Much* are
also obvious. It seems possible that Maurice Baring may
indeed have provided him with the idea for Horne Fisher.
If this is so, there is no difficulty in seeing the personal light this
throws on Horne Fisher's story. It is not necessary to believe
that Baring may have provided Chesterton with information
about the inner life of the Edwardian ruling classes which
enabled him to describe them with an air of knowingness and
self-confidence. Guesses such as this are in the nature of things
unverifiable and, in any case, the novel is certainly not a
roman à clef. But there does remain a sense in which a knowledge
of Baring helps to illuminate the novel. The undercurrent of
melancholy in his otherwise genial temperament, his curious
detachment from English political life, and the strange blend
of contempt and sympathy for his own social class which he
expresses in his novels, these are the hints which may have
coalesced in the creation of Horne Fisher and added a depth
and complexity to his character.[13]

But any discussion of the realism of *The Man Who Knew Too
Much* must go beyond the character of Horne Fisher to the
picture of political life which his story reveals. The catalogue of
almost unrelieved political horrors which his story presents
shows no signs of being a serious historical study in contemporary English politics. Nor do his adventures explore the
theme of the condition of England in the manner of Chesterton's
friend Charles Masterman.[14] What does seem to lie behind the
novel, however, is Cecil Chesterton and Belloc's theory of
politics. The account of Horne Fisher's election campaign in
the seventh chapter might almost be read as a political parable
based on Cecil and Belloc's *Party System*.[15] And when one
recalls that Belloc not only wrote a large number of political
satires to illustrate the same political theory, but that
Chesterton collaborated with him in the actual writing of them
by providing drawings as the novels were planned,[16] one might
expect similarities between *The Man Who Knew Too Much* and

the Belloc novels. And at first sight this does indeed seem to be the case. Horne Fisher's world of stock-market swindles, blackmailing Edwardian financiers and Jewish money-lenders, with its sale of peerages and continuous round of country-house parties, has a strong resemblance to the fictional world which might have been borrowed from Belloc. The motives for the kidnapping of Horne Fisher, for example, are not unlike those which led to the kidnapping of Mr Clutterbuck in a similar situation.[17] And Horne Fisher's career has much in common with that of Bill Bailey in the Belloc novels.

But on closer examination, the similarities between the novels only make the differences in their texture and atmosphere more apparent. Thus one may, if one likes, describe Horne Fisher as anti-Semitic, but there is nothing in his attitude which approaches the vivid and repellent picture of Bill Bailey poring over the Jewish Encyclopaedia to compile statistics for a card-index of Jewish financiers.[18] The cheque for twenty-five pounds which Bailey sends 'to the Jew-baiting organization in Vienna',[19] the number 666 which is sewn carefully on Bailey's shirts,[20] the casual reference to the monstrance in the Duke of Battersea's study which slyly exploits Catholic feelings for the purposes of anti-Semitism[21]—there is nothing corresponding to these things in Chesterton's novel. It may be that Chesterton does occasionally echo Belloc's anti-Semitism in a way that partially justifies C. S. Lewis's comment that Belloc's influence on him was disastrous intellectually,[22] but fortunately Chesterton does not seem to have been an apt pupil. In a curious essay published after Chesterton's death, Belloc expresses a mixture of regret and admiration for the lack of rancour in his political writings which sets them so sharply apart from his own bitter satires:

> He wounded none, but thus also he failed to provide weapons wherewith one may wound and kill folly. Now without wounding and killing, there is no battle; and thus, in this life, no victory; but also no peril to the soul through hatred.[23]

And yet, in spite of Belloc's tribute, there is a sense in which *The Man Who Knew Too Much* is less kindly and more pessimistic than the Bellocian novels. This is perhaps partly explained by the absence of Edwardian society hostesses who temper and humanize the heartbreaking political game which Belloc describes. What one misses in Chesterton's novel and finds in Belloc's novels is the suggestion of a world which lies outside the inanities of politics. Both writers discover essentially the same criminal class at the top of England's social structure. But in the background of Belloc's novels one is always aware of the immemorial and unchanging rhythm of life in an older and more stable social order, which continues and proceeds largely unaffected by the intrigues and corruptions which are the ostensible subject of the novels. This world of obscure and politically innocent country gentry, which Belloc inveighed against in his essays and seems to have secretly envied in his real life, provides a sanctuary to which his heroes can return after their bitter introduction to the political and financial life of London. Young Mr Delgairn in *The Missing Masterpiece*, like Paul Pennyfeather in *Decline and Fall*, is caught up briefly in an adventure he never really understands and eventually returns with relief to the comfortable routine of North Merton House. In the Belloc novels, nothing that happens really changes the political situation. The madness of life at the top is perennial and irremediable, but because it is confined to a single social class, the sickness never spreads and matters never reach a crisis. This is true even of the rare novel which he sets in the future. The Communists and Anarchists who rule the England of 1979 in *But Soft: We Are Observed*[24] behave exactly like their Conservative and Liberal counterparts in the Edwardian novels. But in the first of Chesterton's Distributist novels, there are no sanctuaries of unspoiled rural innocence, and things get increasingly worse with no prospect of their getting much better, as events move inexorably forward towards an apocalyptic conclusion which cannot be escaped.

Perhaps a better clue, however, to the meaning of *The Man Who Knew Too Much* is found in the way in which it is related to the two Distributist novels which follow it. In *Tales of the Long Bow*, there are very few direct references to religion or transcendental values and almost no references to Catholicism. Only in *The Return of Don Quixote* does Chesterton attempt to relate a Distributist novel to Catholicism. The absence of religion from *The Man Who Knew Too Much* is even more striking. Readers who expected to find some allusion to Catholicism in a novel which was published the year of Chesterton's conversion must have been surprised and perhaps disappointed.[25] None of the characters are identified with any church and the favourable references to Catholicism and Catholic countries which occur occasionally in the early novels and more frequently in the essays written during the Anglo-Catholic period are completely absent. Horne Fisher's peculiar blend of Little England nationalism and Distributist agrarian principles has no obvious connection with religious values of any kind. It is true that in the fifth chapter the historical allegory seems to depend on the view that the confiscation of monastic property in the sixteenth century was a turning-point in English history, and the theme of expiation which this chapter develops is certainly Christian in inspiration. But the emphasis is placed on the social meaning of the event. The seizure of the monasteries is interpreted as a social crime analogous to the disinheritance of the poor by modern Capitalism. Horne Fisher cries, 'God save England' as he is dying, and the final sentence of the novel implies a belief in personal immortality,[26] but there is nothing that suggests that the political meaning of the novel is connected with a particular religious belief. In a word, the exclusion of religion in the first of the Distributist novels anticipates the careful distinction between religion and politics which was the policy of *G.K.'s Weekly*. In both cases, the purpose seems to have been the same: to distinguish political views from religious beliefs in order to secure the widest possible hearing for them.

The chief problem in understanding *The Man Who Knew Too Much* has to do with the relation of Horne Fisher's story to the story of Harold March. It is not enough to describe the novel as a study in which the conditions of political life in England are thoroughly and systematically examined, for that evades the question of how the novel works. Nor is Monsignor Knox's suggestion that Horne Fisher is simply another version of the Chestertonian detective particularly helpful, except perhaps as an explanation of the melodramatic element which is found in many of Horne Fisher's adventures.[27] Listing the discoveries of Fisher or attempting a resumé of his political knowledge is also unsatisfactory, for this suggests the novel is a mere collection of political gossip and inside information retailed as a kind of political shocker. In fact it would be more accurate to describe the story as the political education of Harold March. Fisher becomes the mentor of the

D

intelligent but naïve journalist, initiating him into the mysteries of English political life. The narrative method is therefore related to the narrative method of *Manalive*. Each adventure of Fisher works towards the education of March and through him towards the education of the English public. This also explains March's function as a journalist. At the beginning of the novel, he is described as 'the rising reviewer and social critic', who knows 'a good deal about art, letters, philosophy and general culture; about almost everything, indeed, except the world he was living in'.[28] At the end of the novel, he is 'in charge of a big independent paper, with a free hand,' ready 'to open a cannonade on corruption'.[29] The final *volte-face* of the novel might be said to complete his education, and with the outbreak of the revolution and the death of Horne Fisher, March is to be imagined writing the novel in order to accomplish by literature what he was unable to accomplish by journalism, playing the part of a sort of literary Horatio to a modern Hamlet by telling the truth 'to the yet unknowing world'.[30]

But although the adventures create a parallel between him and Fisher, the effect of the adventures on the two men is very different. March's only links with the world of politics are through his friendship with Fisher. His reactions to what he learns range from surprise and distress to shock and horror, but they are always the reactions of an outsider learning unpleasant truths about a remote and alien world.[31] The information he collects is grist for a journalist's mill, but there are no signs that he understands Fisher's position or the deeper significance of what he teaches him. In the second chapter, for example, he learns another lesson about the contrast between ugly private realities and pleasant public appearances and the way in which crime and law can be interchangeable: 'And he told the story of the Irish adventure of his youth because it recorded the first occasion on which he had ever come in contact with crime, or discovered how darkly and how terribly crime can be entangled with law.'[32] For Fisher, however, the story is directly personal, since it is a reminder of his own involvement in a situation from which he can see no escape: 'I am too tangled up with the whole thing, you see, and I was certainly never born to set it right.'[33] In perhaps the most startling of Fisher's adventures and March's lessons, the differences between their reactions are equally significant. When it becomes clear that the Prime Minister, Lord Meriville, has strangled Sir Isaac Hook, March's chief shock seems to be that the Prime Minister could be a murderer, while Fisher characteristically interprets the crime in a personal sense, as the freeing of a family from a blackmailer. It is true that by the end of the novel March reaches the same conclusion which Fisher expresses at the beginning of the novel, but even this identity of views is more apparent than real. At the beginning of the novel, Fisher tells March: 'If you people ever happen to blow the whole tangle of society to hell with dynamite, I don't know that the human race will be much the worse.'[34] At the conclusion of the novel, March picks up this phrase and makes it his slogan for action:

'And do you remember you said that, after all, it might do no harm if I could blow the whole tangle of this society to hell with dynamite?'
'Yes, and what of that?' asked Fisher.
'Only that I'm going to blow it to hell with dynamite,' said Harold March, 'and I think it right to give you fair warning.'[35]

But the moment at which March finally agrees to act on the information he receives from Fisher is the moment at which he finds himself for the first time in opposition to him.

The adventures which Fisher translates into a political primer for March have therefore a complex and personal meaning which March understands only after Fisher's death. For March, Fisher's experience is simply the material for a sensational journalistic coup. For Fisher it is the record of a personal tragedy. What the novel describes is not so much the way in which Fisher shares a collection of political gossip and scandal with a friend, but the way in which his knowledge gradually involves him in a situation which makes action seem impossible and which his friend is unable to understand. The adventures must be seen not as self-contained units without relation to one another, but as an inter-related record of moments in a personal political crisis which can only be understood in reference to each other. A study of this interaction of events is essential to an understanding of his story, and unless one takes it into account, one risks repeating the mistake of March and sharing his incomprehension of what the story means.

In this process, two groups of adventures seem to be particularly important. In the first group, one finds the adventures
described briefly in chapter two and developed at greater length
in chapter seven, and the adventure described in chapter four
which can only be understood in the light of them. The second
chapter recounts Fisher's first disillusionment as Sir Walter
Carey's secretary in Ireland, and the seventh chapter recounts
his political disillusionment in the remote market-town in
western England, where he runs for parliament and successfully
champions 'a new peasantry against a new plutocracy'.[36] The
second group of adventures includes the murder in Prior's
Park, which turns the novel into a historical allegory, and the
account of the revolution in the eighth chapter, in which
Fisher puts into practice the doctrine of expiation which the
historical allegory teaches. In the events described in the first
group of chapters, one finds the explanation for Fisher's pessimism and inactivity; in the events described in the second
group of chapters, one finds the explanation for the change in
attitude which leads both to his final political action and to his
death.

The story of the election campaign against the reform and the
constitutional candidate completes the political education of
both March and Fisher. And to a degree what both men learn
is the same. This might be summed up in the Distributist
commonplace that economic power means political power.[37]
The power which extra-parliamentary financial interests
exercise over both major political parties makes English politics
in its traditional form meaningless and parliamentary reform
impossible. That is why it not only does not matter whether
Eric Hughes or Sir Francis Verner wins the election, it does not
even matter whether Fisher himself wins it. In fact he does win
and proceeds to imitate Belloc's political gesture with improvements of his own.[38] In Belloc's final speech to parliament, he
spoke of his possible resignation and outlined the argument of
The Party System: that the collusion between Liberal and
Conservative front-benches made party differences meaningless
and the parliamentary system hopelessly corrupt. Fisher repeats
this political gesture with improvements of his own. He
discovers in a fortnight what Belloc takes four years to discover,
and contemptuously resigns from parliament without ever
taking his seat in it.[39]

But although much of Fisher's experience is identical with what March learns, there remains a personal element which alone can explain his political inactivity. The clearest example of what this personal element is is found in the account of his imprisonment in the Doric Temple on the island of the ornamental lake.[40] It is this situation which becomes a multi-level symbol both of English politics and of his personal dilemma. The setting has first of all the unreality and bleak desolation which Fisher associates with eighteenth-century scepticism, whose religious symbols point to no further religious reality. 'The eighteenth-century gentleman who built these temples didn't believe in Venus or Mercury any more than we do; that's why the reflection of those pale pillars in the lake is truly only the shadow of a shade.'[41]

But even the unreal art is not what it seems to be: the island is not an island, for an unobtrusive causeway joining it to the mainland makes it a peninsula; and on closer examination, the classical temple is discovered to contain a box-like room which makes it a prison. The temple-prison is therefore an emblem of the present condition of the genuine English aristocracy, whom Chesterton once described as being 'hand in glove with those very money-grubbers and adventurers whom gentlemen have no other business but to keep at bay.'[42]

And although the present temple is temporarily no longer a prison, this, instead of being a sign of new hope, in actual fact marks a further stage in the degradation of the English gentry. The gaoler has been taken prisoner by a thief worse than himself, and the new aristocracy of financiers represents an even lower stage of unreality. Without any historical link to the ornamental gardens and the eighteenth-century landscape, their position is false in a far more complete way than that of the squire with the one guilty secret. The man who acts the part of the reactionary Tory has in fact no claim to his position, and the eighteenth-century architecture and the Gothic mystery suggested by the empty prison are merely the elaborate stage-setting for a vulgar melodrama, in which a shifty stockbroker plays the part of an English squire.

Finally, as the comfortable prison of Horne Fisher, the island-temple represents the way in which he is prevented from acting. The flash of lightning in which he recognizes his brother's face provides a symbolic illumination of his own position. He cannot

speak out against the falsity of English politics, because he is a
prisoner of family loyalty. The group to which he is bound by
ties of personal affection is equally implicated in the evil
deception he has discovered. It is this knowledge which prevents
any political action. Thus speaking in apparent freedom, 'on a
rise of ground overlooking wide green spaces under a blue and
empty sky',[43] he comments on the final meaning of the symbol:

'I have been in that room ever since . . . I am in it now . . . My
life has been a life in that little room on that lonely island. Plenty
of books and cigars and luxuries; plenty of knowledge and interest
and information; but never a voice out of that tomb to reach the
world outside. I shall probably die there.'[44]

There is no essential difference between the political meaning
of the temple-prison and the political meaning of the Irish
adventures. In both cases he is prevented from speaking by a
sense of personal involvement. Talking to March, 'in a little
but luxurious restaurant near Piccadilly',[45] it is clear that he is
still silenced by family and class loyalties: 'And he is my father's
old friend, and has always smothered me with kindness.'[46]
He protects Sir Walter Carey for the same reason that he has
protected his brother and Sir Francis Verner.

The island-prison adventure also explains Fisher's curious
attitude towards Imperialism in chapter four. What is significant in this chapter is the way in which his family affection and
class loyalty are now identified with his love of England. For it
is this sense of personal involvement which gives a peculiar
twist to what would otherwise be a simple restatement of
Chesterton's anti-Imperialist beliefs. Thus up to a certain
point the story repeats Chesterton's familiar and cynical
analysis of the difference between Imperial rhetoric and the
unpleasant realities which the rhetoric disguises. The striking
victory of Lord Hastings which should add a province to the
empire has in fact been won by his Second-in-command who is
given no credit for his achievement by the Imperialist press.[47]
Not only that, but annexation serves no English interests and
takes place at the dictation of England's financial masters
'simply because Nosey Zimmern has lent money to half the
Cabinet'.[48] Even financially it makes little sense; 'everybody
knows adding provinces doesn't always pay much nowadays.'[49]
Fisher, like Chesterton, considers himself a Little Englander,

and he sees the central image of Imperialism in the Arab legend of the Sultan who wanted to build a tower that would rise infinitely above the heavens and was punished for his pride by being hurled down a bottomless well:

And Allah cast him down to earth with a thunderbolt, which sank into the earth, boring a hole deeper and deeper, till it made a well that was without a bottom as the tower was to have been without a top. And down that inverted tower of darkness the soul of the proud Sultan is falling for ever and ever.[50]

All this is very much in line with Chesterton's pre-War assessment of the Imperialist as at best an inconsistent sentimentalist who finds it flattering to offer the subject-peoples a dreary industrial culture, but is afraid to give them the European notion of citizenship for which industrial culture is the mere machinery; '[he] decides to spread the body of Europe without the soul'.[51] At the worst, he sees Imperialists as people who offer foolish and pointless distractions from the pressing political and social problems of England; '. . . if we left the rest of the world alone we might have some time for attending to our own affairs, which are urgent to the point of excruciation.'[52] Although this assessment of the Imperial theory, which Chesterton calls 'the Roosevelt and Kipling theory,'[53] expands the point made by Fisher, it locates the evil in the same insensate pride of which Fisher speaks. Thus the bottomless well, which provides a realistic focus for the story and gives the chapter its title, becomes the image of the growth of the empire, 'growing until it reaches the sky',[54] a growth whose only meaning can be found in a pride which invites its own retribution.

Fisher adds two unexpected qualifications to this critique of Imperialism, both of which are connected to this notion of personal involvement and his view of patriotism as an extension of family loyalty. In the second and seventh chapters he decides that he must preserve the illusion about English politics in order to spare his family and his friends from humiliation; in this chapter he decides that he must preserve the illusion about the Imperialist adventure in order to spare the humiliation of England. Like Conrad's Stein in *Lord Jim*, he argues the need for romantic illusions, because they can be ideals and because in any case they are 'better than the reality'.[55] Hastings's unearned and undeserved reputation among the Arabs is preserved ('His was the one name we had left to conjure with'),[56] just as Sir Francis Verner's unreal reputation in the west country is finally left undisturbed. Fisher's refusal to speak publicly about the political situation is connected with his refusal to do anything which might hurt his own people. This, too, finds its parallel in his attitude towards Imperialism. The Imperialistic system expresses an evil and self-destructive pride, but he will do nothing to hasten its destruction. His explanation of his refusal to act repeats the anti-Semitic diatribe found in his comments on Sir Francis Verner:

> '. . . I don't believe in the Union Jack going up and up eternally like the Tower. But if you think I am going to let the Union Jack go down and down eternally like the Bottomless Well, . . . no, I won't, and that's flat; not if the Chancellor were blackmailed by twenty millionaires with their gutter rags, not if the Prime Minister married twenty Yankee Jewesses, not if Woodville and Carstairs had shares in twenty swindling mines. If the thing is really tottering, God help it, it mustn't be we who tip it over.'[57]

In chapter five, which is entitled 'The Hole in the Wall', one turns from knowledge which prevents political action to knowledge which leads to political action. In this, the most explicitly allegorical of all the adventures, one finds the explanation for the final transformation of Horne Fisher from a reflective man into a man of action. As in *The Return of Don Quixote*, an exercise in antiquarian research leads to the solution of both a private and a social crime, and a romantic drama takes on the colours of real life. The pageant in Prior's Park creates what is called a 'curious psychological atmosphere'[58] in which the characters suddenly have the sense of being part of a story which provides an explanation both of their own lives and of the society in which they live. As they gather beside the ornamental lake, they feel that they are unconsciously acting out a historical allegory with a meaning which is clear, even though they cannot see what it is:

> It was almost as if they were the ghosts of their own ancestors haunting that dark wood and dismal lake, and playing some old part that they only half remembered. The movements of those coloured figures seemed to mean something that had been settled

long before, like a silent heraldry. Acts, attitudes, external objects, were accepted as an allegory even without the key; and they knew when a crisis had come, when they did not know what it was.[59]

Horne Fisher's research provides the explanation of the allegory. The artificial lake disguises a medieval holy-well in which Lord Bulmer's ancestor had thrown the body of the last Abbot and in which a modern murderer has thrown the body of Lord Bulmer. The private crime committed by a Tudor nobleman is symbolic of the social crime of the pillage of the monasteries which had been committed by him and by other members of his class.[60] The death of Lord Bulmer becomes the expiation for his ancestor's crime, but the social crime remains unexpiated. It is at this moment that the allegory illuminates for Horne Fisher the fatality which awaits both him and the class to which he belongs and which can only be averted by a repentance which is expressed by restitution and suffering. Prior's Park, like Seawood Abbey in *The Return of Don Quixote*, is a reminder of the historical origin of the modern social problem. The revolution which Fisher prophesied in the first chapter and which takes place in the last chapter now finds its moral meaning as a form of social expiation.

At the same time, the meaning of Fisher's own action in the revolution becomes clear. His role in the pantomime anticipates his role in the revolution. The figure dressed in penitential sackcloth becomes the expiatory victim who dies to pay for the social crimes of his own class. The same personal involvement which first prevents his acting later becomes his motive for action. A life-time of passive inactivity ends with a political action which gives moral meaning to his death. Harold March sees part of the meaning of the revolution in a world 'full of uproar and volcanic vapour and chaotic light';[61] for Fisher, the meaning of the revolution and all the political and social follies which bring it about is revealed long before it happens in the chill, winter light of a pageant beside a frozen lake:

'And how did you get on the track of all this hidden history?' asked the young architect.

A cloud came across the brow of Horne Fisher.

'I knew only too much about it already,' he said, 'and, after all, it's shameful for me to be speaking lightly of poor Bulmer, who has paid his penalty, when the rest of us haven't. I dare say every cigar I smoke and every liqueur I drink comes directly or indirectly from

D*

the harrying of the holy places and the persecution of the poor. After all, it needs very little poking about in the past to find that hole in the wall; that great breach in the defences of English history. It lies just under the surface of a thin sheet of sham information and instruction, just as the black and bloodstained well lies just under the floor of shallow water and flat weeds. Oh, the ice is thin, but it bears; it is strong enough to support us when we dress up as monks and dance on it in mockery of the dear quaint old Middle Ages. . . . You see I do know a little about our national and imperial history, our prosperity and our progress, our commerce and our colonies, our centuries of success or splendour. So I did put on an antiquated sort of costume, when I was asked to do so. I put on the only costume I think fit for a man who has inherited the position of a gentleman and yet has not entirely lost the feelings of one.'

In answer to a look of inquiry he rose with a sweeping and downward gesture.

'Sackcloth,' he said, 'and I would wear the ashes as well, if they would stay on my bald head when I put them there.'[62]

Not only does this incident give significance to Fisher's final action, but it also helps to explain many of the circumstances which surround it. It throws a particularly interesting light, for example, on the final behaviour of his family circle, which is perhaps the most curious incident in the entire novel. The family loyalty which has prevented him from acting is ultimately vindicated by something which might almost be called a family conversion. One might say that Fisher's final intervention is made possible because his relatives turn out to be patriots as well as scoundrels and hypocrites. This is of course true, but the point to the incident is somewhat more subtle. They are saved not in spite of their hypocrisy, but through their hypocrisy. The gap between appearance and reality is certainly striking enough. Officially they are men who live impossibly heroic lives; in fact the venality and sensuousness which their public masks conceal only becomes fully apparent in the way in which they are described. What is meant by the reference to the Foreign Secretary as 'a wreck of drink and drugs'[63] becomes clear only when one sees his dishevelled face and haggard eyes. The Chancellor's bankruptcy and dissipation become real in the contrast between his festive clothing and his sallow face and sullen manner. The Prime Minister's moral disintegration becomes vivid not because of the reference to the commission he takes on the petrol contract, but because of the weird imagery which describes him as an evil child with a soft voice and a soft step and a fondness for sleep.

In the end, however, it becomes clear that their hypocritical masks present a more accurate picture of the moral reality than their hidden vices. They possess a basic integrity which their moral failure has hidden even from themselves and which in a sense is very close to their official pose of righteousness. In the end they become what their public masks have always proclaimed them to be. The situation is in fact very close to that which one finds in the typical Mauriac novel or in the typical Mauriac literary essay, in which grace works through the very completeness of a moral collapse which makes humility possible: La Pharisienne, whose pretence to a virtue which she lacks becomes her means of salvation, or the guilty hero of *The Scarlet Letter*, whose sin, in Mauriac's words, 'condemns him to sanctity'.[64] Indeed Mauriac's comments on *The Scarlet Letter* serve equally well as a description of this aspect of *The Man Who Knew Too Much*:

> Ce roman nous livre une clef pour pénétrer un mystère impénétrable entre tous aux yeux du croyant: le mystère du mal. Le mal est dans le monde et au-dedans de nous. Mais 'tout est Grâce'. C'est le dernier mot du curé de campagne de Bernanos. Le principe même de notre régénération peut se trouver contenu au pire de nous-mêmes.[65]

In Chesterton's novel, the theme is given a social significance, as Fisher extends to the criminal politicians an understanding and compassion which Chesterton usually reserves for the criminal poor:

> 'Believe me, you never know the best about men till you know the worst about them. It does not dispose of their strange human souls to know that they were exhibited to the world as impossible impeccable waxworks, who never looked after a woman or knew the meaning of a bribe. . . . I tell you it is as true of these rich fools and rascals as it is true of every poor footpad and pickpocket: that only God knows how good they have tried to be. God alone knows what the conscience can survive, or how a man who has lost his honour will still try to save his soul.'[66]

It is therefore perhaps significant that the only traitor in Fisher's family should be the one man who seems to have no obvious moral failings of which to repent. Horne Hewitt has apparently escaped the corrupting influence of political life; he exists only as Fisher's uncle, the colourless country squire, who is 'a good soldier'.[67] And yet eventually even his treachery is brought into the redemptive scheme of the novel. He dies in a duel which is fought to keep the family disgrace within the family circle and to prevent the military plans from reaching the hands of the enemy. But the curious point is that his death, which frees Fisher to perform the action which makes the final victory possible, is something which he brings about himself. It is a form of self-destruction, a kind of parody of Fisher's own death, which forwards the national cause which he has betrayed. By seizing the rotten bar for a weapon, he brings down the Britannia statue which crushes him so that he acts out what Fisher calls 'that appalling allegory'.[68] There is a sense in which the unrepented evil of the 'good' man, like the repented evil of the hypocrite, also 'works together unto good'.[69]

The clearest expression of the theme of expiation is found in the description of Fisher's death. It is at this point that the conflicting attitudes of Fisher and March finally fuse to form a common political view which blends March's language of social regeneration with imagery which recalls Fisher's adventure in Prior's Park. At the crisis of the revolution, when Fisher sends the signal to the western armies, March interprets the scene in terms of the social apocalypse of which Fisher used to dream: he thinks of 'the signs of the last days'[70] and he sees the rocket-flash as 'the apocalyptic meteor of something like a day of judgment'.[71] By sending the signal Fisher at the same time ensures the defeat of the mysterious Eastern armies, whose battery can now be located and pounded to pieces by the artillery of the west country and their Irish allies, and brings about his own death. The imagery also links the frozen lake in Prior's Park which had begun to melt with the entire landscape of the final battle, which has become 'like a lake of ruby light'.[72]

What Fisher's expiatory death brings about, apart from the destruction of the cosmopolitan aliens, is not altogether clear. His relatives in the ruling class have already implemented at least the beginning of a Distributist programme of land reform: 'The experiment of attempting to establish a new peasantry in the west of England, on the lines of an early fancy of Horne Fisher's.'[73] So one may suppose that this policy will be continued and perhaps extended. And although the description of the rocket-blast also suggests that his death helps to inaugurate a kind of earthly paradise, this passage remains true to Chesterton's ambivalent attitude towards the possibility of building a Utopia. For 'the sanguine moment of morning'[74] which seems to last forever in fact only lasts for an instant before darkness returns. The violence and noise which surround the actual moment of his death seem to be an almost literal fulfilment of his words about blowing society to bits with dynamite. But in the moment which precedes it, in the brief vision of a socially transformed universe bathed in a light which is more like wine than blood, there is a suggestion that the death of the best representative of the old order has averted the complete chaos of social disintegration. His death preserves a link between his life and his role as March's teacher. And his final and decisive action illuminates with light as well as destroying with fire:

> Far up in the infinite heavens the rocket stooped and sprang into scarlet stars. For a moment the whole landscape out to the sea and back to the crescent of the wooded hills was like a lake of ruby light, of a red strangely rich and glorious, as if the world were steeped in wine rather than blood, or the earth were an earthly paradise, over which paused for ever the sanguine moment of morning.[75]

In a study of *Tono-Bungay*, David Lodge speaks of the way in which H. G. Wells's imaginative work sometimes disturbingly questions the teaching of his public self.[76] The same comment might be made about *The Man Who Knew Too Much*. It is certainly difficult to discover anything in Chesterton's public pronouncements which corresponds to the political view put forward by the novel. There is nothing in the essays, for example, which prepares one for the strange alliance between politicians and populace which the novel finally suggests. That the discredited politicians whom Chesterton inveighed against in his political journalism should be presented as rallying to the Distributist cause is surprising enough; that they should be the first heroes of the Distributist revolution is almost unbelievable. Even Fisher's detachment and long period of inactivity implies a kind of political patience which seems to be at odds with Chesterton's repeated calls for immediate action. Fisher's story does of course reiterate the political commonplace that knowledge must precede action, which Chesterton expressed in his early fiction. But it also suggests that the opportune moment for action will be created with very little action required on anyone's part. Time itself clarifies political issues and polarizes political forces. What the novel describes is an almost Marxist process, whereby history moves towards an inevitable revolution which those who have most reason to dread, do most to bring about. The financial clique, who stand in the background of the novel, have every reason to preserve the favourable *status quo*, but they are driven by a kind of suicidal instinct to create the unbearable conditions which transform the politicians they have manipulated into patriots and revolutionaries.

It is only if one considers the novel in terms of Harold March's political education that one finds a story which is in keeping with the official Distributist view. And even then there are some surprises. The alignment of forces at the end of the novel which reverses March's political assumptions represents accurately enough Chesterton's own disillusionment with Liberalism. The alliance of the financiers with the Liberal Press which surprises March would surprise no one who was familiar with Chesterton's political journalism. But the tripartite alliance between mutinous Irish regiments, corrupt politicians, and a brutal mob, is as much a shock for any student of Chesterton's writing as it is for Harold March. One might say that the final lesson March's political education teaches is a caution about drawing simple conclusions. But one would also have to add that what the novel finally suggests and what Chesterton's political journalism never makes clear is that when the Distributist revolution happens the Distributist may find that his chief difficulty is recognizing his friends.

Tales of the Long Bow marks a significant departure in Chesterton's novels. In its themes, it belongs to the group of novels which begins with *The Man Who Knew Too Much* and ends with *The Return of Don Quixote*, but in its treatment of social and political themes it is very different. Like *The Man Who Knew Too Much*, it uses the device of eight linked stories to which Chesterton was to return in two of his final novels. But instead of recounting the political experience of a central character and the political education of his confidant, the novel recounts the adventures of the seven members of the League of the Long Bow, a half-comic and completely informal association of friends, each of whom performs an apparently hopeless task which a proverb suggests to be impossible.[77] These eccentric adventures provide the novel with its precarious unity and support its central theme, which is concerned with the restoration of rural England. The appropriateness of stories drawn from homely rural proverbs to a novel about agrarian society scarcely needs to be commented upon. What is more significant is that the same adventures which prove the falsity of proverbial fatalism by 'the doing of things recognized as impossible to do' also help to bring about the apparently equally impossible restoration of an English peasantry. And so the novel ends with the first complete description of a Distributist revolution and a Distributist State.

Another and more curious way in which the book marks a point of departure is the appearance of Chesterton in the novel as the narrator.[78] It is a device he uses again, although far less skilfully, in *The Return of Don Quixote*. It is possible to argue about what he actually achieves by the obtrusive Thackeray style of narration. The relation he forms with the readers can indeed be sometimes irritating, and the repeated references to the 'indomitable'[79] or 'exhausted and broken-spirited'[80] reader become wearisome by repetition. But in the loosely episodic serial publication, the novel gains from the engaging presence of the storyteller. The effect is very similar to that of Chesterton's very successful talks on the B.B.C. in the late twenties and early thirties.[81] There is the same range in tone from self-deprecation and playful irony to serious and earnest concern. The difference is that, unlike the radio talks, he is not merely a voice but almost a character in his own novel. He bids the readers goodbye and invites them back to hear the next episode, and at the beginning of a chapter he often welcomes them back and comments on the story they are about to hear. The most obvious characteristic of his comments is their air of self-mockery. Reading is described as the heavy price one pays to satisfy curiosity,[82] or as a torment to be endured,[83] and his efforts at story-telling as 'singularly unproductive and unprofitable labours'.[84] At the end of the novel, he wonders how many of his audience have left or have fallen asleep,[85] and he speaks of the story as the recounting of a private political dream whose images are '[the] shadows of the shapes in his own private and comfortable nightmare'.[86] At the same time, he insists that the story he deprecates means a great deal to him, even if it does not mean as much to the readers. And after rapidly reviewing the imagery which lies behind several of the adventures,[87] he concludes on a note which blends self-mockery with complete seriousness: 'Images are in their nature indefensible, if they miss the imagination of another; and the foolish scribe of the Long Bow will not commit the last folly of defending his dreams.'[88]

In addition to underlining the connection between the novel and his personal political views and giving the novel the support of his powerful personality, the narrative technique also enables him to turn his irony against the faults and mannerisms of the story he narrates. He becomes the first critic of his own novel. Thus he seems aware that a novel in which a mathematical theory becomes a starting-point for something called 'an astronomical allegory'[89] is a novel in which allegory is carried to extravagant lengths. In earlier novels, characters act out allegories, but never allegories as complicated as this and never with the same fondness for commentary and explanation:

'I understand his astronomical theory a good deal better than he thinks I do. And, let me tell you, his astronomical theory is an astronomical allegory.'

'An allegory?' repeated Crane. 'What of?'

'An allegory of us,' said Pierce; 'and, as with many an allegory, we've acted it without knowing it . . .'[90]

Chesterton the narrator mocks this fondness for allegorical interpretation which characterizes his own story. On one occasion, he even draws the reader's attention to an allegorical setting which isn't there. 'At this point,' he remarks, 'a symbolic cloud ought to have come across the sun.'[91]

The criticism of the narrator is also echoed by other characters. Audrey Smith, who anticipates in a curious way Gabriel Gale's method of sociological painting in *The Poet and the Lunatics*,[92] warns her fiancé that literary conventions can sometimes distort the reality which they are supposed to clarify:

'I told you I was an artist, and didn't know much about literature,' she said. 'Well, do you know, it really does make a difference. Literary people let words get between them and things. We do at least look at the things and not the names of the things. You think a cabbage is comic because the name sounds comic and vulgar; something between "cab" and "garbage," I suppose. But a cabbage isn't really comic or vulgar. You wouldn't think so if you simply had to paint it. Haven't you seen Dutch and Flemish galleries, and don't you know what great men painted cabbages? What they saw was certain lines and colours; very wonderful lines and colours.'[93]

Another unusual feature of the narrative technique is the use of an imaginary social historian to narrate the history of the revolution.[94] When Owen Hood reads this history to his house-party guests at the end of the novel, the characters once again begin to criticize the record of the events in which they have taken part. But this Chinese-box technique is not presented for its own sake, since it contributes directly to the meaning of the novel. The history is first of all an official account of a revolution which has already happened. The events leading to the revolution are carefully recorded in the first seven chapters, and one expects that the final chapter will provide an account of the revolution as it actually happens. This is not the case. For the eighth chapter is set some time after the successful conclusion of the revolutionary war, which is only recalled by the reading of the history and by the occasional comments of Hood and his guests.

The significance of this shift from pre-revolutionary to post-revolutionary times is worth examining. In a way it recalls a similar technique employed by Conrad in *Nostromo*. In both novels, everything seems to be leading to the direct description of a revolutionary war. But at the moment when the adventure reaches its apparent climax, the narrative abruptly ends and the next scene is placed in the calm of post-revolutionary times, in which a somewhat uninformed narrator attempts to reconstruct what has happened. Chesterton's anonymous historian does not bear much resemblance to Conrad's Captain Mitchell, but the effect of their narratives is very similar. The account of the Sulaco rebellion is based on a conventional and superficial knowledge of Costaguanaean politics and the unimaginative and rather stupid official history betrays no misgivings about the triumph of material interests. But this naïve and uncritical acceptance of the surface view of things compels the reader to question the complacent assumptions about modern politics which he may perhaps have shared with Captain Mitchell. The very limitations and distortions of the narrative draw attention to the inner significance of the novel. Chesterton's historian is at once better informed and more intelligent; he is described as being 'a rather clever fellow, detached but understanding and a little ironical on the right side'.[95]

But despite this detachment and ironic intelligence, his failure to understand the significance of the revolution is as almost complete as Captain Mitchell's. The meaning of the 'conflagration in which much of modern civilization had been consumed'[96] is found not in the historian's witty account of military tactics and official fatuities, but in the quiet scene of domestic happiness in which his history is read. By saving English agriculture, the League of the Long Bow makes possible the simple house-party at which the reading of a book is interrupted by random questions about children and gardens. What the novel makes plain and what the historian shows no sign of understanding is that the revolution is justified by the private happiness it secures. 'I shouldn't call that our history,' Elizabeth Hood remarks to her husband. 'I'm devoutly thankful that nobody can ever write our history or put it in a book.'[97] This implies first of all an ironic contrast between the failure of Chesterton's historian and the success of Chesterton the chronicler in understanding the Distributist revolution. For the remark is after all recorded by the chronicler in the book which it is supposedly impossible to write. More importantly, however, the remark suggests the pre-eminence of private over public life, which is the real point of the novel. Indeed Mr and Mrs Hood's rather dull house-party, in which they entertain the revolutionary leaders, is remarkably close to the picture of the post-revolutionary society Chesterton once described in the *New Age*[98] and close also to the Utopia which H. G. Wells had once challenged him to write:[99]

And if I were a poet writing an Utopia, if I were a magician waving a wand, if I were a God making a Planet, I would deliberately make it a world of give and take, rather than a world of sharing . . . in the many Utopian pictures of comrades feasting together, I do not remember one that had the note of hospitality, of the difference between host and guest and the difference between one house and another. No one brings up the port that his father laid down; no one is proud of the pears grown in his own garden.

If ever the actual poor move to destroy this evil [badly distributed property], they will do it with the object not only of giving every man private property, but very specially private property; they will probably exaggerate in that direction; for in that direction is the whole humour and poetry of their own lives. For the Revolution, if they make it, there will be all the features which they like and I like, the strong sense of English cosiness, the instinct for special festival, the distinction between the dignities of man and woman, [the] responsibility of a man under his roof.[100]

The narrative method of *Tales of the Long Bow*, which culminates with the history of the revolution, has therefore several advantages. It creates the comfortable relationship of storyteller and listener, which is ideally suited to a loosely episodic serial novel. It relates the novel more directly to Distributist political views by introducing Chesterton the Distributist as the narrator. It exploits the wide range of tone in narrative voices for the purposes of irony and satire. And it provides a valuable clue to the meaning of Distributist sub-ordination of political life to family virtues.

An understanding of the narrative method is therefore a necessary preliminary to an understanding of the novel's central theme, which is concerned with the relationship of politics to family life. Political activity in the novel is not only directed towards domestic happiness, it is inspired by it. Each of the stories recounted is a love story, and the political adventures are merely the history of the way in which the members of the League fall in love and marry. The Distributist politics of each hero are after all the expression of his love for a particular woman. The story of Captain Pierce provides the most obvious example of a pattern which is repeated throughout the novel. His involvement in politics is entirely incidental to his love for Joan Hardy. The extravagant efforts he makes to supply provisions for her father's inn and the extravagant efforts the government makes to prevent his doing so do indeed help to bring about the revolution. But in themselves, they are simply incidents in a grotesque kind of courtship. Similarly it is only after Owen Hood again meets Elizabeth Seymour that he begins his political campaign against Dr Hunter. Until then, he is content to sit by the river with his attention fixed entirely in the past, like an attenuated version of Horne Fisher. The same is true of Green and Blair and perhaps true of White, all of whom join the revolution only because they have fallen in love.

Even the turbulent career of Enoch Oates seems to have been inspired by a perfectly genuine love for his absurd wife.

This emphasis on family life marks perhaps the most significant difference between *Tales of the Long Bow* and *The Man Who Knew Too Much*. The Distributist ideal of the family and the family farm necessarily involves women. And despite Chesterton's well-known and frequently expressed distaste for women taking part in any kind of political activity, the novel suggests that in the Distributist revolution they will even be involved in the fighting. 'In all wars of peasants defending their farms and homes,' one of the characters remarks, 'women have been very much on the spot.'[101] The role of women in the novel is therefore not so much to humanize the world of politics, but to remind both the heroes and the readers that the values of domestic life are of primary importance in the Distributist state. Politics exist to serve not so much the individual as the family. What Distributism is really concerned with can be seen in the glowing pictures of bizarre romances and happy marriages. Government has no other function than to make this kind of life possible. As Blair explains, 'You can't have the family farm without the family. You must have concrete Christian marriage again.'[102]

But a close examination of 'the concrete Christian marriages' in the novel reveals some curious and unexpected anomalies in the Distributist ideal. Despite the frequent references to the new equality of the English people, all the characters accept the assumptions of a hierarchical society and of sharply-marked class distinctions with complete unselfconsciousness. Joan Hardy's comment on her father's attitude towards her marriage is characteristic: 'He says he doesn't believe in people marrying out of their class; but that if I must marry a gentleman he'd rather it was somebody like you, and not one of the new gentlemen.'[103] Moreover the social types that are left out of the novel are as significant as the ones that are included. The absence of representatives of the working classes is perhaps explained by the novel's emphasis on the land question, since one might argue that the appearance of factory workers is logically deferred to *The Return of Don Quixote*, which deals explicitly with the industrial side of the Distributist programme. But one might have expected someone to represent the rural population in what is after all supposed to be the story of an agrarian revolution. There is, of course, Archer the gardener. But as an expatriate Cockney who only takes up gardening as a kind of hobby and perversely refuses to become a member of the post-revolutionary peasantry, he is perhaps a rather unsatisfactory example. And one misses, too, what might be called the Wellsian small shop-keepers and business men, who, one would have thought, would have been as much at home in this novel as they were in *The Napoleon of Notting Hill*.

The social and political backgrounds of the social types who found the Distributist families are curious to say the least. They include a retired lawyer, an Anglo-Indian Colonel, a Flying Officer, an eccentric Vicar, and a young don who has made his reputation with a recondite mathematical theory, as well as an aeronautical engineer who invents secret weapons, and an American millionaire. Take them how you will, they are an odd collection of social types to bring about the Distributist revolution. The law, the military, the Established Church, pure and applied science, and American Capitalism: it is not the kind of social arithmetic one would have expected from the champion of the common man. The list could scarcely be improved if one were writing a left-wing parody of a reactionary alliance.

And nothing of the little which is said about the political views of the members of the League does anything to quiet one's misgivings. Colonel Crane describes himself quite simply as a Tory and traditionalist. Robert Owen Hood, as his name suggests, inherits a family tradition which is vaguely revolutionary; but this is somewhat undercut by his antiquarian interests and his hatred of industrialism as such. Despite his claim to be a radical (or perhaps because of it), his political position seems to be at least as conservative as the Colonel's. When they do disagree it is only in having different reasons for arriving at the same conclusion, as their comments on Pierce's marriage to the innkeeper's daughter make abundantly clear:

> The Colonel blinked a little. 'Well, times change,' he said. 'I suppose I'm old-fashioned myself; but speaking as an old Tory, I must confess he might do worse.'
>
> 'Yes,' replied Hood, 'and speaking as an old Radical, I should say he could hardly do better.'[104]

None of the other members of the League begins with an identifiable political philosophy, unless Parson White's perennial and obscure quarrel with Lord Arlington about rural problems is meant to represent a primitive form of the Distributist belief which they all eventually accept.

In fact the marriages of the revolutionary council present the strongest evidence of the traditionalism and class-consciousness of the new movement. Viewed politically and socially, the marriages, far from altering political conservatism, serve only to strengthen and reinforce it. Colonel Crane's wife, it is true, enjoys the reputation of being a somewhat Bohemian painter, and even continues her career after her marriage. But she is also a cousin of Mr Vernon-Smith of Heatherbrae and is therefore related to the most conventional and stolid middle-class element in the Colonel's conventional and wealthy middle-class suburb. Owen Hood, Wilding White, and Bellow Blair, each of them marries daughters of the oldest and most respectable families in their respective neighbourhoods. White's wife, 'the daughter of a country gentleman',[105] is almost a caricature of the formidable county lady, organizing village fêtes and directing them with a firm hand. Blair's wife is the daughter of an impoverished Irish squire whom he describes as a princess from a Celtic poem. The marriage of Hood, ostensibly the least class-conscious of the group, provides the clearest evidence of the social tone of the marriages. There is no hint that the old Radical considers class a matter of little importance. Indeed there is scarcely a reference to his wife that is not also a reminder of her social position:

But though she was not old she had always been a little old-fashioned; for she came of a forgotten aristocracy whose women had moved with a certain gravity as well as grace about the old country houses, before coronets were sold like cabbages or the Jews lent money to squires. But her husband was old-fashioned too; though he had just taken part in a successful revolution and bore a revolutionary name, he also had his prejudices; and one of them was a weakness for his wife being a lady—especially that lady.[106]

The marriage of Enoch Oates, perhaps because he is an American, is not commented upon. But the marriages of Green and Pierce seem at first to be more unconventional and more democratic. Marriages to a publican's and a farmer's daughter might seem to be a good illustration of the way in which Distributism occasionally breaks down barriers of class. But the effect is rather spoiled by the frequent hints that they have not really married very far beneath themselves. We learn that Joan Hardy's father enjoys the status not indeed of a gentleman, but 'at least of a yeoman'.[107] Marjory Dale's father, one of the first of the new peasants, is a person of substance before the marriage and is 'already respected in that county',[108] and we are no sooner told that Marjory milks cows than we are quickly reminded that she 'was not in the common connotation what is meant as a milkmaid'.[109] There is even a somewhat patronizing suggestion that the Distributist farmers are rapidly on the way to becoming squires: 'These new peasant farmers must be treated like small squires and not like tenants or serfs.'[110] Everything considered, the marriages of middle-class eccentrics to the daughters of wealthy farmers or impoverished squires does not seem to indicate a particularly hopeful beginning for an egalitarian society.

The essentially conservative character of the League marriages becomes clearer when one looks at the social backgrounds of their opponents. The most obvious thing that can be said about the enemies of the revolution is that they are all of them social outsiders. Rosenbaum Low is another crude caricature of a Jewish financier, who, from Chesterton's point of view, is by definition a rootless person. Lord Normantowers' obscure social origin is sufficiently indicated by the preposterous title, which he seems to have chosen in a pathetic attempt at what the psychologists call compensation. Dr Hunter moves rapidly from class to class, without ever quite belonging to any of them. It is significant that the narrator speaks of 'the dubious and wavering atmosphere' of his world,[111] and that Pierce dismisses him contemptuously as 'a quack doctor on the make'.[112] It is true that Lord Eden, the Prime Minister, has a fixed social position as a member of the aristocracy, but he is representative of an old but stagnant social class which has betrayed its trust by following fashion instead of preserving tradition. That may be why his appearance combines 'a factitious air of youth'[113] with a lined and wrinkled face which gives 'almost a shock of decrepitude'.[114] Taken as a group, the opponents of the League are in fact very similar to the alien alliance which confronted Horne Fisher and his friends. They are perhaps more urban and less eastern than the Oriental cosmopolitans that Fisher had to fight, but the east-west geographical symbolism is the same, with the Distributist experiment established once more in western England and the opposing armies attacking from the east.

But if the popular conception of the Distributist ideal is partly compromised by the Distributist marriages, it is far more seriously damaged by the part played by Enoch Oates in the novel. The implications of this curious episode are far-reaching indeed. That an American millionaire should be the *deus ex machina* of the Distributist revolution is astonishing enough, but what is especially odd is that Oates is the kind of millionaire that Chesterton always claimed to find particularly odious. His fortune has been made, as we are told with a disarming candour, by what amounts to 'robbery on a large scale'.[115] And his social type is defined in terms which would seem to put him beyond the Chestertonian pale: 'He was a Puritan and a Prohibitionist and a Pacifist and an Internationalist; in short, everything that is in darkness and the shadow of death.'[116] At least as unlikely a champion for the Distributist State, one would have thought, as Horne Fisher's relatives. The explanation which is given for this improbable change does not altogether succeed in making it believable, although the half-ironic use of the language of religious conversion is certainly significant:

'It's something to produce a penitent millionaire. And I do believe that poor Enoch Oates has seen the light (thanks to my conversations at lunch); since I talked to him, Oates is another and a better man.'

. . .

'His heart's in the right place. It's on his sleeve. That's why I preached the gospel to the noble savage and made him a convert.'
'But what did you convert him to?' inquired the other.
'Private property,' replied Pierce promptly. 'Being a millionaire he had never heard of it.'[117]

In fact the role of Enoch Oates suggests an inconsistency in Distributism which is symptomatic of an inner lack of confidence. It suggests a moral inconsistency, because Distributism, which exists largely as a remedy to the evils of Capitalism, is now represented as being financed by money which is derived from the worst kind of Capitalism. It would seem to be a degradation of the Distributist State that it should become for Chesterton's Oates the same kind of rich man's hobby that

Sulaco became for Conrad's Holroyd. One would think that money accumulated by grinding the faces of the poor in America is no less poisoned than money accumulated by grinding the faces of the poor in England. Rosenbaum Low's millions would do just as well. It is as if the moral meaning of Oates's wealth is never seriously considered, so that one is disturbed by the echoes from Ruskin which one does not hear:

One mass of money is the outcome of action which has created,— another of action which has annihilated,—ten times as much in the gathering of it; such and such strong hands have been paralysed, as if they had been numbed by nightshade: so many strong men's courage broken, so many productive operations hindered; this and the other false direction given to labour, and lying image of prosperity set up on Dura plains dug into seven-times-heated furnaces. That which seemed to be wealth may in verity be only the gilded index of far-reaching ruin; a wrecker's handful of coin gleaned from the beach to which he has beguiled an argosy; a camp-follower's bundle of rags unwrapped from the breasts of goodly soldiers dead; the purchasepieces of potter's fields, wherein shall be buried together the citizen and the stranger.[118]

Finally it is inconsistent that the good nature which is supposed to explain Oates's generosity in giving away his money should survive undamaged the long years of crime during which he acquired it.

The inconsistency suggests an inner lack of confidence because it implies that the success of the Distributist revolution depends on the unlikely financial support of the very enemy it seeks to destroy. For the novel makes clear that the agrarian state would never be introduced by the revolution if it had not already been set up in microcosm by Enoch Oates's millions. The peasants whose support is decisive at the critical moment of the war have after all been created by Enoch Oates years before the war begins. Because of the lavish financing of the Distributist experiment, western England is already a Distributist state before the war which is supposed to introduce Distributism. What the novel implies is that without the support of modern Capitalism there is no possibility of mounting an effective attack on Capitalism. The hope that promises that this might happen is equivalent to the despair that answers that it will never happen.

A partial explanation of what seems to be an inexplicable

volte-face in Chesterton's political thinking can perhaps be found in the record of his first visit to the United States in 1920.[119] *What I Saw in America* provides the first evidence of the new and surprisingly sympathetic view of American businessmen, which receives another expression in the character of Enoch Oates. In this travel-book, Chesterton argues that in contrast to their counterparts in Europe, American businessmen possess an engaging idealism which makes them more interested in making money than in having money.[120] The moral implications of what they do seem never to occur to them, so that amid cruelty and social injustice they preserve a kind of unworldliness which amounts to a kind of innocence. Indeed Chesterton's account of his meeting with Henry Ford[121] reads very much like the chronicler's account of the first meeting with Enoch Oates. And it does make a certain amount of sense, as well as adding a touch of grim irony to the novel, that the financiers should be ruined by a financier, and particularly by a financier they despise and hope to make use of. In a sense the situation is merely the reverse of the one described in *The Man Who Knew Too Much*. Horne Fisher receives unexpected help from the politicians in order to defeat the financiers, and the members of the League of the Long Bow receive help from a financier in order to defeat the politicians. And although one may doubt whether the Henry Fords and the Enoch Oateses are the democratic rough diamonds Chesterton describes, the accuracy of his critique of American business is not the essential point at issue. The dream that Distributism might receive this kind of eccentric and suicidal support may indeed be preposterous, but there is a valuable and subtle insight into human complexity in the picture of a man who keeps his self-respect and basic kindness after a life-time of cruelty and social irresponsibility.

A more complete and perhaps more satisfactory explanation of Oates can be found in the theory of nationalism elaborated in the novel. Colonel Crane's metaphor for nations as tribes with nose-rings and tribes without nose-rings implies the complete impossibility of judging another people. Oates is saved from censure not because he is a millionaire, but because he is an American. The suggestion is that no nation is capable of understanding another nation. Therefore no one can speak with any assurance about the faults of any people except his own. The faults and the qualities of Oates can be evaluated only by

Americans. The apology to Oates and the invitation to him to
join the League represent the translation of this theory into
action; they can receive help from him, because they believe
they have no way of judging foreigners. Political and economic
systems which seem to contradict everything the League stands
for escape condemnation by being incomprehensible. The
League of the Long Bow with its English puns and English
proverbs must remain a national and consequently a private
joke, and the corollary of this somewhat smug insularity is a
complete and radical agnosticism about foreigners and foreign
politics.

The novel presses this political and perhaps moral relativism
to its logical conclusion. Enoch Oates's final enthusiasm for
something called alternately a United States of Europe, a
Universal Peasant Republic, or a World State of Workers on
the Land, receives no encouragement from the founders of the
League. Distributism, it seems, is not for export. The agrarian
revolution which saves English agriculture has no necessary
relevance to the kind of revolution that might be needed in
Lithuania, Spain or Asia—to use some of the examples Hilary
Pierce actually cites. Each country must come to its own
political and economic arrangement. The logic of the novel's
politics is that of an extreme sort of non-intervention in foreign
affairs:

'What's the good of talking to me about a World State,' growled
Hood. 'Didn't I say I preferred a Heptarchy?'
'Don't you understand?' interrupted Hilary Pierce excitedly.
'What can we have to do with international republics? We can turn
England upside down if we like; but it's England that we like, which-
ever way up. Why, our very names and phrases, the very bets and
jokes in which the whole thing began, will never be translated.'[122]

The Distributist state must never become the Distributist
empire. Chesterton remains loyal to the anti-Imperialism of his
first novel: it is as if the League of the Long Bow is determined
not to repeat the folly of Notting Hill. The variety and colour
expressed by the existence of separate nations also implies the
variety and colour of separate national political and social
systems, which no foreigner can ever fully understand or
presume to judge. Thus the meaning of Enoch Oates's role in
the novel is explained by a peculiar theory of nationalism. As
the product of another culture, he remains a puzzling and

ultimately incomprehensible phenomenon. It is this suspension
of understanding and judgment which enables him to play an
important and unexpected role in the novel. A liability is
turned into an advantage.

With the exception of this theory of nationalism, the political
content of the novel offers few surprises. This is particularly
true of the treatment of Socialism, which follows entirely
familiar lines. In effect, the novel merely dramatizes the
argument which Chesterton had expressed as early as 1909 in
the *New Age* and which he outlined in *The Flying Inn*.[123] The
governing classes accept Socialism in theory but take care that
they administer it, so that what is established is not Socialism
but the Servile State. Pure Socialism can in fact never be
established because of a human need for property, and the
establishment of what is supposed to be Socialism marks the
furthest extension of tyranny. The anti-Socialist slogan 'Don't
Nationalize but Rationalize' with which the politicians win
one election is simply reversed in order to win another. And as
one of them comments, 'It comes to the same thing.'[124] The
scene in which Lord Eden explains his plan for land nationaliza-
tion is therefore largely a repetition of what Chesterton had
written fifteen years before:

> 'Damn it all!' said the Prime Minister, with his first flash of
> impatience and sincerity. 'Can't you see you'll get twice as much as
> before? First you'll be compensated for losing your castle, and then
> you'll be paid for keeping it.'
> 'My Lord,' said Lord Normantowers humbly, 'I apologize for
> anything I may have said or suggested. I ought to have known I
> stood in the presence of a great English statesman.'
> 'Oh, it's easy enough,' said Lord Eden frankly. 'Look how easily
> we remained in the saddle, in spite of democratic elections; how we
> managed to dominate the Commons as well as the Lords. It'll be the
> same with what they call Socialism. We shall still be there; only we
> shall be called bureaucrats instead of aristocrats.'[125]

The cynical exposition of what is meant by 'true Socialism' is
the least interesting feature of Lord Eden's strange character.
Far more significant is the way in which he is used to connect
Tales of the Long Bow with *The Return of Don Quixote*.[126] In a
curious way, he provides the intelligence and the memory which
link the two novels. For although *The Return of Don Quixote* was
published after *Tales of the Long Bow*, it takes place in a fictional

time which precedes *Tales of the Long Bow*. And although the
two novels are quite distinct works of fiction, the reader is
able to bring to his reading of one novel the knowledge he has
gained from a reading of the other. In this way a note of
dramatic irony is added to the later novel. For the reader who
remembers Lord Eden's bitter opposition to the League of the
Long Bow understands at once that the League of the Lion in
The Return of Don Quixote is doomed from the moment Lord
Eden appears as its champion. Moreover Lord Eden's own
memory is as important as the memory of the reader, for he is
the only character with a memory that goes back to the time of
The Return of Don Quixote and beyond it to the Edwardian years
of his youth; and he is the only character with intelligence
enough to understand the significance of what he remembers:

> He was the only man there who understood that the England
> about him was not the England that had surrounded his youth and
> supported his leisure and luxury; that things were breaking up, first
> slowly and then more and more swiftly, and that the things detach-
> ing themselves were both good and evil. And one of them was this
> bald, broad and menacing new fact: a peasantry.[127]

Thus by a characteristic paradox Chesterton's novels are en-
riched by a character's memory of the past and the reader's
memory of the future.

One recalls that Maurice Baring makes use of a similar
though far more elaborate and demanding literary device in
his early chronicle novels.[128] As in Chesterton, an understanding of one novel is improved by a knowledge of another.
Thus the meaning of the conclusion of *Cat's Cradle* depends
partly at least on a knowledge of *C*. The apparently casual
reference to Bernard lunching with Leila Bucknell is meant to
trigger the reader's memory and enable him to understand
that the tragedy of *C* is about to be repeated. The value of the
tenuous link which Chesterton provides between the last two
of the Distributist novels is more difficult to evaluate. But it
seems clear that, in creating an additional irony, it also draws
attention to the way in which the novels deal with complementary sides of Distributist politics. The almost exclusive
emphasis on the land programme in the *Tales of the Long Bow*
is balanced by that on the industrial politics in *The Return of
Don Quixote*. Read in isolation, there is danger that each novel

will distort the meaning of Distributism; the presence of Lord
Eden in both of them is a reminder of the two sides of the
Distributist programme and their relationship to each other.

No study of *Tales of the Long Bow* would be complete which
did not consider the strangely poignant note of melancholy
on which the novel ends. The final comment on the successful
revolution and the successful establishment of the Distributist
State seems to throw the entire achievement into doubt. That
this comment is made by Owen Hood, the most idealistic
member of the League, is all the more astonishing. The affirmation of the seriousness of political concern is undercut by the
affirmation of the transitoriness of all political achievements.
The lighthearted breaking of proverbs which results in the
creation of the agrarian state will be remembered only in a
book of comic literature in which a frivolous story-teller entertains an equally frivolous audience:

'All our battles began as jokes and they will end as jokes,' said
Owen Hood, staring at the smoke of his cigar as it threaded its way
towards the sky in grey and silver arabesque. 'They will linger only
as faintly laughable legends, if they linger at all; they may pass an
idle hour or fill an empty page; and even the man who tells them
will not take them seriously. It will all end in smoke like the smoke
I am looking at; in eddying and topsy-turvy patterns hovering for
a moment in the air. And I wonder how many, who may smile or
yawn over them, will realize that where there was smoke there was
fire.'[129]

Hood's melancholy summing-up of the agrarian achievement
echoes in a particularly appropriate way the question which
Auberon Quin asks at the conclusion of *The Napoleon of Notting
Hill*: '. . . if what is achieved by all these efforts be only the
common contentment of humanity, why do men so extrava-
gantly toil and die in them? Has nothing been done by Notting
Hill that any chance clump of farmers or clan of savages would
not have done without it?'[130] But in the first novel Quin is
answered by Wayne, who has already asserted the value of his
comic epic, even though it has ended in failure:

'. . . the doom of failure that lies on all human systems does not in
real fact affect them any more than the worms of the inevitable
grave affect a children's game in a meadow. Notting Hill has fallen;
Notting Hill has died. But that is not the tremendous issue. Notting
Hill has lived.'[131]

In *Tales of the Long Bow,* failure is anticipated at the moment of complete success. But instead of glorying like Wayne in the temporary triumph of the human spirit over the brutal inevitability of failure, Hood can see only the absurdity and apparent pointlessness of the endeavour. It is surely significant that the character in the novel, who in his idealism most closely resembles Wayne, should express the scepticism which is characteristic of Auberon Quin. In a perceptive essay, written in the early twenties, Shaw describes the melancholy he notes in the post-War writings of Chesterton: 'Something—perhaps the youthful sense of immortality, commonly called exuberance—has lifted a little and left him scanning the grey horizon with more sense that the wind is biting and the event is doubtful.'[132] This may be so. The comment is certainly accurate as a description of the post-War essays, but when applied to *Tales of the Long Bow* it is a serious understatement of the case. It is not the doubtfulness of the event which the novel questions, but the value and meaning of the event once it has been gained.

The Return of Don Quixote was serialized in *G.K.'s Weekly* from 12 December 1925 to 13 November 1926,[133] and was published as a book in 1927. It completes much of what Chesterton's early fiction expresses by developing themes first dealt with in *The Napoleon of Notting Hill* and *The Ball and the Cross,* and it completes the themes dealt with in the Distributist novels by balancing the exclusively agrarian emphasis of *Tales of the Long Bow* with an emphasis on the meaning and implications of industrialism. More tightly constructed than any other of the novels, it is written with remarkable care and skill, and in spite of the complexity of its design there are few details which do not contribute to the unity of the whole. The more general allegory of the early novels and the more narrowly political allegory of the early Distributist novels now achieve a point of equilibrium. For the second time Chesterton appears in one of his novels in the role of chronicler, and although he makes a less successful use of this narrative method than he does in *Tales of the Long Bow,* he derives many of the same benefits from it, particularly in the use of the familiar authorial voice to help hold together a novel which is broken into serial parts as small as a half-chapter in length.[134] Finally Chesterton is more successful in this novel than in any other in turning his vivid sense of colour to the symbolic and political ends of his fiction.

In her biography of Chesterton, Maisie Ward devotes these three sentences to the novel:

Don Quixote is a fantasia about the future: in which the study of heraldry leads to the discovery of England and the centuries of her happiness and of her faith. Increasingly Gilbert saw the only future for his country in a re-marriage between those divorced three hundred years ago: England and the Catholic Church. *Don Quixote* is among the less good of his books, but like all the works of these years it is saturated with Catholicism.[135]

It is difficult to understand how Mrs Ward arrived at this inaccurate and misleading evaluation of the novel. In fact the setting of the story is far more contemporary than futuristic: the slight element of fantasy is subordinated to an action which is supposed to take place soon after the Great War. It is significant that the turning-point of the novel is provided by a general strike which is very similar to the general strike of 1926, which occurred during the serialization of the novel.[136] As for Michael Herne's 'study of heraldry', it would be described more accurately as a cram-course, first in a particular period of European history and secondly in a particular kind of medieval law. What it leads to is not 'the discovery of England and the centuries of her happiness and of her faith', but the discovery that modern Syndicalism is far closer to medieval social thought than his own neo-medieval movement and that the chief results of his medieval fantasies had been the creation of what can only be described as a Fascist state.[137] Not only that, but the action of the novel and any discoveries that are made originate not in Herne's hastily conducted research, but in Olive Ashley's amateur play and in her search for the lost illumination colour. It is appropriate that Mrs Ward should conclude her comments on the novel with a critical estimate which places it among 'the less good' of Chesterton's books.[138] Perceptive readers are more likely to see it as the culmination of Chesterton's fiction and to accept the judgment that it is perhaps the best and most interesting of all his novels.

Perhaps the best example of the complexity of the novel and its successful recapitulation of earlier themes is the way in which its political meaning is expressed through a series of complex human relationships. The story of the antagonism between

Michael Herne and John Braintree recalls the conflict between MacIan and Turnbull. Once again the romantic idealist quarrels with the scientific materialist. Although it is also true that Herne's politics blend Adam Wayne's neo-medieval-ism and MacIan's romantic Jacobitism, and that Braintree's Syndicalism adds something like Raymond Percy's social conscience to Turnbull's revolutionary Socialism. On the other hand, the contrast between Herne's humourless fanaticism and Douglas Murrell's ironic detachment recalls the central conflict of *The Napoleon of Notting Hill*. But in fact there are no adequate parallels to the grouping and re-grouping of the characters in the novel. Murrell, for example, is as much a foil to Braintree as he is to Herne, since his knowledge of the English poor is set in direct contrast both to Braintree's theoretic knowledge and, by implication, to Herne's antiquarian research. At the same time, Braintree and Herne each throw their own particular light on the flaws and qualities of Murrell's own political position.

The subsequent reversal of political viewpoints adds a further complexity to the novel. Braintree's Syndicalism is finally identified as the authentic medievalism which Herne was trying to express through the political movement which opposed Braintree. At the conclusion of the seventeenth chapter, Murrell is revealed as the ironic Sancho Panza and the embodiment of the comic spirit, and Herne as the modern Don Quixote and as the embodiment of romantic idealism:

> The bones of the gaunt, high-featured face, the flame-like fork of beard, the hollow and almost frantic eyes, were in a setting that startled with recognition. Rigid above the saddle of Rosinante, tall and in tattered arms, he lifted that vain lance that for three hundred years has taught us to laugh at the shaking of the spear. And behind him rose a vast yawning shadow like the very vision of that leviathan of laughter; the grotesque cab like the jaws of a derisive dragon pursuing him for ever, as the vast shadow of caricature pursues our desperate dignity and beauty, hanging above him forever threaten-ing like the wave of the world; and over all the lesser and lighter human spirit, not unkindly, looking down on all that is most high.[139]

At the same time, Herne himself insists both at the judgment-scene and at the end of the novel that Murrell is Don Quixote: 'It is you who lead and I who follow. You are not Sancho

E

Panza. You are the other.'[140] The real work of chivalry is performed not by Herne in the medieval pageant at Seawood Abbey, but by Murrell in the commonplace setting of a sea-side town and by Braintree in the grimy industrial town of Milldyke.

Moreover each of these shifting alliances is finally determined by the part played by women in the novel. Indeed in no novel of Chesterton is the role of women as important or as decisive as it is in *The Return of Don Quixote*. It might of course be said that the marriages are very similar to the marriages in the earlier novels. Certainly there are a number of parallels to the kind of balance which the marriages seem to represent, whether one thinks of MacIan's marriage to Beatrice and Turnbull's marriage to Madelaine in *The Ball and the Cross* or whether one thinks of the series of marriages announced at the end of *Manalive* and *Tales of the Long Bow*. In each instance, marriage expresses a re-established harmony: the end of strife in *The Ball and the Cross*, the conversion to Smith's philosophy of optimism in *Manalive*, and the restoration of the domestic virtues in *Tales of the Long Bow*. In *The Return of Don Quixote*, the marriages also represent the conventional happy endings of romantic comedy. As in Olive Ashley's sentimental play 'Blondel the Troubadour', which controls so much of the action of the novel, the marriages belong to an atmosphere 'accompanied by faint music and evening light, which corresponds to the grouping of figures near the footlights'.[141] Politically, the marriages bear a special resemblance to the marriages of *Tales of the Long Bow*. In both novels, political action is inspired by romantic love.

The distinctive element to the role of women in *The Return of Don Quixote* might be described as twofold: an emphasis on their individual character and an emphasis on their part in shaping the action of the novel. Not only does Olive Ashley write the play which inspires the central action of the novel, but she also sends Douglas Murrell on the quest for the illumination colours, which originates the secondary plot as well. Rosamund Severne plays an equally important part in bringing about the neo-medieval revolution. Everything Herne does is related directly to her, and it is clear that he would do nothing without her flair for practical action: in Murrell's words, she is 'a Man of Action'.[142] In *Tales of the Long Bow*, women provide the inspiration for political action, but remain essentially passive; in *The Return of Don Quixote*, they exercise an active and often independent political role. Consequently, unlike the heroines of the earlier novel, they bring to their marriages far more than the political implications of their social background. Each of them is simultaneously a sharply individualized character with a strong personality and a clearly defined political type.

That is why the marriages are as significant psychologically as they are politically. Olive Ashley's mysticism and passion for art complement Braintree's somewhat cheerless and theoretic cast of mind; Rosamund's love of action and social intrigue complement Herne's diffident and reflective character; and Dr Hendry's daughter provides a personal loyalty and moral commitment which Murrell needs and lacks. Politically, the balance is equally significant. Olive's marriage to Braintree creates an equilibrium between positions which are classically Rightist and Leftist: a romantic idealism tending towards the pageantry of Fascism corrects and is corrected by a scientific materialism tending towards a barrenly ideological Socialism. Rosamund's marriage to Herne reverses this order, since her practical energy, which originally provides the dynamic for Herne's romantic political movement, eventually provides the dynamic for his preoccupation with matters of individual injustice. The marriage of Dr Hendry's daughter to Murrell is the least obviously political in significance, although it might be argued that the transformation of the uncommitted Tory into a kind of amateur social reformer is partly explained by her direct experience of the kind of social distress which he had previously ignored.

The focus of the novel, however, is provided by two quite distinct but related actions. The first of these is Olive Ashley's play 'Blondel the Troubadour'; the second is her search for the lost illumination colour. Everything in the novel is connected to one of these lines of action, the first of which provides the chief element of allegory, and the second, the cluster of images and symbols by which the allegory achieves its final meaning.

It is Chesterton as narrator who comments on the importance of Olive Ashley's play to the central action of the novel. 'That alone,' he explains, 'could have rendered possible or credible the central incident in the story called "The Return of Don Quixote".'[143] No claim, however, is made for the play as a

work of art. The chronicler speaks of it as typical of the kind of
romantic drama popular in the pre-War years. Written by an
amateur for amateurs and meant for private production, it is,
like the plays of which it is representative, important not in
itself, but for its effect on those who take part in it. 'Such was
the play of "Blondel the Troubadour" ', he comments, 'not
altogether a bad specimen of the sentimental and old-fashioned
romance, popular before the war, but now only remembered
because of the romantic results which it afterwards produced
in real life.'[144]

It should also be noted that the image of the amateur theatre
is one that Chesterton returned to often in his life and writings.
There is the toy-theatre with which his father entertained him
as a child and which he describes at such great length in the
Autobiography;[145] and there are the plays which Chesterton
wrote and produced for the entertainment of his friends and
their children in his own home and to which he devoted hours
of careful preparation.[146]

The relevance of the play to the novel, although never
explicitly commented upon, is nonetheless sufficiently clear.
There is no need to underline the obvious point that it presents
the essential action of the novel in miniature. As a political
drama, it is concerned with the conflict between public and
private duty. Blondel's search for King Richard ends with the
King's refusal to return to England, because of the complete
breakdown of political life and the impossibility of his reforming
it. Blondel, who has sacrificed his romance to what he regards
as his public duty, interprets the King's decision as the sacrifice
of public duty to private romance. The play ends with the
reconciliation of the King and Blondel with the women they
love in much the same way that the novel ends with the
reconciliation of Braintree and Herne with Olive Ashley and
Rosamund Severne. But what the play chiefly foreshadows is
the political career of Michael Herne. Thus the King's abdication speech, which is spoken by Herne at the climax of the play,
is repeated by him at the climax of the novel. In both instances,
it is a pronouncement on the ineffectualness of romantic
politics in dealing with the political realities of modern
England; and in the second instance, it also identifies Herne's
failure to realize his romantic dream with Don Quixote's
failure to live in the world of romance:

The evil kings sit easy on their thrones
Shame healed with habit; but what panic aloft
What wild white terror if a king were good!
What pestilence of protection blanching all!
Men easily endure an unjust master,
But a just master no man will endure,
His nobles shall rise up, his knights betray him
And he go forth, as I go forth, alone.[147]

The theme expressed in these lines recalls *Manalive* and the way in which Innocent Smith's terrifying goodness involves a sort of secular judgment on all the characters he comes in contact with. More importantly, the lines anticipate the scene of Chesterton's last and unfinished play, *The Surprise*, in which the puppet-show, which is a romantic comedy in the first act, turns into a tragedy in the second act, when the life-size puppets come to life and repeat the same story with minds and wills of their own.[148] The relation of the play to *The Return of Don Quixote* is very similar. From the moment when Herne, with the encouragement of Rosamund Severne, refuses to return to ordinary life and ordinary clothing, the play begins to repeat itself in everyday life and everyday life begins to take on the colour of a tragic drama. The somewhat preposterous League of the Lion is as much a fantasy as it is a reality, but with the financial support of Lord Eden and his friends, it quickly becomes the 'famous revolution, or reaction, which transformed the face of English society and checked and changed the course of its history'.[149] The elaborate reconstruction of what is supposed to be a medieval political and social system with its colourful pageantry of a monarch and King-at-arms is essentially a translation of Olive Ashley's sentimental romance into contemporary political terms.

The moral failure of politics which are an extension of romantic drama is, however, never in any doubt. The presence of Lord Eden as the sponsor of the movement makes this clear from the beginning. For readers who recall *Tales of the Long Bow* it is at once obvious that the situation is analogous to the one described in the earlier novel with only the terms reversed. Herne's League of the Lion is the weapon with which Eden tries to defeat Braintree's kind of Socialism, just as Eden's kind of Socialism is the weapon with which he tries to defeat the Distributist League of the Long Bow. Eden's action provides a clue to the moral meaning of the conflict. The effect of his appearance in the novel is to identify Herne's romantic medievalism with the bogus Socialism of *Tales of the Long Bow*. And there is an interesting corollary to this identification, which suggests the close relationship between the agrarian movement of the earlier novel and the industrial movement of the later. At the end of *The Return of Don Quixote*, Herne sees Syndicalism as the expression of all that is valuable in the neo-medievalism which Lord Eden has exploited. At the beginning of the novel, the reader sees that Lord Eden's attack on Syndicalism suggests that Syndicalism and agrarianism are two aspects of a single political cause. The defence of human values in industrial England is a continuation of the defence of human values in rural England in the earlier novel, on another front, but against the same enemy.

Although Eden provides a link between the industrial town of Milldyke and the little farms of western England, the political meaning of his intervention is also defined by its relationship to Imperialism. The novel looks backward to the historical past as well as forward to the fictional future. Eden believes that the ruling classes are threatened by the new Socialism of Braintree, which has caught the popular imagination in a way which the old Socialism never did. In this situation he turns to the medieval movement of Herne which he hopes to use as a substitute for Imperialism. Like Imperialism, it is simultaneously a popular and an anti-popular movement, a circus which entertains the populace and at the same time diverts their attention from the political realities which it leaves unchanged. It has therefore the double advantage of distracting the people from the real social problems and defeating the one political movement which is likely to solve them:

'Did you ever know a party meeting that knew what it was voting about? They called themselves Socialists or something and we called ourselves Imperialists or something. But, as a matter of fact, things had got quieter and quieter on both sides. But now that this man Braintree has turned up, talking all their nonsense in a new sort of way, we don't seem to have any of our nonsense to call up against him. It used to be the Empire. But something has gone wrong with that; the damn Colonials would come over and people saw them, and there you are. They don't talk as if they wanted to die for us, and nobody seems to want very much to live with them.

But whatever it was, all that sort of picture and poetry of the thing seems to have given out on our side; just at the moment when something picturesque turns up on the other side.'[150]

Olive Ashley's play, transformed by Herne's antiquarian research, provides Eden with the 'picture and poetry' which Imperialism no longer possesses. But the League of the Lion, despite its similarity to Auberon Quin's Charter of the Cities, has a very different political meaning. Like Auberon's medievalism, it begins as a kind of game and by its appeal to idealism and romance it ends by creating a genuine enthusiasm. But whereas Auberon's charter is a private joke which happens to be taken seriously, Herne's League is a serious popular movement which happens to fall into the hands of a dangerous enemy of the people. To find an analogy to the situation, one would have to imagine Adam Wayne as the unconscious tool of the financial interests he opposes.

But the gap between what the League means for Herne and what the League means for Eden does create a kind of dramatic irony which is similar to the comic conflict between Wayne and Auberon Quin. The contrast between the theatrical appearance and the sinister political reality which lies behind it adds a note of poignancy both to the politician's cynicism and the idealist's fanaticism. Sometimes the contrast is implied, as for example, when Herne's painfully earnest explanation of his motives is followed by the scene in which Eden explains what the new movement means to him: 'Give the people plenty of sports—tournaments, horse-races—*panem et circenses*, my boy—that will do for a popular side to the policy. If we could mobilize all that goes to make the Derby we could fight the Deluge.'[151] At other times, the contrast between the two views is built into a single scene, such as the description of Herne's coronation, which the chronicler describes first as it appears to him and then as it appears to Lord Eden:

But Herne sat on his high throne above all the coloured crowd, and his eyes seemed to inhabit the horizons and the high places. So have many fanatics ridden high on clouds over scenes as preposterous; so Robespierre walked in his blue coat at the Feast of the Supreme Being. Lord Eden caught sight of those clear eyes, like still and shining pools, and muttered: 'The man is mad. It is dangerous for unbalanced men when their dreams come true. But the madness of a man may be the sanity of a society.'[152]

Herne's medievalism is, however, much more than a foil to
Eden's cynicism. Although it is ultimately revealed as an
illusion, it is also the central force which connects the
characters in the story and enables them to understand the
events in which they have taken part. Eden and his friends are
finally exposed by the movement they have manipulated, and
Herne finally acquires through it the political knowledge which
it originally conceals.[153] Not only that, but throughout the
novel it exercises a decisive influence on both its supporters
and its opponents. And it is from their changing attitude
towards it that the novel achieves its unity and its final political
synthesis.

For Olive Ashley the medieval league has both a personal
and a political significance. Personally, she sees it first of all as
the fulfilment of the inner vision of romance which she tried to
express through her play. Herne's claim to her political loyalty
depends, therefore, at the beginning, at least, on his ability to
understand and to interpret her incoherent romanticism. In a
passage which echoes in a curious way the words of the
mysterious guide in MacIan's dream, she tries to explain what
she means by this personal ideal:

'I don't know what King it is who ought to come back, any more
than anybody else does,' answered Olive steadily. 'King Arthur or
King Richard or King Charles or somebody. But Mr Herne does
know something about what those men meant by a king. I rather
wish Mr Herne really were King of England.'[154]

Politically, however, she sees medievalism as a sort of religion.
The private dream becomes a religious cause to which everything, including her love for Braintree, must be sacrificed. The
reality of kingship to Herne first becomes clear to her when he
rebukes Archer and defends Braintree:

For one instant the impression, or illusion, was stunning and
complete. He had spoken spontaneously and simply out of himself;
but it might have been a reincarnation. So exactly might Richard
the Lion Heart have spoken to a courtier who imputed cowardice
to Saladin.[155]

But it is Herne's attack on the social system which has ruined
Dr Hendry which makes her love for Braintree seem a betrayal
of filial piety and the national cause:

She seemed to have come suddenly to the end and edge of something; to a challenge and a choice. She was one of those women who cannot be stopped from hurting themselves, when once their moral sense is strongly moved. She needed a religion; and chiefly an altar on which to be a sacrifice. . . . She could not any longer maintain her merely romantic parley with the enemy, unless she was prepared honestly to go over to him. If she went over, she would go over for ever; and she had to consider what exactly she would leave behind. If it had been merely the whole world, or in other words society, she would not have hesitated; but it was England; it was patriotism; it was plain morals. If the new national cause had really been only an antiquarian antic, or a heraldic show, or even a sentimental reaction such as she might once have dreamed of, she could have brought herself easily to leave it. But now with her whole brain and conscience she was convinced that it would be like deserting the flag in a great war. Her conviction had been finally clinched by the denunciation of Hendry's oppressors in human and moving terms; the cause was the cause of her father's old friend and of her father.[156]

Braintree's own attitude towards medievalism is also curiously complex. In the reconstruction of a medieval social order and the return of kingship, he sees a serious threat to the egalitarian society he is trying to build. He is the first person to understand the serious political implications of the play and the serious political force represented by Herne.

'I don't like Kings,' replied Braintree rather roughly. 'I don't like knights and nobles and all that parade of armed aristocracy. But that man likes them. He doesn't only pretend to like them. He is not a snob or a silly flunkey of old Seawood. He is the only man I have ever seen who might really defy democracy and the revolution. I know it simply from the way he strode about that silly stage and spoke.'[157]

Nonetheless Braintree never fully understands the medieval league. Although he appreciates the sincerity of Herne and recognizes the dangers of his movement, he shows no signs of understanding either the appeal of romantic idealism or the way in which it is exploited by Lord Eden and his friends. The failure to estimate accurately the practical effectiveness of the league means that he is totally unprepared for the vigorous measures Herne takes to break the strike. Similarly his failure to understand that medievalism might eventually turn against

E*

the ruling class which supports it means that he is merely
bewildered by Herne's attack on Capitalism and defence of
Syndicalism.[158]

Braintree's inability to understand romantic politics is in
fact part of a larger failure in understanding. Douglas Murrell
demonstrates how little Braintree knows about the workers he
leads.[159] And it is significant that he knows nothing about
Herne's love for Rosamund until Olive Ashley tells him. As his
name suggests, he is the ideologist who understands nothing
which cannot be brought into his complete but narrow system
of political thought. In his own way, he is more isolated from
the world of actuality by Syndicalism than Herne is by
medievalism.

The shrewdest and most illuminating reaction to the medieval movement is provided by Douglas Murrell. The ironic
detachment, which makes him seem to be another version of
Auberon Quin, is blended with a sort of transcendent common-
sense, which gives his political comments a special value.
Consequently his criticism of Herne's new order goes much
further than Braintree's. His misgivings are based on an insight
into the English national character and the English historical
tradition. And although his criticism partially echoes the non-
Intervention theory of *Tales of the Long Bow*, it also detects the
incipient Fascism which lies behind the medieval pageantry:

'These high-handed ways don't suit us a bit, either revolutionary
or reactionary. The French and the Italians have frontiers and they
all feel like soldiers. So the word of command doesn't seem humi-
liating to them; the man is only a man, but he commands because
he is a commander. But we are not democratic enough to have a
dictator. Our people like to be ruled by gentlemen, in a general sort
of way. But nobody could stand being ruled by one gentleman. The
idea is too horrible.'[160]

Murrell also recognizes the danger that Herne's fondness for
simplifying political issues will result in a permanent and
embittered division between Left and Right. It is a criticism
very similar to Chesterton's own criticism of Baldwin's policy
after the General Strike,[161] but the analysis is more important
as a critique of doctrinaire policies, which can occur in any
historical epoch, than as a topical allusion to the repressive
policies of a particular political regime at a particular
historical moment:

'Everything is too simple to him. Even his success is too simple. He sees everything in black and white; with the need of restoring holy order and a hierarchy of chivalry on the one side and nothing but howling barbarians and blind anarchy on the other. He will succeed; he has already succeeded. He will hold his court and impose his judgment and bring the mutiny to an end; and you will not see that a new sort of history will have begun. . . . You are making something new; at once a sword that divides and a shield with two sides to it. It is not England; it is not ourselves. It is Alva a hero for Catholics and a hobgobblin for Protestants; it is Frederick the Father of Prussia and the murderer of Poland. When you see Braintree condemned by this tribunal, you won't understand how much is being condemned with him; how much that you like as much as I do.'[162]

The relation of the medieval league to Herne and Rosamund's love for each other is of course the final and most important question. What none of the characters ever completely understands, but what the narrator makes increasingly clear, is that Herne's apparently impersonal passion for reconstructing a medieval social order is really an expression of his infatuation for Rosamund Severne. It is this fact which ironically undercuts every attitude towards the League. The national political cause for which Olive Ashley deserts Braintree turns out to be as private a matter as two people in love. The man whom Braintree considers a fanatical reactionary and Murrell a Mussolini figure creating a permanent rift between Left and Right turns out to be a man who is suicidally in love.

No-one is more completely deceived than Herne himself. 'I am not a man,' he says, 'I am here only a mouthpiece to make clear the law; the law that knows nothing of men or women.'[163] He sees himself as the mere spokesman of the new order and as a man whose very personality has been replaced by the kingship he embodies. Explaining the measures that must be taken to deal with Braintree, he says quite simply: 'And as the law makes me the executive officer, I have really no will in the matter.'[164] And during the actual trial-scene, he makes the same claim to impersonality in words, which, like Olive Ashley's, once again link the political romanticism of the novel to the romanticism of MacIan and the words of his sinister guide:[165] 'It is not I who speak: it is the Law.'[166] In fact there is no political decision he takes which does not depend ultimately on Rosamund's approval, from the decision to continue the play in everyday life as a house-party masquerade to the decision to accept the kingship of western England and even perhaps to the decision to give judgment against Rosamund's father and his friends: 'He had hardly realized what personal romance was inspiring the impersonal romance of his historical revolution.'[167]

Herne's unconscious dependence on Rosamund does not, however, deprive his medievalism of its political significance, for Rosamund is equally dependent on him for her political views. Each one needs the other. And it is from this situation that the real political danger comes. For although everything Herne does is inspired by Rosamund, everything Rosamund thinks is derived from Herne. And in reflecting his political views, she also intensifies and distorts them. Because of her inspiration, the imaginative dream is transformed into a practical reality. But it is also her love for immediate and drastic action that threatens to turn medievalism into a kind of Fascism: 'Many have imagined,' the narrator comments, 'that feminine politics would be merely pacifist or humanitarian or sentimental. The real danger of feminine politics is too much love of a masculine policy. There are a good many Rosamund Severnes in the world.'[168] A subtle indication of the way in which this interaction leads to extremism is suggested by the scene in which Rosamund, full of 'rage and fury',[169] asks Herne what answer he will make to Braintree's defiance. There is no indication that she originates the plan, but in breaking Herne's dreamy mood she provides the dynamic for its implementation: 'He looked round slowly in his rather short-sighted fashion; only the pause before he spoke expressed the change in his feelings on hearing the voice that hailed him.'[170]

Even in the trial-scene, when Herne condemns her father, there are indications that he has not really escaped her influence and become at last the voice of impersonal truth and justice he has always claimed to be. There is after all no reason for him to think that the remorseless application of the law will offend Rosamund, even though it destroys her father. From what one knows about her character it is more likely to fascinate than repel her. Perhaps Herne instinctively understands this. Certainly if he had done anything else, he would have alienated her permanently. Even the obvious effort which he makes to be impartial and the over-simplified judgment which he finally gives are signs of Rosamund's influence. As the chronicler remarks: 'Perhaps it was a little overdone; the words with which he went on were rather too dead and distinct.'[171] The verdict loses none of its importance in the novel as a summing-up of Distributist principles if one also sees it as a final and paradoxical proof of the way in which Herne is motivated by his love for Rosamund Severne.

But the complete meaning of the transformation of Olive Ashley's romantic play into Herne's romantic politics, only becomes fully apparent when one considers the imagery connected with Olive Ashley's search for the crimson illumination colour. The Dr Hendry chapters, which recount Murrell's first involvement in a social question, provide both the clearest example of the way in which the symbolism of the novel works and the best indication of the novel's meaning.[172]

On a literal level, the errand Olive Ashley sends Murrell on is concerned with finding a particular colour she needs for her medieval illuminations. But the political and symbolic implications of the errand become increasingly apparent. The colour is from the first associated with the world of romance and everything about it makes a particular symbolic point. Thus it is important that the new industrial combines which dominate English life are unable to produce the paint, and it is also important that it can only be found in a medieval book, in which it is the colour of the many-headed monster of the Apocalypse, whose tint 'glowed across the ages with a red that had the purity of flame'.[173] Olive attempts to describe it in these words, 'a red vivid as if it were red-hot, and yet as delicate in its tint as a clear space in the sunset'.[174]

It also has an enormous psychological importance to Olive as a link with her pre-Raphaelite childhood in which she acquired her romantic temperament and her peculiar bias against modern progress. The ultimate explanation for the personal importance of the colour is therefore found in her memories of her father, a painter and a friend of William Morris:

To him was due the fact that all her first thoughts about things had been coloured. All those things that for so many people are called culture and come at the end of education had been there for her from the beginning. Certain pointed shapes, certain shining

colours, were things that existed first and set a standard for all this
fallen world, and it was that which she was clumsily trying to express
when she set her thoughts against all the notions of progress and
reform. Her nearest and dearest friend would have been amazed to
know that she caught her breath at the mere memory of certain
wavy bars of silver or escalloped edges of peacock green, as others
do at the reminder of a lost love.[175]

But the political symbolism of Murrell's adventure only
becomes clear when the search for the lost colour becomes a
search for Dr Hendry. He provides another link with the world
of Olive's childhood, because, like her father, he is a friend 'of
the old group that worked with William Morris'.[176] He is also a
craftsman who has succeeded in manufacturing the pigments
needed for reproducing medieval colour. The large London
shop which sells red chalks and red ink does not sell Hendry's
Illumination Colours because the large combine, which has
driven Hendry out of business and now controls all the
manufacturing of paint, has no interest in preserving the paints
used by the pre-Raphaelite artists. Like the empire which
annexes Juan del Fuego's Nicaragua in *The Napoleon of Notting
Hill*, big business does not in fact preserve the talents of the
people it destroys. The disappearance of Dr Hendry's shop and
the poverty which he and his daughter suffer are therefore
both an illustration of the way in which industrial monopolies
impoverish life and an indictment of their cruelty.

Equally significant, however, for the central theme of the
novel, is the way in which even the smallest details of Dr
Hendry's situation take on a symbolic meaning. Thus his
insistence that the colour Olive wants is opaque rather than
transparent is at once an example of his pedantic meticulousness
and his pathetic vanity, and a means of making a symbolic
point which is important for the final meaning of the novel:

'The thing to remember, first of all, of course, is that this type of
colouring is in its nature opaque. So many people confuse the fact
that it is brilliant with some notion of its being transparent. I myself
have always seen that the confusion arose through the parallel of
stained glass. Both of course were typically medieval crafts, and
Morris was very keen on both of them. But I remember how wild
he used to be if anybody forgot that glass is transparent. "If anybody
paints a single thing in a window that looks really solid," he used
to say, "he ought to be made to sit on it." '[177]

As the novel develops, this distinction between the opaque and the transparent becomes emblematic of two opposed views of life. The opaqueness of Olive's crimson illumination paint represents the secular and somewhat negative political values which have only a limited significance, and the transparency of stained glass represents the religious and more positive transcendent values, through which the orders of nature and grace achieve a kind of harmony.

The colouring of the monster in the illuminated drawing is opaque because the romantic politics of Olive and Herne are not completed by the theological view which gives romanticism its final meaning. Olive's explanation to Rosamund outside Seawood Abbey at the end of the novel makes this clear:

'There may be people to whom it's senseless to talk about a flower of chivalry; it sounds like a blossom of butchery. But *if* we want the flower of chivalry, we must go right away back to the root of chivalry. We must go back if we find it in a thorny place people call theology. We must think differently about death and free will and judgement and the last appeal. It's just the same with the popular things we can turn into fashionable things; folk-dances and pageants and calling everything a Guild. Our fathers did these things by the thousand; quite common people; not cranks. We are always asking how they did it. What we've got to ask is why they did it.'[178]

The final contrast in the novel is a contrast between two sets of images. The first are represented by the opaque red of the monster in Olive's illuminated book and the dragon in the garden of the Seawood country-house, and the second are represented by the transparent windows of the library-chapel in which Herne carries out his medieval research and the fragments of stained glass in the small leaden cage which forms an image of St Francis and 'a burning red angel'.[179] But the figure of the beast of the Apocalypse and the dragon in the garden are incomplete without the figure of Saint Michael who defeats them. By themselves they represent the negative quality of romantic politics:

'We have only the dragon left. A hundred times I've looked at that dragon and hated it and never understood it. Upright and high above that horror stood St Michael or St Margaret, subduing and conquering it; but it is the conqueror that has vanished. . . . There burned in this court a great bonfire of visionary passion which in the spirit could be seen for miles and men lived in the warmth of it; the positive passion and possession, the thing worth having in itself. But now the very best of them are negative; attacking the absence of it in the world. They fight for truth where it isn't. They fight for honour where it isn't. They are a thousand times right; but it ends in truth and honour fighting each other, as poor Jack and Michael fought.'[180]

The transparencies of the stained glass windows of the library, which Olive identifies with the windows of the former chapel, and the stained glass lantern, which hangs outside Rosamund's home in Limehouse, are symbolic of a world of nature which is perfected by grace. In a moment of recognition, Olive imagines that the walls and windows of the chapel are watching and waiting for her search for medieval colour to become a search for medieval theology. The windows themselves seem to be trying to explain the meaning of medievalism:

That pointed and tapering tracery, of which she had talked lightly to Monkey long ago, the dark glass of the windows, dense with colours that could only be discovered from within—suddenly told her something; a paradox. Inside there was light and outside there was only lead. But who was really inside?[181]

And in the final scene of the novel, Olive Ashley's medieval illuminations and Herne's medieval politics are identified as part of the same search for colour. They are now compared with a light which, like the tabernacle lamp in Waugh's *Brideshead Revisited*, is a sacramental symbol of the divine reality which gives the world of nature its ultimate meaning. Herne sees the stained glass lantern as a sign of the 'great thirst for colour, which had filled his life, fed as from a goblet of flame'.[182] The final difference between the opaque and the transparent is found in the presence or the absence of the interior reality:

Somehow this childish transparency seemed like a password and a signal of all that he had once sought to do on a great scale or Olive Ashley on a small one; and yet with some secret and vivid difference; that the lamp was lit from within.[183]

The symbolic distinction therefore offers a valuable clue to the meaning of the final synthesis of the novel. The opaque illumination colour which Murrell obtains from Dr Hendry and brings to Olive Ashley is a symbolic preparation both for the political failure of romantic medievalism and for the final transformation and completion of the romantic Catholicism represented by the transparent stained glass windows.

It may seem that Dr Hendry's adventures partially vindicate Maisie Ward's reading of the novel. The leaders of the medieval league all eventually move towards Catholicism. Olive and Rosamund actually become Catholics, and there is a hint that Herne may follow their example. Seawood Abbey, the seat of the medieval revival, becomes a monastery once again, and the library in which Herne conducts his research presumably becomes the monastic chapel which it used to be. One might be tempted to agree with Maisie Ward's view that the novel implies that the only hopeful political future consists in an identification between England and Catholicism.

But such a reading, however plausible, leaves too much out of account. Above all it fails to recognize the distinction between the personal and the political meaning of the novel. It is surely significant that the conversion of the medievalist leaders to Catholicism takes place only after the collapse of the medieval league. In each case, it is associated with a turning away from political life to personal and individual action. Rosamund becomes a nurse in a Catholic settlement in the London Docks, and Herne becomes a Don Quixote figure who deals only with individual problems of social injustice. The only information provided about Olive Ashley is that she marries Braintree. Conversion is presented as the personal fulfilment of those who have learned the impossibility of finding a political solution in romanticism. Chesterton's own comments on the novel would seem to bear out this interpretation. In fact his explanation of what he calls the point of the novel contains no reference to Catholicism at all.[184] Instead his comments on Herne's abdication emphasize only the argument for Syndicalism and the failure of the medieval league:

He lays down the theory of the Guild which justifies Braintree and the theory of Forestalling which condemns the whole world which supports him and especially the father of his betrothed. Even he is not such a lunatic as not to know that he has broken his own life and leadership; the whole of that world deserts him and he finds himself repeating the attitude of the King in the play as he had acted it; he declares that a King is powerless against the pressures and wickedness of the world and that a man could do more good as a knight errant, dealing with individual cases as they came.[185]

The absence of any direct reference to the religious conversions in what is supposed to be a summary of the last five chapters of the novel is not a matter of evasiveness. The implication is rather that the novel maintains the same careful distinction between politics and religion that Chesterton maintains in *G.K.'s Weekly*, where the personal religious convictions of a Papist are never confused with the purely political convictions of a Distributist.[186] Chesterton made no secret of his religious views either as an Anglo-Catholic or as a Catholic, but he made it perfectly clear that Distributism has no necessary connection with Catholicism. Both in the novel and in the newspaper in which the novel was serialized, there is never any suggestion that the acceptance of Distributist politics means acceptance of the Catholic religion. And that is why it is important to do what Maisie Ward fails to do and distinguish the political from the religious meaning of the novel.

This distinction is never a difficult one to make. Thus the Dr Hendry symbolism which connects medievalism with Catholicism also connects medievalism with Syndicalism. The central image of the crimson illumination colour from which the symbolic contrast between opaque secularism and transparent Christianity is developed is also the starting-point for a chain of imagery which moves outwards from the medieval pageant of the romantics to the industrial situation of modern England and the political preoccupations of John Braintree. The coal miners' strike is also a strike of 'the affiliated Unions connected with the by-products',[187] and it is made clear that the by-products of coal are more important than the coal itself. It is also pointed out that the inferior paints which provide the unfair competition to Dr Hendry's private shop are made from coal by-products. More than that, we learn that the fortunes of Lord Seawood, Sir Howard Pryce, and Lord Eden all depend on industries connected with the derivatives of coal, one of which is the Coal-Tar Colour and Dye Company, which enjoys a monopoly of the manufacture of paint and which ruins Dr Hendry. Murrell's quest for the red colour of the dragon becomes an economic and sociological study of the way in which Seawood Abbey, where the owners of the mines and the paint factories are found, the Imperial Stores in London, where their paints are sold, the shabby seaside town, to which Dr Hendry has fled, and the town of Milldyke, in which Braintree's strike begins, are all part of the same symbolic web of industrialism, which Herne calls a 'sort of spider's web of worry and misery . . . spread over all the unfortunate mass of mankind'.[188]

The images which help to trace this symbolic circle are worth noting. And among the imagery which does most to clarify the central political meaning of the novel, perhaps the most important is the imagery associated with Dr Hendry's theory of universal colour-blindness. This eccentric theory is first of all an indication of what Dr Hendry has endured from the modern industrial state. It is at once a symptom of his mental derangement and an indictment of the mad society which brought this derangement about. More significantly, his theory provides an explanation for the madness of society which is symbolically true. Understandably enough, perhaps, the doctor never gives a coherent statement of what he means by universal colour-blindness, but he does speak of the two principles of pathological psychology; the first is that a sickness may affect an entire population; the second is that 'maladies affecting the chief senses are akin to maladies of the mind'.[189] The drabness and tawdriness of industrial life which people tolerate are indications that they have lost their sense of colour. A people who prefer the cheap and inferior paint of the Imperial Stores to Dr Hendry's true colours seem at first to be mad; in fact they are merely colour-blind. Only a few individuals, such as Olive Ashley, escape the universal sickness: 'This friend of yours, now, I think you said she was the daughter of my old friend Ashley. Now there you have an exceptionally sound stock still surviving. Probably with no trace of the affliction at all.'[190]

There is no need to comment on the obvious relevance of the theory to Olive Ashley's search for colour and Michael Herne's attempt to restore the colour of romance to modern life. What is not so obvious and what needs to be underlined is the way in which the theory of colour-blindness is linked to the imagery which suggests a kind of blindness even among the lovers of colour, and a clear-sightedness and true sense of colour in Braintree, the character who seems least sensitive to the need for it.

Thus it is surprising how much imagery of sight is associated with Herne and how frequently this imagery suggests not the clarity of vision of a man who feasts on colour, but the myopia of a man who is in some sense blind. References to his defective sight in a literal and metaphorical sense occur in many passages. He sees things either at a visionary distance or in his own inner imaginative world, but he seldom sees things as they are. On the one hand, there is the reference to his being 'blind with inner light';[191] on the other, there is the description of him on coronation day sitting, 'on his high throne above all the coloured crowd, and his eyes seemed to inhabit the horizons and the high places'.[192] In the library, he stares, 'into the depths of the distance with blind but shining eyes';[193] and we are told that he is short-sighted, that his eyes are blank, and, more significantly, that 'he did not see the world to scale'.[194] Only in the presence of Rosamund does his vision acquire a kind of lurid clarity. When she invites him to take part in theatricals, the description is once again given in terms of sight: 'Mr Herne's eyes seemed to alter their focus, as if fitted with a new lens, to lose the distance and take in the foreground; a foreground that was filled with the magnificent young lady.'[195] But the ultimate effect of the new clarity of sight which his infatuation with Rosamund creates is a more total and complete kind of blindness. At the moment when he recognizes and declares his love, he tells her: 'Your eyes blind me.'[196] Moreover Rosamund herself is guided by the myopic man who follows her. And this influence, too, is described by similar imagery: 'Quite suddenly, and perhaps accidentally, there had become clear to her very single eye something like a ray of light that she could follow; something that she could understand.'[197]

Among the medievalists, only Olive Ashley seems to escape the general weakness in sight. And there is one occasion when she seems, momentarily at least, to share Herne's and Rosamund's affliction. Watching Douglas Murrell driving the hansom cab down the western road at sunset, she does not at first recognize him, and, as if blinded by the romantic setting, she thinks of the return of the legendary king: 'He seems to be behind a horse,' said Olive in a low voice. 'That low sun dazzles my eyes . . . Can it be a Roman chariot? I suppose Arthur would *really* be a Roman?'[198]

It is Braintree who reveals in his political activity the clear-sightedness which the medievalists lack. What the novel suggests is that both the recovery of sight and the recovery of colour will be brought about by Syndicalism. The recurring nostalgia for the return of the king which characterizes romantic politics in Chesterton's fiction receives its most harshly realistic rebuttal in Braintree's answer to Olive Ashley. He presents a picture of human equality in which free men see Richard Coeur de Lion without romantic illusions:

'Perhaps,' she answered. 'He and his virtue might come back.'
'When he comes back he will find the country a good deal changed,' said the Syndicalist grimly. 'No serfs; no vassals; and even the labourers daring to look him in the face. He will find something has broken its chain; something has opened, expanded, been lifted up; something wild and terrible and gigantic that strikes terror even into the heart of a lion.'
'Something?' repeated Olive.
'The heart of a man,' he replied.[199]

The imagery associated with Braintree suggests a final paradox. There is a sense in which the character who is least affected by the political blindness of the romantics does most to accomplish the romantic task of restoring colour to modern life. Throughout the story, Braintree wears a red tie as a sign of his commitment to the revolutionary movement. The significance of the repeated references to its colour becomes clear only at the end of the novel. On an earlier occasion, Murrell compares the fourteenth-century red of Olive's illuminated dragon with the twentieth-century red of Braintree's tie; in the final episode, Olive identifies Braintree as the man who successfully accomplishes what the romantics fail to accomplish and his colour as the equivalent to the illumination colour that has been lost. What Murrell does for Dr Hendry by his romantic adventure Braintree does for him by a political action which remedies the social causes of his unhappiness:

'What a strange story all this is. . . . I mean ever since I started poor Monkey running after red paint. What a rage I was in with you and your red tie; and yet, in a queer sort of way, it turns out to have been the same sort of red. I didn't know it and you didn't know it; and yet it was you who were working back blindly for the colour that I was after, like a child after a sunset cloud. It was you who were really trying to avenge my father's friend.'[200]

It is therefore a serious misunderstanding of a novel to interpret it in Maisie Ward's fashion as an example of Catholic propaganda. Olive Ashley's marriage to Braintree may suggest a synthesis between the important but somewhat arid values of Syndicalism and the important but somewhat chimerical values of romance. Presumably Rosamund and Herne do good work at their Catholic settlement, and Olive Ashley certainly becomes a Catholic. But Braintree, whose policy for industrial England is the only political policy which the novel affirms, shows no signs of becoming a Catholic. Rosamund's comment on the marriage might be taken as emblematic of the balance between personal religious convictions and public Distributist principles which Chesterton expresses in the novel: 'They are married now and they seem to agree about almost everything. I wonder how much there really was for good people to disagree about in those quarrelsome old times.'[201]

5 The Late Novels

The sharp decline in literary quality which characterizes the final group of novels is reflected in the difficulty one has in discovering their precise meaning. This is particularly true of *The Poet and the Lunatics*, which is perhaps one of the least easy of Chesterton's novels to evaluate. Not that there is any difficulty in defining the theme which runs through the novel, since each of the eight chapters deals with a different kind of madness. Nor is there any difficulty in recognizing the central character, who clearly belongs to a long line of Chestertonian artist-poets whose apparent madness is the true norm of sanity. In fact Gabriel Gale is one of a group of characters that begins with Adam Wayne, in *The Napoleon of Notting Hill*, continues with Syme, the poet-detective of *The Man Who Was Thursday*, Innocent Smith, in *Manalive*, and Herne, in *The Return of Don Quixote*, and concludes with the heroes of *Four Faultless Felons*, and with Mr Pond, the shrewd and apparently simple-minded detective of Chesterton's last romance. Like each of these characters, Gale creates the familiar contrast between the madness of a world which claims to be sane and the sanity of a character whom the world thinks to be mad.

This contrast between a misleading appearance of simplicity and an inner reality of mental alertness also bears a strong resemblance to the basic idea of the Father Brown stories. Gale's method of detection, like Father Brown's, consists in following moral clues and interpreting moral atmospheres. He is also like Father Brown in seeing himself as a kind of anti-Sherlock Holmes figure: 'I know the sort of proofs you want,' he says on one occasion, 'the foot-prints of the remarkable boots, the bloody finger-print carefully compared with the one at Scotland Yard, the conveniently mislaid matchbox, and the ashes of the unique tobacco. Do you suppose I've never read any detective stories?'[1] Even Father Brown's method of discovering criminals by becoming like them in every way, save in the final

act of choice, finds its parallel in Gabriel Gale's method of
helping the madmen whom he meets: 'He thought he could
cure cracked people by what he called sympathy. But it didn't
mean what you would mean by sympathy; he meant following
their thoughts and going half-way with them, or all the way
with them if he could.'[2]

There is therefore no difficulty in understanding either the
theme of the novel, which is expressed with perfect clarity by
the title, or the meaning of the hero, who is quite clearly
another version of the fool figure which seems to have held a
permanent fascination for Chesterton.[3] The real difficulty in
understanding is concerned with a twofold problem of interpretation. For there is an ambiguity both in the subject and in
the construction of the book. In few other novels is it more
difficult to distinguish the political and personal meaning of the
story; and in no other novel is it more difficult to decide
whether one is dealing with a loosely constructed and badly
unified novel of eight chapters, or a collection of eight short
stories, whose single hero and theme provide a surprising degree
of unity.

Certainly there is no doubt that the novel possesses a political
and social as well as a personal significance. The varieties of
madness which Gale encounters have all of them a political
meaning, even when their meaning seems to be primarily
personal. The novel begins with the stock Chestertonian situation of the deserted countryside, which might be read as the
setting for *Tales of the Long Bow*, and ends with an account of an
attempt to combat the plutocrats who have destroyed a corner
of rural England, which might be read as a continuation of *The
Flying Inn*. Both the second and the seventh chapters deal with
the explicitly political question of the meaning of liberty, and it
is no coincidence that Ivanhov, the central character of the
former, has written a treatise on 'The Psychology of Liberty',
and that Phineas Salt, the central character of the latter, finds
himself unable to follow his career of writing, because of his
notion of liberty. Other chapters, however, are more difficult to
place. The central and perhaps the most successful story in the
book deals with the philosophical problem of solipsism, which
is personal in the fullest sense of the word, since it recounts the
story of a mental crisis very similar to the one which almost
resulted in Chesterton's own madness.[4]

Other stories seem to be chiefly concerned with the way in which curious crimes are sometimes the result of curious views of life. 'The Shadow of the Shark', for example, is primarily the story of the murder of an eccentric millionaire by a fanatical scientist; and 'The House of the Peacock', apart from its curious setting, reads very much like a standard Father Brown story. Occasionally, too, a more idiosyncratic meaning under-cuts the social significance of what seems to be an obviously political story. Thus 'The Finger of Stone' begins as an ap-parently conventional study of the conflict between science and religion in a French village, but turns out to be far more concerned with the symbolical meaning of a peculiar kind of realism in art. Even Gale's involvement in rural politics is subordinated both to his loyalty to John Hurrel and to his love for Lady Diana Westermaine.

The first and final chapters, which provide the novel's frame, seem clear enough. One begins in romantic-epic fashion in the middle of a situation which is only explained and resolved in the final adventure. The meaning of the events outside the inn is provided in the final chapter, which combines a flash-back account of the origin of Gale's friendship with Hurrel with an account of the outcome of his love for Lady Diana. But it is also true that the six stories which these two chapters enclose do little to advance the action. And, indeed, with the exception of one very effective scene in the middle of the novel, there are few clear references to Gabriel Gale's own story.[5] The six adventures which take place after his meeting with Diana and before his rescue of her in the last chapter might be described as a kind of comic interlude or, as the sub-title of the novel suggests, as mere episodes in his life. From the point of view of Gale's own problem, they are simply random events which provide a way of marking time for the four years during which he waits for Hurrel's death.

Gale's role as the confidant of madmen does however give the stories within the frame another, although incomplete, thematic unity. The varieties of madness which he encounters are after all not entirely unconnected. Considered in relation-ship to each other, they form an imperfect but recognizable pattern. There is, for example, an obvious connexion between chapter two and chapter seven, since both study the meaning of human limitations, first in the story of an attempt to escape

them through self-destruction and then in the story of a
successful escape from them by way of acceptance. The
'madnesses' of chapters three and four are also related, for they
turn out to be respectively the madness of a materialist and the
far more terrifying madness of the idealist. Even the fifth and
sixth chapters, which seem totally unrelated to the other stories
or to each other, possess a tenuous link, since the first is concerned with the denial of objective truth and the second with
the denial of objective evil.

Gale's role in the stories must be seen in the context of this
curious philosophical unity. In each chapter, the kind of
madness presented implies an opposite and positive quality of
sanity which is embodied in the character of the apparently
mad poet. He is as much the foil as the detective, since his very
presence provides the necessary contrast. And the cumulative
effect of the series of contrasts between his sanity and the
madness of his antagonists also helps to move the novel from the
individual to the social plane. Ivanhov's theory of radiating
anarchy implies the need for Gale's notion of a limited and
ordered liberty; Dr Wilkes's kind of materialism, whose
'dreadful dry light shed on things must at last wither up the
moral mysteries as illusions',[6] suggests the need for his philosophy of reverence for the 'common objects' of everyday life.
The list might be extended from chapter to chapter. The
strange isolation of the philosophical idealist, whose egoism
makes him the centre of the universe and the entire external
world a mere projection, finds its opposite in the philosophy in
which Gale takes into account the pain and suffering of
ordinary people. Similarly Humphrey Crundle's contempt for
the superstitions of ordinary folk stands in contrast to his
respect for even this primitive dread of real evil. And in the final
adventure, Phineas Salt's original craving for an unlimited
choice of fantasies is contrasted with the poet's romance of
limited and prosaic things. Thus the kinds of madness which
Gale encounters become representative of a general social
malaise which his philosophy would cure, so that in spite of the
apparently negative and random quality of the novel, one might
be tempted to give it the title which Chesterton gave to his
first book of positive social theory and call it *The Outline of
Sanity*.

But although Gale represents the norm of sanity throughout

the adventures and the obvious irony of the book turns on the difficulty of distinguishing the mad person who seems sane from the sane person who seems mad, there is also a sense in which the madmen themselves contribute directly to the picture of social sanity. For there is a real correspondence between Gale's many-faceted view of life and the varieties of madness, each of which isolates and exaggerates an element which is a necessary part of sanity. Gale is able to understand these peculiar lunacies not only because he possesses something called 'a sort of psychological imagination',[7] but also because he can to a degree sympathize with each of them. The 'streak of sympathy' he claims to have with each form of madness implies that there is an element in each of them with which he agrees. The passion for abstract liberty which eventually destroys Ivanhov may be a political as well as a personal tragedy, and the philosopher may be the archetypal figure of extreme Liberalism, but Gale goes a long way towards approving what he stands for. Even Dr Wilkes's materialism is favourably commented upon, so far as it involves the acceptance of the world of things as they are. And Gale argues, somewhat unconvincingly, that the under-graduate's error is very close to the centre of everyone's thought. He also draws attention to the way in which Pardou's mad theory of realism is partially vindicated, since it depends upon an unusual awareness of the strangeness of man: the petrified corpse in the market place is mistaken for one of the sculptor's more grotesque works of art. It is also significant that Gale, after revealing that Crundle is a murderer, should give the speech for the defence when Crundle's friends have deserted him. His approval of Phineas Salt's retreat from the world of literature to the circumscribed world of the lower middle-class may be interpreted as a Tory argument against social mobility, but it is clear that his approval of it is unqualified, since he describes Phineas as the man who went sane.

A more detailed study of the stories of Ivanhov and Salt in the second and seventh chapters provides perhaps the best illustration of the way in which the personal and the political themes are related and the best clue of the relation of the adventures to Gale's own story. Such a study also indicates the way in which the meaning of the novel is expressed through a blend of action and commentary on the action.

The Ivanhov story is presented by means of a number of

vivid but apparently disjointed images. What is most striking about this series of rapidly changing pictures is the way in which they repeat a pattern in colour. The story begins in the morning with a description of the brown birds' attempt to kill the yellow canary which has been 'liberated'. It continues with the long passage which describes Ivanhov as he is seen from the woods, throwing open window after window, and finally breaking open the sky-light and standing on the roof with his arms outstretched and his lemon-coloured dressing gown and yellow hair flowing in the wind. And it concludes with a triptych of afternoon pictures, in colours which are at once similar to and very different from the bright morning colours and the hard white sunlight with which the story begins.

There is first the twilight scene in which Gale sees the goldfish, which, in spite of their name, seem to him to bear little resemblance to the yellow of gold. Like 'little living flames' they are in his own words, 'a much more gorgeous colour than gold'.[8] This is followed by the curious picture of Gale as a figure standing on the wall, with his yellow hair made lighter by the moon: 'The moonshine made a halo of pale yellow round the head; and for a moment they thought it was the Russian, standing on the wall as he had stood on the roof.'[9] The final picture is provided by the description of the dead goldfish lying beside the shattered bowl. Although this scene also takes place in moonlight, the change in colour is now brought about not by the moon but by death: 'At that time it was already dark, with a rising moon; and what forms I could see scattered in the shadow seemed almost grey, and even outlined in lines of grey light, which might have been moonlight, but I think was the corpse-light of phosphorescence.'[10]

The significance of this pattern in colour needs little elaboration. Nor is it necessary to look for a source of Ivanhov's vaguely-sketched story. His name and his slightly bogus manner recall Conrad's Ivanovitch, 'the heroic fugitive' of *Under Western Eyes*; his escape from prison and his theory of anarchy recall the story of Michael Bakunin;[11] while his social grace and his position in English society suggest the well-known Edwardian figure, Prince Kropotkin.[12] More probably he is like the people he resembles, an example of the Russian national type which Chesterton somewhat ironically describes in his *Autobiography*.[13]

But for the purposes of the story, the identification of the Russian with the series of coloured pictures is more important. Thus he is first identified with the canary which he has let out of its cage:

'He's like that yellow bird,' said Gale vaguely. 'In fact, he is a yellow bird, with that hair and the sun on him. What did you say you thought it was—a yellow hammer?'[14]

The suggestion of a liberation which is also an annihilation is also suggested by the picture of the opening of the windows, in which yellow once again appears against the quiet pattern of green and grey and brown. When the window breaks the vine, we are told that 'it had the look of the snapping of some green chain securing the house like a prison. It had almost the look of the breaking of the seal of a tomb.'[15] The meaning of this as an emblem of the revolutionary ideal in an expanding universe becomes clearer when one recalls the earlier passage, in which Mallow employs a metaphor from painting to speak of his love for Laura in terms of the Chestertonian theory of limits: '. . . but I radiate inwards, so to speak; that is why I paint all my pictures of this little corner of the world. If I could only paint this valley, I might go on to paint that garden; and, if only I could paint that garden, I might be worthy to paint the creeper under her window.'[16] It is equally significant that in the only conversation of Ivanhov which is recorded he boasts of the superiority of photography to painting and speaks of the development of colour photography as an example of the way in which science offers the possibility of an unending improvement of the very instruments of art.

The meaning of the identification of Ivanhov with Gale is more difficult to evaluate. Their similarity in appearance is partly a sign of their similarity in mood. It is a similarity which is expressed somewhat obliquely through the resemblance between the yellow-hammer bird and the canary; 'and as to being a hammer, yellow or otherwise, well, that also is an allegory'.[17] Gale's desire for revolutionary action in his youth enables him to sympathize with the Russian's nihilism: 'I used to want a hammer to smash things with.'[18] It is true of course that Gale insists that the resemblance is less important than the difference: ' "Perhaps I'm rather like him," said Gale quietly. "Perhaps I'm just sufficiently like him to learn not to be like

him, so to speak." '[19] But there is no doubt that his sympathy for
the Russian is almost as great as his disapproval. Thus his
comment on the dynamite explosion which kills Ivanhov is less
significant for the way in which it relates the death to the escape
from the Siberian prison than for its note of exultation: ' "It was
only the prison gun," he said, "the signal that a prisoner has
escaped." '[20]

The clearest indication, however, of the difference between
Gale and Ivanhov is provided by the image of the goldfish in
the bowl. Presumably, Gale would understand the appeal of the
Russian's McLuhanesque image of the modern age: 'When a
man has his eyes and ears at the end of long wires; his own
nerves, so to speak, spread over a city in the form of telephones
and telegraphs.'[21] He would also have some sympathy with the
view that the limitations of city life might require the remedy of
aviation through space, 'a sea you can never find the end of'.[22]
It is certainly clear that he understands and at least partially
accepts his view that the goldfish bowl is an image of the human
condition: 'There really is a round prison. The sky itself,
studded with stars, the serene arch of what we call infinity—'[23]
But he cannot approve the breaking of the bowl, for this is a
sign of an inhuman desire 'to be outside everything'. The
Liberal within Gale, and perhaps within Chesterton, is willing
to interpret the freeing of the canary as at worst 'a disputable
kindness'.[24] But the Tory within him, which rejoices both in the
variety and even in the imperfection of things, must deplore the
smashing of the goldfish 'prison', which is in fact 'their only
possible house of life'.[25] And it is entirely in keeping with
Chesterton's social thought that what Gale most resents about
Ivanhov's action is the way in which it deprives the goldfish of
their colour, changing the gorgeous orange and scarlet of living
prisoners into the uniform grey of the liberated dead.[26] In a
sense, this difference expresses the difference between Ivanhov's
two books. Gale shares the love of liberty which leads him to
write 'The Psychology of Liberty', but disapproves of the spirit
behind the other and unfinished work, which, we are told, is 'to
embody some mathematical theory about the elimination of
limits'.[27]

The chief interest of the Phineas Salt story is the way in which
it complements the story of Ivanhov. Although the chapter is
less well constructed and makes far less use of symbolic effects,

its meaning is clearly the direct antithesis of the earlier adventure. Instead of a quest for unlimited freedom which ends in death, it deals with a quest for the most limited kind of freedom which only begins after a symbolic death. The madness of a man who rejects human limitations is contrasted with the sanity of a man who accepts them. Thus the parallel between Gale and the hero is repeated.

It is not merely that both men are poets but that their careers resemble one another even in detail. Not only do they both write poetical dramas, but they both have the same publisher, the same theatrical manager and, apparently, many of the same friends. They are also both romantics, although admittedly in rather different ways. But apart from a common interest in poetry, their public reputations are very different, Gale being better known as a painter, and Salt being better known for the preposterous self-dramatizations which lead to the inevitable comparisons between himself and Byron and D'Annunzio. But the similarity is nonetheless sufficiently complete to be called a 'brotherhood in folly'[28] and expressed in a sympathy which extends to complete approval. At the end of the chapter, Gale tells Salt that he understands him, 'because I think I should have done the same thing myself'.[29] Salt's story is therefore important not only as a complement to Ivanhov's adventure, but also as the presentation for the first time of a system of values which Gale can endorse without qualification.

The story itself presents few problems in interpretation. One might indeed be tempted to call it a parody of the stock romantic adventure. It begins with Salt's flight to the sea and his symbolic drowning, and ends with his reappearance in the character of his prosaic brother, the shopkeeper of Croydon. But although it seems clear that Salt's story begins at the point at which Ivanhov's ends, it also seems clear from the way in which Gale's commentary echoes the earlier story that the problem he solves by a symbolic rebirth is the same as the problem Ivanhov fails to solve by suicide:

'The poet Phineas Salt was a man who had made himself master of everything, in a sort of frenzy of freedom and omnipotence. He had tried to feel everything, experience everything, imagine everything that could be or could not be. And he found, as all such men have found, that that illimitable liberty is itself a limit. It is like the circle, which is at once an eternity and a prison.'[30]

Perhaps the most curious feature of the story is the use it makes of a scriptural theme of rebirth. The references to St Thomas of Canterbury, the allusions to spiritual childhood, and the suggestion of a religious conversion, give the story a moral seriousness which is difficult to explain. There is even the suggestion that the happiness which Salt discovers in the simplicity of a shopkeeper's life is somehow equivalent to a kind of interior transformation. This at least seems to be the meaning behind the window-display of sweets which reveals his identity to Gale. A true shopkeeper would arrange them with an eye to the view from the street; the artist arranges them with an eye to the view from within. More importantly, however, the contrast between the dingy and commonplace exterior and the vivid and glowing interior reality becomes a symbol of the interior happiness which Salt has found. The flight from artistic success to the apparent ugliness of suburban life is presented as the recovery of spiritual childhood and innocence, a kind of religious transformation and rebirth. Gale describes Salt's return to his social origins in explicitly religious terms:

'What comes next? I tell you there are only two steps possible after that. One is the step over the cliff; to cease to be. The other is to *be* somebody, instead of writing about everybody. It is to become incarnate as one real human being in that crowd; to begin all over again as a real person. Unless a man be born again—

'He tried it and found that this was what he wanted; the things he had not known since childhood; the silly little lower middle-class things; to have to do with lollipops and ginger-beer; to fall in love with a girl round the corner and feel awkward about it; to be young. That was the only paradise still left virgin and unspoilt enough, in the imagination of a man who has turned the seven heavens upside down.'[31]

The social implications of this curious identification of suburban life with religious conversion are also worth considering. A biographical critic would mark that the Wellsian note of sympathy for the trivialities of middle-class life is presented with a tenderness which seems nostalgic enough to be personal. In fact the misgivings which the story implies are deeply Tory misgivings about the wisdom of social mobility of any kind. It suggests that social happiness and indeed personal happiness consists in remaining within the social class to which one is born. It is not the least surprising feature of the chapter that the limitations within which both Gale and Salt rejoice should turn out to be the sharply marked limitations of social class. What the story celebrates is not so much the emptiness of 'life at the top', but the happiness which comes with the acceptance of what seems to be one's station in life. What life at the forge is for Dickens's elder Pip in *Great Expectations*, life at a suburban shop is for Chesterton's Phineas Salt in the first of his later novels. The problem of the alienated hero which both authors describe is remarkably similar; what they disagree about is the possibility of finding a possible solution.

But the most successful blend of social commentary and personal preoccupations is found in the frame-story which also provides the most biting example of satire in the entire novel. It seems at first that Hurrel's scheme for redeveloping the country inn by turning Gale's painting to commercial use offers a very plausible solution to something which is evidently a very real problem. And indeed there seems to be no reason why modern business methods cannot be applied to solving a problem which modern business has helped to create, so that Hurrel might become simply an English version of Enoch Oates. It is true that Dr Garth betrays puzzled misgivings from the first, but these have more to do with Hurrel's apparent role as Gale's keeper than with the ethics of his business methods. The inn-keeper and the squire, who are most directly involved, accept the plan with enthusiasm. And it must be admitted that, apart from the aesthetic distaste for vulgarity and brashness, the novel presents no literal argument against its practicality. Only on the level of symbol and allegory is the case against it clearly stated.

That the successful businessman should turn out to be ineffectual is entirely in keeping with a view which Chesterton expresses throughout all his writing, and particularly in his fiction, where the millionaire is always a fool or a criminal. Characteristically, in the early Father Brown story, 'The Paradise of Thieves', the Tuscan poet Muscari warns his friend Ezza about the dangers of a financial career: 'You're too strong-minded for business, Ezza. You won't get on. To be clever enough to get all that money, one must be stupid enough to want it.'[32] And this view is also common to Chesterton's literary circle. In Belloc's novels, the financially successful are the most repellent of his characters, and in Baring's novels, the characters themselves often express a dislike for the business

F

ethos: 'We do not care for money,' the hero of his Russian novel explains. 'We treat it like what it is—dirt.' And again: 'Do you remember what Swift said? "One has only to look at the people God has given money to, to see what He thinks of it." '[33] But the view suggested by the symbolism of the frame-story goes even further than this. The businessman is now presented as a homicidal maniac and the very type of extreme madness. As Gale explains: '. . . of all the maniacs I have tried to manage, the maddest of all maniacs was the man of business.'[34] The grizzly symbolic comment of Hurrel's plan to help the inn-keeper and the squire is suggested by his attempt to murder them: whatever the speciousness of modern business, it eventually results in death.

The development of this symbolism follows lines which Chesterton's earlier novels have made all too familiar. Predictably the inn is called the Rising Sun and the irony of the name is heavily and repeatedly underlined. Thus Hurrel's plan to make the valley prosperous and the inn fashionable depends ultimately on Gale repainting the faded emblem of hope:

A new bridge of the most artistic woodwork seemed already to point across the river to the open road; a new and higher class of rents seemed already to be dotting the valley with artistic villages; and a new golden sign of the Rising Sun, with the signature of Gabriel Gale, already blazed above them, a symbol that the sun had risen indeed.[35]

But the suicide-murder transforms the sign into a classical symbol of despair, darkening and as it were cancelling out the image of hope with an image of self-destruction: 'the black figure of a man dangling from the painted gallows of the Rising Sun',[36] and finally the subsequent painting of the picture of St Peter's conversion at sunrise gives the symbolism an explicitly Christian meaning.

This imagery is also used to express the social meaning of the story. In a passage which might have been borrowed from *The Flying Inn*, Gale speaks of his painting as a means of reviving the dead rural traditions represented by the country inns: 'But one's life would be well spent in waking up the dead inns of England and making them English and Christian again. If I could do it, I would do nothing else till I die.'[37] There is scarcely a passage in the story which is not in some way connected with the same image. The contrast between Gale's view of life and Hurrel's, for example, is expressed in the scene in which Diana Westermaine sees the two men as figures in a living picture, in which Gale becomes a type of the new creation which dominates the darker reality represented by Hurrel:

... she could still see the sign itself shining with its new accretion of colours, and the tall, actively moving figure, shining also with sunlight, and from that distance altogether dwarfing the small and dingy figure near his feet. There returned on her still more strongly the vision of a true creator, making pure colours in the innocent morning of the world.[38]

And when Gale stands on his head, the incident is followed by a comment on the death of St Peter and the meaning of the humility which is opposed to despair:

'I've often fancied his [St Peter's] humility was rewarded by seeing in death the beautiful vision of his boyhood. He also saw the landscape as it really is: with the stars like flowers, and the clouds like hills, and all men hanging on the mercy of God.'[39]

Hurrel's second attempted murder provides further examples of the same imagery. Daylight is followed by darkness and a dramatic storm; the newly painted sign is once again blotted out by another apparent suicide; and, in language which recalls the Despair Canto of *The Faerie Queene*,[40] Gale compares himself both to a sentinel who has deserted his post and to a Judas who has betrayed his trust: 'I followed my own will till it went within an inch of murder; and it's I who ought to be hanging from the wooden sign, if hanging weren't too good for me.'[41]

The weakness of the imagery is that it never leads to anything. The occasions on which there are sunrises of hope and the sunsets of despair are as numerous as they are pointless. It is, for example, difficult to argue that a great deal is gained by Gale and Diana's inevitable parting at sunrise and meeting again years later at sunset. The creation of these careful balances is both unnecessary and contrived, and the significance of incidents which Chesterton calls symbolic coincidences[42] does not justify their repetition. One might argue that the meditation at the end of the Saunders chapter ('At least I know now that I have not dreamed of everything.')[43] helps to make Gale's love for Diana seem more real, so that one can forgive the allusion to the 'memory [of] slopes of another garden against another storm'.[44] But it is hard to defend the recapitulation of imagery at the end in the frame-story. The gratuitous return to the Rising Sun inn in the final chapter or the cryptic comment to the innkeeper about duties in Wimbledon may add a further balance to the imagery, but it adds nothing to the novel, except the promise of a social Apocalypse which in fact never takes place:

> 'It is Wimbledon that has skies of a strange and unique character at the present time. The sunsets of Wimbledon are famous throughout the world. A storm in Wimbledon would be an apocalypse.'[45]

Nor does the account of Gale's career as a social reformer given in the frame-story provide the significance which the imagery lacks. The career is in fact an extraordinarily limited one. The satirical drawings may be a form of political protest, but it is a protest which never extends beyond his own rural valley. The 'rack-renters and usurers',[46] who are the targets of his satire, are apparently only local tyrants, and there is no suggestion that the campaign, even if it were successful, would have had any larger social effect. We are told that he was 'very much of a revolutionary',[47] but we are given no indication of the kind of revolution he is looking forward to or indeed any indication of the way in which his activity is supposed to bring it about.

Nor does the plot to imprison Gale in the mad-house do much to give the frame-story a social significance. The situation is curiously similar to the one described in *The Ball and the Cross*, with Dr Simeon Wolfe and Dr Starkey substituted as later and slightly anti-Semitic versions of Dr Quale and Dr Hutton. But one has only to note the parallel to recognize the difference. The incident has none of the disturbing allegorical overtones which characterize the earlier novel. Instead of the Orwellian nightmare of the world as a universal madhouse and science as a diabolical force, one is presented with a rather tame attempt to silence the hero and to kidnap his fiancée.

On the other hand, Gale's motive for silence might seem to suggest the social theme of *The Man Who Knew Too Much*. Like Fisher, he is restrained from public action by personal loyalty. And there is a similar conflict between private duty and public

responsibility. While Hurrel lives, Gale's promise to protect him
from what he calls 'the infernal brutality of officials'[48] prevents
his acting. The solemn biblical form in which the promise is
given emphasizes its importance: 'God do so to me and more
also, if aught but death part thee and me.'[49]

But once again the differences are more significant than
similarities. Fisher's sullen silence is the result of no explicit
commitment to his friends, and he is the only judge of when the
time for action comes. Moreover the long period of silence is
also a time of preparation, during which he completes March's
political education and waits for events to clarify themselves as
they move rapidly towards a crisis. Gale's wait has a very
different meaning. The four-year period which elapses between
chapter one and the conclusion of the novel is described as 'a
sort of armed truce'.[50] Adventures do indeed take place during
his 'brief absences'[51] from his self-imposed duty as keeper of a
private madhouse, but they do nothing to prepare for the final
action of the novel. Moreover the final action has none of the
social significance which gives Fisher's participation in the
revolution its public importance. Apart from rescuing Diana
Westermaine and capturing a handful of criminals, Gale
accomplishes nothing.

Indeed it is difficult to think of any way in which his career
affects the world in which he moves. One cannot even speak
about a deliberate retreat from the problems of the age or about
his despair of finding a solution, for apart from the brief episode
of the satiric drawings, there is no indication that he is ever
seriously engaged in solving them. What his adventures provide
is a rapid sketch of the way in which the world has gone wrong.
What they fail to provide is any suggestion of the way in which
it can be set right. No indication is given of the way in which an
essentially private vision of social sanity can be translated into
a public reality.

It may be that this failure to suggest a social remedy marks a
turning-point in Chesterton's fiction. The world of the novel is
sufficiently similar to the world of the Distributist novels. There
is the same desolate countryside, the same decaying and
embittered rural gentry, and the same comfortable and mindless suburban class. But one waits in vain for the events of the
novel to bring about a change. In *Tales of the Long Bow*, a social
diagnosis is followed by a sort of cure; in *The Return of Don*

Quixote, the diagnosis of a political problem is followed by a positive failure to find a solution. *The Poet and the Lunatics* fails to consider even the possibility of a social cure. It is this and not the absence of official Distributism which is surprising. The society in which Gale moves in the beginning of the novel is essentially the same as the society in which he finds himself at the end, for he has done nothing to alter it.

This failure to suggest a positive social remedy may be connected with the uncharacteristic note which is introduced by the arrest of Dr Starkey and Dr Wolfe. It would not be too much to say that the implications of this curious incident suggest a change in Chesterton's attitude towards the state. That Gale should send a telegram to Dr Garth is understandable enough, for this is a gesture equivalent to Horne Fisher's asking for the help of March. But that he should send 'one or two telegrams to persons in rather responsible positions'[52] is another matter. The incident may be trivial, but it is inconceivable that it could have happened in any of the earlier novels. The Chestertonian hero seldom sends for the police.

It is of course true that Syme, in *The Man Who Was Thursday*, becomes a member of an organization called the philosophical police force. But he does so only because he is convinced that the real power is in the hands of the anarchist conspirators in the scientific and artistic worlds, compared to whom the defenders of order are almost helpless: '. . . he always felt that Government stood alone and desperate, with its back to the wall. He was too quixotic to have cared for it otherwise.'[53] And throughout the novel, like every Chesterton hero, he is a fugitive: one of the hunted, not a hunter. Even Father Brown, in spite of what the Marxist critics have to say about crime fiction,[54] is no exception to this rule. Not only does he frequently leave the scene of the crime before the police arrive, but he shows no real interest in apprehending criminals and very rarely makes use of any official help. The chronicler of *The Return of Don Quixote* expresses the characteristic Chestertonian view when he speaks of Herne and Murrell's trouble with the police as being 'in itself almost a sign of sanctity'.[55]

This distrust of the state does not mean that Chesterton was against authority for the sake of being against authority. Nor can it be explained in terms of a Liberal's fondness for championing the under-dog. What he makes clear both in his fiction and in his other writing is his conviction that the least suitable people are likely to hold the positions of authority, and that the perennial problem in politics is the giving of power to the people who are least likely to seek it.[56] That is why he usually presents himself as the spokesman for the inarticulate majority against the insolent minority which oppresses them.[57] Charles Williams has expressed the truth of the matter perfectly in his lecture on Chesterton's poetry, and what he has to say about Chesterton's verse applies equally well to his fiction:

All the magnificent imagery of forlorn hopes and last charges and final stands and broken swords which Mr Chesterton has strewn about his poems does not conceal the fact that he is, on the whole, on the side of the big battalions. Nor would he desire to conceal it; on the contrary, he asserts it—it is his claim and his song throughout. He is on the side of God and the people. But, in a sense, both of his great allies are voiceless and unarmed. It is he who is their song and weapon; and his weapon is his song. It is always the few whom he attacks, the politicians, the usurers, King Dives.[58]

That is what makes the arrest of the doctors in *The Poet and the Lunatics* surprising. Although it might seem to be an unimportant incident, and although the doctors richly deserve their punishment, it remains true that for the first time the hero appears to be on the side of the 'few in possession'. Any study of the novel must note the apparent lack of unity expressed by the vagueness of its design, and the apparent lack of interest in positive social remedies expressed by the absence of Distributism. These are indeed differences which set it apart from the work which immediately precedes it, and may be signs of an artistic falling-off. But the picture which remains disturbingly in one's mind, long after one has completed one's study of the novel and noted its defects and qualities, is the picture of Gale silently watching Dr Starkey moving his head from left to right like a trapped animal, as the plain-clothes detectives shift and close round him.[59]

Four Faultless Felons might be described as an unusual blend of *The Club of Queer Trades* and *The Man Who Was Thursday*. Instead of a club made up of men who have invented eccentric trades, we have a club made up of men who have invented eccentric crimes; and instead of detectives who look like anarchists, we have heroes who look like four different kinds of criminals. Even the division of the book recalls the early novel, with the six chapters of *The Club of Queer Trades* replaced by four stories, each of which is six chapters in length.

The novel is in fact unusually well constructed. And the four stories follow a remarkably similar pattern. The first two chapters introduce a half dozen characters in a distinctive setting, the third or fourth chapter, the complication, and the fifth chapter, the dénouement, which is followed in the sixth chapter by a brief epilogue. The frame-story also shows signs of careful construction. The incident which encloses the four stories takes place in the club to which the four heroes belong and in which they narrate their adventures to Asa Pinion, the American journalist, who, in turn, is supposed to have recast them in the form in which they are eventually published. Although the stories which they tell the journalist provide him with illustrations of the principle of the club, the frame-story itself also provides an illustration of the same principle. Count de Marillac's reputation as a gourmet turns out to be a disguise for an unusual kind of asceticism, and Pinion's reputation as a brash and unscrupulous sensation-monger turns out to be a disguise for the very real courtesy by which he gains his journalistic coups.[60] Thus the stories are at once extended footnotes on Pinion's interview with Marillac and a proof of the success of his method of journalism. And their subjects provide further links with the curious situation described in the frame-story, since the first and fourth stories deal with forms of journalism which are scarcely less fantastic than Pinion's own, and the second and third with the same kind of asceticism which makes an anchorite like Count de Marillac pretend to be a man of the world.

The stories themselves deal with familiar Chestertonian political and social themes. They begin with a parable on the meaning of modern Imperialism and conclude with an elaborate allegory on the meaning of modern revolution. The central part of the book shifts the emphasis from politics to sociology. In the second story, the familiar conflict between the urban and the agrarian is presented in terms of the antagonism between a progressive doctor's enthusiasm for modern science and industrial progress and a romantic poet-painter's enthusiasm for liberty and rural England. And in the third story, a curious social parable presents the case for repentance in modern business.

There are several unusual features to the stories. Few of them
suggest social and political remedies on a large scale, and the
solutions which they do suggest are tentative and cautious. It
is as though the novel had set out to qualify and partially
correct themes from the earlier fiction. Neither religion nor
politics are treated in a general way. Distributism and
Catholicism play no obvious part in any of the stories, and the
novel makes no obvious call to action. Like an essay in fiction,
it instructs without overtly propagandizing, and although it is
one of the least ambitious of the novels, it succeeds in drawing
attention to the aspects of post-War political and social life
which seem to have preoccupied Chesterton. In a word, if one
were to make a case for the mellowing of Chesterton's political
and social thought in his later fiction, it might be largely
based on this novel.[61]

Perhaps the most unexpected feature of the first story, 'The
Moderate Murderer', is that it should be a parable about the
dangers of reactionary extremism. Like 'The Bottomless
Well', in *The Man Who Knew Too Much*, the events take place
in a vaguely near-Eastern setting, in the imaginary Colony of
Polybia, 'a strip on the edge of Egypt'.[62] And it is interesting
that it is like the earlier story, too, in the way in which it offers
no direct criticism of Imperialism. It is not that the existence
of the empire is accepted uncritically, but that the existence of
the empire is merely the starting-point for a story which is
chiefly concerned with the dangers of a foolish kind of journalism and the difficulties of protecting patriotism in a disinte-
grating political system.

The situation of the hero of the story might also seem to
suggest the situation of Horne Fisher. But John Hume's curiously detached attitude towards imperial politics resembles
Horne Fisher's only superficially. Like Fisher, he is a man
unable to act who does finally move towards action. But his
political position is very different. Instead of suffering from a
personal involvement in the situation he wishes to correct, he
suffers from a sort of emotional exhaustion. Fisher's knowledge
and affection make him protect a system he knows to be
corrupt; Hume's 'deadly weakness'[63] is an inability to hate
something which he knows to be hateful, because he believes
that the only available alternative will be worse. Seeing
Imperialism as a discredited system, which is believed in only

F*

by the most naïve readers of the popular press, he finds that he
dislikes the enemies of Imperialism and their substitute for it
even more. Politically he describes himself simply as a moderate.[64] The wounding of Lord Tallboys serves the practical
purpose of saving his life, but it also in a sense represents Hume's
intermediate political position and is emblematic of his attitude
towards Imperialism. For although he recognizes its defects,
he is willing to wound it with hard truth in order to save it
from death.

The fact is that he has no political allies. With a Liberal's
suspicion of Imperialism, he has none of a Liberal's confidence
in the native nationalists, whose demand for self-government he
dismisses out of hand: 'I find it very hard to believe that these
people cannot live or breathe without votes, when they lived
contentedly without them for fifty centuries when they had the
whole country in their own hands.'[65] Moreover he distrusts the
nationalist leaders, whom he describes as frauds. Unlike the
English, they understand the political reality of the country,
but this only means that the choice is between blackguards
and idiots. Another curious feature of his political position is
his way of judging opinions by the people who hold them.
Thus he admits that everything that Dr Gregory tells Barbara
Traill is true, but because the doctor is a revolutionary agitator
and an enemy of England, nothing that he says is to be
believed. Truth requires more than verbal accuracy; one must
also be able to trust the person who tells it, and since Dr
Gregory embodies Chesterton's obsession with Germans and
Jews in much the same way that Dr Gluck does in *The Flying
Inn*, this is obviously impossible: 'I shouldn't believe that man,'
Hume warns Barbara, 'not even if you believe all the things
he said.'[66]

What the story dramatizes therefore is the danger of something which it calls political innocence. Only the friends of a
country understand it well enough to criticize it. But the
silence of the English press about the real shortcomings of
Imperial policy means that the political innocents learn about
them from the enemies of England. As a result of a bad kind of
journalism, the 'liars' of *Tales of the Long Bow* have become
the deceivers of 'The Moderate Murderer': '. . . it's a very
dangerous condition of the Press and the Public when only the
liars tell the truth.'[67] In fact the story makes the somewhat banal

point that the truth suppressed by a well-meaning friend provides the obvious material for the calumny of an enemy.

But the most curious feature of the story is its concern for the patriotism of what it calls the comfortable classes. It is less concerned with revealing the uglier truths about Imperialism than it is with warning about the dangers of such a revelation. The wrong kind of disillusionment can be more dangerous than the wrong kind of ignorance:

> That most necessary and most noble virtue of patriotism is very often brought to despair and destruction, quite needlessly and prematurely, by the folly of educating the comfortable classes in a false optimism about the record and security of the Empire. Young people like Barbara Traill have often never heard a word about the other side of the story, as it would be told by Irishmen or Indians or even French Canadians, and it is the fault of their parents and their papers if they often pass abruptly from a stupid Britishism to an equally stupid Bolshevism.[68]

The relationship of patriotism to Imperialism provides an element of inconsistency which the story never entirely resolves. There is as it were a constant and unconscious contradiction between what might be called its poetic and its official meaning. An incident which illustrates this confusion is provided by Barbara's conversation with Dr Gregory. In this scene, the setting becomes part of the argument: the pyramids seem to identify the fate of England's empire with the fate of ancient Egypt, and the inevitable sunset seems to foreshadow retribution on a catastrophic scale:

> . . . he lifted his green umbrella and pointed with a momentary gesture at the dark line of the desert and the distant Pyramid. The afternoon had already reddened into evening, and the sunset lay in long bands of burning crimson across the purple desolation of that dry inland sea.
>
> 'A glorious Empire,' he said. 'An Empire on which the sun never sets. Look . . . the sun is setting in blood.'[69]

This incident is never properly integrated into the official meaning of the story, so that the emotion which the passage undoubtedly evokes is at odds with the explanation that is finally given for it. Both the reader and Barbara Traill are encouraged to believe that the governor's scheme for solving the social problems of Polybia and eastern Egypt is 'a fair and final settlement'.[70] One is asked to accept Imperialism as a sort of *faute de mieux,* and at the same time one must believe that Dr Gregory's prophecy of disaster is also true, because he is described as a liar who speaks the truth. The way in which both statements can be simultaneously affirmed is never really explained.

Dr Snow's commentaries on the Apocalypse provide another example of the same thing. Although a comic figure, there is a solemnity about his sayings which gives them a curious impressiveness which moves Barbara in spite of herself:

> She still had only a confused idea to what the old clergyman was saying, but she began to feel a vague element of poetry in it. At least it was full of things that pleased her fancy like the dark drawings of Blake, prehistoric cities and blind and stony seers and kings who seemed clad in stone like their sepulchres the Pyramids.[71]

And Dr Snow's view is surprisingly similar to that of Dr Gregory. Like Gregory, he links the dissolution of the empire with its origin and prophesies a violent political catastrophe: 'The foundations were traced in blood and in blood shall they be traced anew. These things are written for our instruction.'[72]

The solution which Lord Tallboys ultimately suggests does nothing to undercut these powerfully poetic pictures of a doomed empire. In fact Tallboys himself is the solution, and it is difficult to accept him as the solution to anything. The preposterous name, the pompous rhetoric, the deafness which plays such an important part in the crisis of the story, and the slightly period clothing are consistent with a picture of a late Victorian bewildered by the modern violence and the treachery which he is unable to understand. But they scarcely form a credible picture of the kind of man who is capable of solving a problem which the story makes clear is almost insoluble. 'Tallboys is no fool,'[73] John Hume tells us. That is exactly what we find impossible to believe. The comment which is supposed to reassure the reader not only fails to do so, but is so patently false that it throws doubt on the reliability of all the earlier judgments. The plans for moderate measures lose their effectiveness when one remembers that they are the plans of Lord Tallboys. A pedantic and ineffectual governor assisted by a deputy who is a murderous reactionary, under the shadow of an ironic pyramid, in an empire whose foundations are traced in blood, and whose sun sets in an ocean of blood, these are the real elements of Chesterton's imperial fable. Whether they do justice to the idealism and the genuine achievements of Imperialism is a question which must be left for historians to answer. But what is indisputable is that the poetic logic of the story does not lead to the official conclusion which Chesterton gives it.

'The Honest Quack' is the first of two stories in which the emphasis shifts from politics to a kind of social allegory. There is no difficulty in recognizing Walter Windrush as another of the artist-poets who seem to have been Chesterton's favourite *alter egos*. Like all his predecessors, he is identified with romanticism, being, as we are told, 'a man in the old tradition of Shelley, or Walt Whitman',[74] and like theirs, his poetry has a broad political meaning, since, for him, '[it] seemed almost synonymous with liberty'.[75] The discovery of the corpse hidden in the tree and the efforts made to certify Windrush as a lunatic in order to save him from being arrested as a murderer provide the actual plot of the story. And the conflict, such as it is, develops from the good-natured antagonism between Windrush and Dr Judson. It is in fact the familiar story of the conflict between romance and science. Dr Judson is described partly as a kind of Ivywood figure, who is devoted to a 'modern organization and machinery and the division of labour and the authority of the specialist',[76] and partly as a genuine and dedicated man of science, like Green and Blair in *Tales of the Long Bow*. Symbolically, he stands in the same relation to Windrush that Dr Garth stands to Gale, as the embodiment of the practical side of life which complements and is complemented by romance.

But the serious interest of the story is provided by its allegorical meaning. It is a matter of slight significance that the plot seems to be derived entirely from *The Poet and the Lunatics*[77] and from the Murrell chapters of *The Return of Don Quixote*.[78] And there is perhaps some interest created by the light-hearted satire on science, although the story of the imaginary malady of Duodiapsychosis is neither particularly original nor amusing. Certainly it is unlikely that any reader will be greatly exercised in trying to decide whether Windrush is a madman or a murderer. The real interest of the story is in fact limited to its curious insistence on the need to protect the tree from the city.

This allegory may be interpreted in different ways. It is first of all and most obviously an allegory on a meaning of rural England. The wall Windrush builds around the tree represents the futility of the attempt to protect the country from the encroachments of the city. It is also an allegory on the difference between use and value. The conversations between the doctor and the poet always return to the same point:

'But what's the *good* of it?' Judson would cry out of the depths of dark exasperation. 'What's the *use* of having a thing like that?'

'Why, no use whatever,' replied his host. 'I suppose it is quite useless as you understand use. But even if art and poetry have no use, it does not follow that they have no value.'[79]

Thus all the efforts to find a use for the tree are self-defeating, whether they are Doone's attempt to use it as the hiding-place for a corpse, or Branden's attempt to use it as the solution to a murder mystery, or Judson's own attempt to use it as the starting-point for a frivolous scientific theory. The only person who remains unaffected by these fantasies is the poet who sees no use in the tree at all. In a word, the allegory draws the same contrast which one finds in C. S. Lewis's *Abolition of Man* between those who accept nature and those who attempt to exploit it.

By the end of the story, the allegory has acquired a more universal and perhaps more predictable meaning. The story is related to the fall of man, and the tree represents the forbidden tree in the Garden of Eden. Windrush's happiness and innocence are the reward for his child-like sense of wonder:

'You scientific men are very superior, of course, and there is nothing legendary about you. You do not believe in the Garden of Eden. You do not believe in Adam and Eve. Above all, you do not believe in the Forbidden Tree.'

The doctor shook his head in half-humorous deprecation, but the other went on with the same grave fixity of gaze.

'But I say to you, always have in your garden a Forbidden Tree. Always have in your life something that you may not touch. That is the secret of being young and happy for ever.'[80]

The allegory does not however conclude with this simple affirmation of Windrush's view of life. The values of common-sense and practicality represented by Dr Judson are affirmed as well. The intellect and the imagination are equally

important. As in all the examples of the Chestertonian dialectic
from Adam Wayne and Auberon Quin to Herne and
Braintree, the opposing forces represent two aspects of a single
reality. And as in all the later novels, human friendship
represents the force which resolves the conflict. Enid Windrush,
looking back at the struggle between her father and Dr Judson,
interprets it as a prefiguring sign of this eventual reconciliation:

> She wondered whether the whole of her riddle would not have
> been clear to her, from first to last, if she could have read it in those
> two dark figures dancing and fighting on the sunlit road against the
> white cloud; like two living letters of an alphabet struggling to spell
> out a word.[81]

What in fact the allegory finally implies is a blending of the
orders of nature and grace. The balance achieved by Christian
marriage transforms the garden into the centre of a new
creation. Enid and Dr Judson are perhaps not altogether
convincing as symbolic versions of Adam and Eve, but the
description of the garden in the morning sunlight and wind
with which the story ends does succeed in indicating the kind
of new beginning in which nature once again becomes symbolic
of the supernatural:

> On the top of the once accursed tree a small bird burst into song,
> and at the same moment a great morning wind from the south
> rushed upon the garden, bending all its shrubs and bushes and
> seeming, as does the air when it passes over sunlit foliage, to drive
> the sunshine before it in mighty waves. And it seemed to both of
> them that something had broken or been loosened, a last bond with
> chaos and the night, a last strand of the net of some resisting Nothing
> that obstructs creation, and God had made a new garden and they
> stood alive on the first foundations of the world.[82]

The social and theological elements which are only implicit
in the second story become quite explicit in the third. For the
most significant feature of 'The Ecstatic Thief' is the way in
which it applies the theological notion of sacrifice and repentance to a particular problem in the social order. What the
story recounts is an attempt of a modern business to come to
terms with its past. Although the past of the Nadoway
Company is never described in any detail, one gathers from
Alan Nadoway's rhetorical comments that it is thoroughly
disreputable:

'Cleansing the name of Nadoway—because the name of Nadoway stinks to the ends of the earth! Because the business was founded on every sort of swindling and sweating and grinding the faces of the poor and cheating the widow and orphan. And, above all, on robbery—on robbing rivals and partners and everybody else, exactly as I have robbed that safe!'[83]

The three Nadoway brothers represent three distinct attitudes towards the past. John, the eldest son, who inherits the business, and Norman, the Anglo-Catholic priest who attempts to reform it, both agree that the past is a shameful one and both reject what they call the old ways of doing things. But although they also agree to put into practice a plan of bonuses and co-partnership, they agree for very different reasons. Norman, who, like Raymond Percy in *Manalive*, works in a London slum and lectures on Political Economy, sees the reform of the business in terms of a kind of applied theology: the reforms are simply another opportunity for putting Christian Socialism into practice. He wants to do for the workers in his father's company what he has been trying to do for the workers in his parish. John's rejection of his father's methods and acceptance of his brother's revolutionary ones have little to do with motives of Christian Social justice, since his sole concern is the tarnished respectability of the family name. What he argues for is a sort of moral and economic relativism according to which new conditions require new moral and economic standards. There is in fact no essential difference between his business outlook and his father's. He is a later version in the altered conditions of the twenties of what his father had been in the very different conditions of late Victorian times.

But it is the attitude of Alan Nadoway which provides the real theme of the story. It should be noted first of all that his belief in the need for expiation in no way undercuts Norman's belief in the need for reforms. Presumably he would agree that Norman's plans are as good as they seem to be; presumably, too, he would approve of any scheme that would make the business more human. But he insists that the company must undergo a process of repentance and expiation which is analogous to the conversion of an individual, before any reform can be effective.

Instead of ignoring the past, he attempts to change it. The allegory which he acts out has the twofold character of restitution and sacrifice. The symbolic restitution consists chiefly in a kind of alms-giving, and the sacrifice consists in the restitution being made to look like theft. In this way, as a representative of the family, he attempts to reverse his father's commercial ethic. The theft which masqueraded as respectability is expiated by virtue masquerading as theft. For him, social justice consists in redressing a cosmic balance. Saving appearances is not enough. The apparently just suffering of the innocent must redeem the apparently just prosperity of the guilty.

The frequency with which biblical imagery is used suggests that the act of expiation is also an act of religion. Thus he describes the new respectability of the business as a sort of Pharisee's virtue, a whited sepulchre which disguises the corruption within: 'And I knew that within, it was full of dead men's bones, of men who had died of drink or starvation or despair, in prisons and workhouses and asylums, because this hateful thing had ruined a hundred businesses to build one.'[84] More than that, his impersonal love of social justice is also inspired by a personal love for his father, whom he sees as the victim of the evil success of the business, and for whom his expiation is a vicarious sacrifice: '. . . I prayed, for one passionate instant, that my miserable death might avail to deliver him from that hell.'[85]

It is not difficult to find literary parallels for this theory of repentance. The situation which Alan Nadoway attempts to solve is, for example, not very different from the situation which Conrad describes at the beginning of *Nostromo*, in his fable of the doomed treasure hunters who are eternally hungry and thirsty because they are unable to perform an act of repentance, 'where a Christian would have renounced and been released'.[86] And in Chesterton's own fiction, a similar theme is found in the Prior's Park chapter of *The Man Who Knew Too Much*. A more curious parallel can be found in the novels which Maurice Baring published in the twenties and the early thirties. Although these novels are never concerned directly with the question of social reform, the theme of each of them turns on the need for sacrifice. Blanche Clifford finds release from her unhappiness only when she turns it into a form of expiation,[87] and C's tragedy consists in his inability to accept his anguish.[88] The theology of creative suffering is perhaps most clearly developed in *Daphne Adeane*,[89] where Fanny Choyce's life unconsciously repeats the pattern of retributive suffering undergone by the dead heroine.

For Baring, as for Chesterton, the sacrifice must be inspired by supernatural grace if it is to be efficacious. That is why Christopher Trevnan's protest about the British policy during the Armenian massacres has no real value. As Yakove explains to him, 'I say it is a pity not because I do not admire people who sacrifice something for an idea, but because I am not sure your nature can bear the consequences: Your ideas spring from rage and are spurred by reaction and so may easily turn to sourness instead of balm. And the essence of sacrifice is balm.'[90] For Baring the chain of selfishness, which he believed to be implicit in most human action, could be broken only by a heroic acceptance of suffering, which was made possible only by grace.

But Baring's fictional studies of the working of grace, which impressed French critics such as Charles Du Bos, Gabriel Marcel, and François Mauriac, do not provide an exact parallel to Chesterton's treatment of the theme.[91] The sacrifice which the Baring heroes and heroines make never provides an escape from suffering, and although it results in a kind of stoical peace, the peace is incommunicable. Nor do the novels suggest a way in which the sacrifice can have social consequences, since it has little effect on the external side of the life of the person who makes it and none on the society in which the person lives.

It therefore seems very unlikely that the theme of expiation in Chesterton's fiction owes much to Baring's novels. The differences in their treatment of it are far more striking than any similarities. The real interest in the comparison lies in the difference between Baring's essentially individualistic theological preoccupations and Chesterton's emphasis on the social and political side of the same doctrine. And it scarcely needs to be emphasized that the theme is not original to either author. One might, for example, cite the example of George Eliot to show how it can inspire the work of a writer who no longer accepts the theology on which it is based. And indeed Maggie Tulliver's insight in *The Mill on the Floss* that personal happiness cannot depend on the unhappiness of others or Dorothea's decision in *Middlemarch* to perform an act of disinterested goodness are in a way closer to the situation which Chesterton describes in his novel than anything one finds in Baring's fiction.

The social meaning which Chesterton gives to the theme of repentance does however mark a new moment in his political fiction. Although Distributism is neither mentioned nor alluded to in the story, the insistence that any programme of social reform must fail which does not have the profoundly religious character of sacrifice has surely some bearing on Chesterton's own programme for social reform. It is the apparent absence of this element in Christian Socialism which the story obliquely criticizes, and one may suppose that its absence from Distributism would be a defect as well. In other words, there is a more directly religious note in this story than is found in any of the earlier fiction.

'Oh, don't you understand? Don't you understand how shallow all these moderns are, when they tell you there is no such thing as Atonement or Expiation, when that is the one thing for which the whole heart is sick before the sins of the world? The whole universe was wrong, while the lie of my father flourished like the green bay-tree. It was not respectability that could redeem it. It was religion, expiation, sacrifice, suffering. Somebody must be terribly good, to balance what was so bad. Somebody must be *needlessly* good, to weigh down the scales of that judgment.'[92]

But although the precise theme is new, its development follows familiar lines. Perhaps the most significant of these is the association of religion with romance. In *The Return of Don Quixote*, romanticism is linked both with a failure in politics and a successful quest in religion; it is at once the cause of a political disaster and a religious conversion. Although romantic politics prove unable to solve the social problem they help to illuminate, they offer a solution to the religious crisis which they help to create. In 'The Ecstatic Thief', the pattern is much the same. Alan Nadoway's social scheme contains the same romantic defect which flaws Herne's League of the Lion. Like Herne, he remains convinced of the truth of his theory and, like him, too, he discovers that the practical effects of his theory ultimately cause more harm than good. The conclusion he draws however is rather different. Whereas Herne turns from politics to individual good works, Nadoway decides that individual efforts are futile and that expiation, if it is to be effective, must be carried out by institutions and by rule.[93]

The romanticism which helps explain the form in which Alan expresses his sacrifice also prepares the reader for his ceremonial courting of Millicent Milton. For it is the romanticism which each recognizes in the character of the other which forms the basis of their love. It is this absurdly theatrical but nonetheless appealing quality which Millicent sees both in Alan and in the house which his father built:

> With all its grotesqueness there had always mingled in her mind something almost operatic and yet genuine; something of real sentiment or passion that there was in the Victorian nineteenth century, despite all that is said of Victorian primness and restraint. It was that essentially innocent, that faulty but not cynical thing, the Romantic Movement. The man standing before her, with his quaint and foreign half-beard, had about him something indescribable that belonged to Alfred de Musset or to Chopin. She did not know in what sort of harmony these fanciful thoughts were mingling, but she knew that the music was like an old tune.[94]

The romantic side of Millicent's own character which appeals to Alan has a more obviously social meaning. The attraction is after all a typical one: the son of a nineteenth-century business-man wants to marry the daughter of a decayed aristocratic family. The emblem of this appeal is the brooch with the Chaucerian inscription, 'Amor Vincit Omnia' which he gives her. But the romanticism with which it identifies her is slightly bogus, for the brooch is described as 'sort of imitation fourteenth century'.[95] Perhaps more significantly, the brooch also identifies her with the social type represented by the prioress: a woman who combines frivolous but genuine religious sentiment with the self-assurance of an English lady:

> 'Why, the Prioress is an immortal portrait in a few lines of a most extraordinary creature called the English lady. You can pick her out in foreign hotels and pensions. The Prioress was nicer than most of those, but she's got all the marks; fussing about her little dogs; being particular about table-manners; not liking mice killed; the whole darned thing even down to talking French, but talking it so that Frenchmen can't understand.'
> He turned very slowly and stared at her.
> 'Why, *you're* an English Lady!' he cried as if astonished. 'Do you know they are getting rare?'[96]

And so the story ends somewhat inconclusively with the religious theme of social expiation apparently resulting in nothing except the conventional ending of a conventional love story. Nonetheless the final scene in the garden during which Alan quotes Chaucer to Millicent is in its own way significant. For in what are called the noble words about the sacrament of marriage, we do have at last something like a successful blend of religious and romantic sentiment.

And without moving his eyes or hands away from where they rested, he repeated the opening words of Theseus in the Knight's Tale about the sacrament of marriage, and as he spoke those noble words as if they were a living language, I will so write them here, to the distress of literary commentators:

> '. . . The first Mover of the Cause above
> When he first made the fair chain of love
> Great was the effect and high was his intent:
> Well wist he why, and what thereof he meant.'

And then he bent swiftly towards her; and she understood why that garden had always seemed to hold a secret and to be waiting for a surprise.[97]

'The Loyal Traitor', the fourth story in the novel, is a purely political parable. The action follows the same pattern as the earlier stories: virtue is once again given the appearance of vice, and it comes as no surprise to learn that the man who seems to have betrayed both his own country and his own friends is a patriot. But there is also a way in which the particular twist given to the plot recalls *The Man Who Was Thursday*. The imaginary conspiracy of the Anarchists is replaced by the imaginary Revolutionary Movement of the Word, and instead of an Anarchist Council made up of six detectives in masks, we have a revolutionary council made up of one man wearing four successive masks. The exact meaning of the story is nonetheless difficult to define. Despite the witty disclaimer that the action does not take place in the Balkans, 'where so many romancers have rushed to stake out claims ever since Mr Anthony Hope effected his *coup d'état* in Ruritania,'[98] the story does have a distinctively Ruritanian flavour. But it is perhaps more accurately described as a satire on modern journalism and a study of modern political life.

As an analysis of contemporary politics, it bears a certain resemblance to Baring's *Friday's Business*. Chesterton's Pavonia,[99] like Baring's imaginary state of Kossovia, seems to be located somewhere in Central Europe. And the ironical description of Pavonian political life describes perfectly the situation one meets at the beginning of Baring's novel:

. . . it is enough to secure the reader's respect and interest to know that it was a thoroughly modern and enlightened community, which had advanced in every science and perfected every social convenience until it was within reasonable distance of revolution; not a potty little palace revolution, in which a few princes are murdered, but a real, international, universal social revolution; probably beginning with a General Strike and probably ending with bankruptcy and famine.[100]

But the political arithmetic in the two novels is very different. Baring makes some attempt at realism, and the four political groups who make successive bids for power are immediately recognizable in terms of the political division between Right and Left in the early thirties: with the 'Fakelist' semi-military clubs and the Monarchist party on the one hand, and the Communist and Liberal Parties on the other. Chesterton makes no attempt at this kind of verisimilitude. Pavonia may indeed be a microcosm of post-War political life, but there is no reason to believe that the story is a realistic study of political life, or far less, that it offers detailed blue-prints for political reform. It would occur to most readers that there are clearly few countries in modern Europe that could be frightened into reform by a political threat that exists only in the imagination.

The chief interest of the four revolutionary parts which John Conrad plays is the picture they provide of the four political types which Chesterton regards as necessary for a revolution. The poet Sebastian, whose appearance and whose theory of poetry recall Lucian Gregory, provides the movement with its romantic idealism. Professor Phocus, with his European reputation as a scholar of 'vast learning and laborious accuracy',[101] provides it with an aura of social respectability: 'He was the scientific world: the world of colleges and committees.'[102] And if Sebastian and Professor Phocus are supposed to represent the imagination and the brains which are necessary for a revolution, Lobb and General Casc represent the material interests which make imagination and brains a real threat.

As a revolutionary millionaire, Lobb partly recalls Sunday and his South African and American Capitalist friends, who dabble in Anarchy as a kind of nihilistic hobby, and partly Enoch Oates, whose support of the League of the Long Bow makes the Distributist revolution possible. That Lobb should be Jewish fits in perfectly with Chesterton's belief that Jews, and particularly, Jewish financiers, are equally disposed to become capitalists or revolutionaries. The Distributist tenet that Capitalism and Communism are essentially the same thing has as its corollary the belief that the Jewish Capitalist finds his counterpart in the Jewish revolutionary.[103] Thus Simon's analysis of Lobb implies the familiar racial theory of the Jews as a rootless and therefore politically dangerous people:

'Avarice is not a Jewish vice; it's a peasant's vice, a vice of people who want to protect themselves with personal possessions in perpetuity. Greed is the Jewish vice: greed for luxury; greed for vulgarity; greed for gambling; greed for throwing away other people's money and their own on a harem or a theatre or a grand hotel or some harlotry—or possibly on a grand revolution. But not hoarding it. That is the madness of sane men; of men who have a soil.'

'How do you know?' asked the King with mild curiosity. 'How did you come to make a study of Jews?'

'Only by being one myself,' replied the banker.[104]

The material basis of the revolution is completed by General Casc, the dictator from the neighbouring country, who is supposed to supply the military expertise and the soldiers, which are essential for the revolution. The importance of military genius is expressed in words which echo Chesterton's criticism of Carthage in *The Everlasting Man*.

'Money doesn't fight. Men fight. If the time comes when men won't fight, even money won't make them. And somebody has got to teach them how. How are your revolutionary armies going to be drilled? Will Mr Sebastian drill them to recite poems? Will Mr Lobb drill them to fill in pawntickets?'[105]

What one is chiefly concerned with, however, is not the composition of a revolutionary movement, but the nature of modern journalism. The point to the story is not the existence of a revolutionary threat, nor even the fact that there is no revolutionary threat, but that in the unreal world which one calls the modern state an imaginary conspiracy can be as effective as a real one. The story is concerned with a satiric

situation very similar to the one Evelyn Waugh describes in
Scoop. John Conrad's achievement in inventing the revolutionary council is much the same as Jakes's achievement in
inventing a Balkan war. Waugh's journalist, one recalls, was
sent to report a revolution in one of the Balkan capitals and,
although he arrives in the wrong country, he nevertheless
sends a thousand-word story about the barricades in the
streets ('machine guns answering the rattle of his typewriter as
he wrote')[106] which creates a new revolution:

> 'Government stocks dropped, financial panic, state of emergency
> declared, army mobilized, famine, mutiny and in less than a week
> there *was* an honest to God revolution under way, just as Jakes had
> said. There's the power of the Press for you.
> 'They gave Jakes the Nobel Peace Prize for his harrowing
> descriptions of the carnage—but that was colour stuff.'[107]

In Chesterton's novel an additional irony is provided by the
resemblance between the imaginary conspirators and the actual
rulers. There is a sense in which the four conspirators are
projections of the fears and guilts of the four members of the
ruling junta. For although there is in fact no real revolutionary
council, there is a real revolutionary situation. The readiness
of the ruling council to accept the existence of the revolutionary
council is an admission of the existence of the social injustices
which makes a revolution necessary: the four revolutionaries
form a mirror as it were in which they see the distorted images
of themselves. That may be why each revolutionary possesses
both the qualities and the exact degree of importance which
belongs to his counterpart. The imaginary General Casc and
Lobb are the most important members of their group: the real
General Grimm, the head of the Secret Police, and Simon,
the Jewish banker, are the most important members of theirs.
King Clovis is as apparently ineffectual and as ultimately
important as the poet Sebastian; and the similarity between the
positions of the Prime Minister and Professor Phocus is
suggested by the similarity of their appearance and manner:
the pince-nez and the fussiness of the one are matched by the
spectacles and the pedantry of the other. Thus the description
of the relative power of the different members of the junta
describes equally well the relative power of the members of the
revolutionary council:

It has already been explained that Pavonia was governed on enlightened modern principles. That is to say, the King was popular and powerless; the popularly elected Premier was unpopular and moderately powerful; the head of the Secret Police was much more powerful, and the quiet and intelligent little banker, to whom they all owed money, was most powerful of all.[108]

The ironical similarity also adds point to the way in which the rulers are duped. It is doubly appropriate that their opposites should deceive them with the same kind of journalistic trick with which they are accustomed to deceive their own people, and that they should be victims of the unreal world of journalism which they have helped to create:

'. . . you've no notion how easy it is to bamboozle a really enlightened, educated modern town, used to newspapers and all that. It was only necessary for each person to have a vast, vague reputation, more or less foreign. When Professor Phocus wrote learned letters to the papers, with half the alphabet after his name, nobody was going to admit they had never heard of the famous Professor Phocus. When Sebastian said he was the greatest poet in modern Europe, everybody felt that he ought to know. And if you get three or four names of that sort nowadays, you have got everything. There never was a time in history when the few counted for so much, and the many for so little. When the newspapers say "The nation is behind Mr Binks", it means that about three newspaper proprietors are behind him. When the professors say "The opinion of Europe has now accepted the Gollywog theory", it means that about four professors in Germany have accepted it.'[109]

Even more interesting is the effect of the revolutionary movement on the four rulers. It might be said that it makes them at once much worse and much better than they are. It makes them much worse, because it reveals the truth about their actual political positions. The Prime Minister's reputation as a radical is suddenly seen to be a sham; 'The new revolutionary movement had suddenly revealed him as a rather obstinate capitalist, turning, as it were, his sturdy figure black against the red glare.'[110] General Grimm's inability to deal with a genuine military threat also becomes clear for the first time; and the absurdity of Simon's confidence in the power of money is also revealed. And even the King's ineffectualness is at last seen as a sort of irresponsibility.

But the threat of revolution also makes them much better

than they were. It brings to the surface a latent nationalism which they have almost forgotten, and, by making them aware of the profound love they have for the country they have misgoverned, it transforms a group of selfish egoists into a band of patriots. The scene in which they make this discovery is interesting for a student of Chesterton's fiction not only because it defines patriotism in terms of the threefold appeal of a shared history, literature, and landscape,[111] but also because, for the first time in any of the novels, both a Jewish financier and a discredited politician are given credit for possessing what Chesterton regarded as the basic national virtue:

There was nothing in that room that did not in some way recall the unreplaceable achievement of a special civilization; the busts of Pavonian poets, who could have written only in the Pavonian tongue, filled the niches and corners of the room; the dark glimmer of the bookcases told of a national literature not to be lightly lost or possibly replaced, and here and there a picture like a little window gave a glimpse of the distant but beloved landscapes of their native land. Even the dog that lay before the fire was of the breed of their own mountains, and there was not a man there so mean—no, not even the politician—as not to know that by all these things he lived and with all these things he would die.[112]

Even more significant from the point of view of the development of Chesterton's fiction is the role the king plays in resolving the political crisis. At the moment when he decides to act, he acts as the embodiment of the nation, so that the reform of Pavonia and the success of John Conrad's revolution of the 'Word' ultimately depend on his word. It might of course be argued that King Clovis's decisive role in the story is simply another expression of a view which Chesterton held throughout his life and expressed frequently in his fiction. Maisie Ward tells how he wept at the news of Queen Victoria's death and in later years he refused to publish any article in his own paper which seemed critical of the monarchy.[113] There are occasional satiric jibes at Edward VII in his writings, but even these are friendly and good-natured.[114] More characteristic is his praise of George V in the *Autobiography*[115] and the leading article he wrote in *G.K.'s Weekly* at the time of his death, in which he describes him as 'a good man who was called to a great office'.[116]

And there is certainly nothing in anything that Chesterton

wrote which suggests a criticism of the monarchy as such. In fact it is always presented as the one part of the English Constitution which is largely unaffected by corruption and therefore seems to offer the possibility of bringing about reform.[117] That is why the return of kingship is one of the political dreams which haunts the imagination of his heroes from Wayne and MacIan to Herne and John Conrad. The initial situation is always the same: a king attempts to intervene on the side of the people and is thwarted by the plutocrats. What his fiction constantly presents is the incident which Chesterton makes the centre of his *Short History of England*: the moment when Richard II, 'the crowned sacramental man',[118] offers to lead the peasants' revolt:

The King was no more than a boy; his very voice must have rung out to that multitude almost like the voice of a child. But the power of his fathers and the great Christendom from which he came fell in some strange fashion upon him; and riding out alone before the people, he cried out, 'I am your leader'; and himself promised to grant them all they asked. That promise was afterwards broken; but those who see in the breach of it the mere fickleness of the young and frivolous King, are not only shallow but utterly ignorant interpreters of the whole trend of that time. The point that must be seized, if subsequent things are to be seen as they are, is that Parliament certainly encouraged, and Parliament almost certainly obliged, the King to repudiate the people.[119]

The change in King Clovis from a weak and ineffectual constitutional monarch to a popular leader is therefore entirely consistent with Chesterton's political thought. What is new and surprising is that the King is for the first time successful, and that the impossible dream is at last a reality instead of the ultimate illusion.

Another change of emphasis which 'The Loyal Traitor' suggests is its more cautious attitude towards revolution. In *The Man Who Knew Too Much*, Horne Fisher is willing to see the whole of society blown to bits with dynamite; in *Tales of the Long Bow*, the revolution which introduces the Agrarian State is accepted as an obviously good thing; and although *The Return of Don Quixote* deals with the subject of revolution only incidentally, it is nonetheless clear that one is supposed to welcome the kind of revolution which Braintree is working for. But in *Four Faultless Felons*, one is encouraged to look beyond a revolution which begins with a general strike to the bankruptcy and famine which will follow it. In fact what one is asked to approve is not the revolution, but the avoidance of revolution. The measure of the success of John Conrad's programme of gradual reform is that it saves Pavonia from the kind of revolution which takes place in General Casc's country, which, 'after some months of very bewildering civil war, had ended in the victory of one out of the six revolutionary generals fighting each other in the field'.[120]

It is of course true that Chesterton, even in his early writing, sometimes distinguishes between two kinds of revolution. Thus, for example, in an early essay, he contrasts a fire in Beaconsfield which destroys a pile of new lumber with the bonfire which destroys a pile of rubbish. The first fire, which takes place at night, represents the meaningless destruction of good things; the second fire, which takes place on the day of George V's coronation, represents the necessary destruction of worthless things. And the two fires become the images of two contrasting revolutions:

And then I saw in my vision, that just as there are two fires, so there are two revolutions. And I saw that the whole mad modern world is the race between them. What will happen first—the revolution in which bad things shall perish, or that other revolution, in which good things shall perish also? One is the riot that all good men, even the most conservative, really dream of, when the sneer shall be struck from the face of the well-fed . . . and the other is the disruption that may come prematurely, negatively, and suddenly in the night; like the fire in my little town.

It may come because the mere strain of modern life is unbearable; and in it the things that men do desire may break down; marriage and fair ownership and worship and the mysterious worth of man. The two revolutions, white and black, are racing each other like two railway trains; I cannot guess the issue . . .[121]

Although this passage assumes that one of the two revolutions will eventually take place, there is no doubt that it also expresses a fear of the indiscriminateness of a certain kind of revolutionary violence. Similarly in the third appendix to *What's Wrong With the World*,[122] he argues that a sweeping redistribution of property can be brought about by a programme similar to George Wyndham's Land Act, and 'without any more confiscation'.[123] More to the point, there is some evidence that he was increasingly repelled by the course which revolutions were taking in post-War Europe, and, more particularly, repelled by the course which the revolution was taking in Russia.[124] In a word, 'The Loyal Traitor' presents in fiction an attitude which was always to some extent present in Chesterton's other writing.

The Paradoxes of Mr Pond, the last of Chesterton's novels, was published posthumously in 1937. It follows the familiar form of eight linked short stories, which began with *The Man Who Knew Too Much* and concluded with *The Poet and the Lunatics*. Although the stories are supposed to be based on Mr Pond's conversations with either Sir Hubert Wotton or Captain Peter Gahagan, they are told by an anonymous narrator who claims to remember Mr Pond as an old friend of his father's, but who plays no direct part in any of the stories he narrates, and whose whole function, it would seem, is to give the conversations the shape of fiction. Thus in the fifth chapter, he describes his work in these terms: 'Mr Pond then proceeded to narrate his little experience, which, when purged of Gahagan's interruptions and Pond's somewhat needless exactitudes, was substantially this.'[125]

Although many of the themes of the novel are political, it is impossible to discover any central theme which gives the novel its unity. Generally one moves from the contemporary politics of the early thirties to the politics of the War or pre-War days, which are used to illustrate or interpret them. Thus in a typical story, a conversation about the Nazi persecution of the Jews becomes the starting-point for a story about the anti-German feeling in England during the First World War.[126] The meaning of this somewhat formless collection of stories is therefore difficult to define. Its political interest seems to depend partly on the character of Mr Pond himself, the first bureaucrat to be the hero of a Chestertonian romance, and partly on the way in which the stories qualify political themes which were developed more completely and perhaps more satisfactorily in the earlier fiction.

Certainly *The Paradoxes of Mr Pond* cannot be described as the triumphant conclusion to Chesterton's novels, and indeed one must have serious misgivings in describing it as a novel at all. The slight degree of unity which it does possess seems to depend almost entirely on its political meaning, and some of the stories have at best a tenuous connection with politics, and others no apparent connection at all. Thus in chapter two, 'The Crime Captain Gahagan' might be read as a light satire on American journalism and post-War drama, or it might be interpreted as a detective story which turns on the modern fashion of clipped speech and inaccurate reporting, but it has no obvious political meaning. It might be argued that the sixth chapter, 'The Ring of Lovers', advances whatever plot the novel may possess by bringing Gahagan's love-story to a conclusion, but its only general interest is the picture it presents of the difference between public lives and private realities. So, too, with the seventh and eighth chapters. 'The Terrible Troubadour' has little serious point of any kind, except perhaps as a curious retelling of Poe's *Murder in the Rue Morgue*, and 'A Tall Story' is chiefly interesting as an illustration of the way in which Chesterton re-evaluated his feelings about anti-Germanism and anti-Semitism.

But although half the novel is concerned with matter that has no immediate bearing on political or social questions, certain aspects of the book are of considerable interest to a student of Chesterton's fiction. 'The Three Horsemen of Apocalypse', for example, presents his first fictional study of the Polish question, and 'When Doctors Agree' presents a curious study of the dangers of a post-Christian society. It might of course be said that the interest of these two stories is at least partly biographical, since they seem to record in a unique way Chesterton's post-War journey to Poland[127] and possibly and more curiously a visit to Professor John Phillimore in Glasgow.[128] But like many other of the stories, they are also interesting for the unexpected foot-notes which they provide to the earlier fiction and for the indication which they give of the direction in which his political thought was moving during the last years of his life.

The most curious feature of 'The Three Horsemen of Apocalypse' is not that it seems to celebrate the virtues of Poland uncritically, but that it celebrates these virtues in an indirect way. There is indeed a vivid picture of the Polish marshes, but there is no picture of Poland itself, which in fact is only seen through the eyes of the German army. So, too, with the Polish poet and singer, Paul Petrowski: although he is the central figure in the story, he is never directly presented. It seems clear that as a national poet and as an international singer ('he sang his own patriot songs in half the concert halls of the world'),[129] he is reminiscent of Paderewski, the well-known Polish political figure, who was also famous as a musician. But the chief subtlety of the story is that although the historical setting is left deliberately vague, it seems to take place some time before the First World War. Thus one is compelled to assume the existence of the Polish nation at a time when it had no legal existence.[130] Perhaps, however, the clearest comment on the political view which the story expresses is provided in an essay which Chesterton wrote in April 1919, and which might be mistaken for an essay based on Conrad's *Autocracy and War*:[131]

. . . We know that a flood threatens the West from a meeting of two streams, the revenge of Germany and the anarchy of Russia; and we know that the West has only one possible dyke against such a flood, which is not the mere existence, but the might and majesty of Poland. We know that without some such Christian and chivalric shield on that side, we shall have half Europe and perhaps half Asia on our backs.[132]

What the story emphasizes, however, is the antagonism between Poland and Germany. This conflict is represented by Marshal Von Grock, who is at the army base at one end of the causeway, and Petrowski, who is in prison in Poznań, at the other end of it. It would be easy to interpret the role of Petrowski as a development of the role of Sebastian in *Four Faultless Felons*. Like Sebastian, he is the poet of revolution, and is at once an idealist and a man of action: 'the torch and trumpet of revolutionary hopes' and of 'prodigious importance in practical politics'.[133] But unlike Sebastian, he presents an immediate danger to the social authority which Von Grock, with a soldier's instinct, immediately understands: 'He did not scoff at visions; he only hated them. He knew that a poet or a prophet could be as dangerous as an army.'[134]

But the conflict between Germany and Poland is actually carried out by Germans. The three horsemen are after all the German messengers who ride to Poznań carrying contradictory orders regarding Petrowski, and if two of them are presented as the odious Prussians of Chesterton's wartime propaganda,[135] the third is the representative of German culture and indeed of German romance. Thus it is significant that Arnold Von Schact, who represents the central and moderate German tradition, should be the second of the three riders. For in the story he is destroyed by the Prussian extremists, and his death has the twofold effect of bringing about the destruction of the plans of the men who murder him and of saving the life of the Polish poet. More particularly, his death results in the death of his own murderer and the furtherance of the Polish cause.

This seems to be the explanation for the way in which the German romantic tradition is linked by imagery to the Polish national cause. The prince who orders the amnesty is described in terms of allusions to Goethe and Greek literature and his passion for music. And we are told that the messenger whom Von Hocheimer murders looks like 'the very embodiment of all that more generous tradition of Germany'.[136] It is at this point that the dead Arnold is transformed into a hero of romance: 'The moon made a sort of aureole of the curled golden hair of young Arnold, the second rider and the bearer of the reprieve . . . Under such a glamorous veil of light, he might almost have been in the white armour of Sir Galahad.'[137] Thus the conflict between the romance of Polish nationalism and the inhuman realism of Prussia is expressed not so much by the direct conflict between Grock and Petrowski, but by the contrast between Grock and the dead Arnold:

> Grock had taken off his helmet again; and though it is possible that this was the vague shadow of some funereal form of respect, its visible effect was that the queer naked head and neck like that of a pachyderm glittered stonily in the moon, like the hairless head and neck of some monster of the Age of Stone. Rops, or some such etcher of the black fantastic German schools, might have drawn such a picture: of a huge beast as inhuman as a beetle looking down on the broken wings and white and golden armour of some defeated champion of the Cherubim.[138]

One may therefore see the murder of Arnold as the emblem of the view of German history which Chesterton inherited from Belloc.[139] The Prussians are as much the enemies of Germany as they are the enemies of Poland. Arnold and Petrowski are so closely identified that whatever happens to one affects the other. That is why, for example, Sergeant Schwartz, thinking of the death of Arnold, thinks of the death of Petrowski, and in doing so expresses the truth: 'He had helped to kill a Pole.'[140]

There is a similar irony to Grock's comment on Arnold's death, which suggests the suicidal character of the Prussian spirit. Throughout the story, Grock is described alternatively as a creature of stone and as a hideous predatory bird; in his pronouncement on the death of Arnold this imagery finally coalesces into an image of the Prussian ego. The image which stands behind this comment is of course the national emblem of Germany, the two-headed imperial eagle, which Chesterton had used effectively in his poem on Poland[141] and which Conrad had used for somewhat more polemical purposes in *Autocracy and War*.[142] For Grock, death is 'the fact of all facts',[143] and a death which is willed and accomplished provides a way of escaping from the human condition, in which, so long as life lasts, repentance is always possible, and grace is able to create a new life. Ironically, however, the two-headed eagle, looking backwards and forwards, also symbolizes the self-destructive meaning of Prussia. Grock's messengers, like the two heads of the eagle, destroy the older and more humane Germany represented by Arnold, but they also destroy themselves. The first rider, who looks backwards and murders Arnold, is killed by the third messenger who looks forward and mistakes him for the man who has been murdered. Unknown to himself, Grock is describing the futility of the German will:

Grock said no prayer and uttered no pity; but in some dark way his mind was moved, as even the dark and mighty swamp will sometimes move like a living thing. . . .

'After and before the deed the German Will is the same. It cannot be broken by changes and by time, like that of those who repent it. It stands outside time like a thing of stone, looking forward and backward with the same face.'[144]

The death of the German romantic also becomes a kind of Christian allegory. Arnold is identified with the chivalry of Petrowski and Petrowski in turn is identified with the chivalry of Poland. And so the vicarious death of the young German which enables the Polish patriot to live also brings life to the Polish nation itself. More than that, Petrowski's 'death' and 'life' are given a Christian meaning as a kind of imitation of the death and resurrection of Christ. Both the poet and the nation he represents 'rise from the dead'. This mystical significance of

G

Polish nationalism is an idea which was often expressed by
Polish writers, from Adam Mickiewicz and Andrzej Towiański
to Apollo Korzeniowski, the father of Joseph Conrad.[145] It is
difficult to know whether Chesterton was aware of this Polish
literary tradition, but as someone who prided himself on his
knowledge of Polish history[146] and who visited Poland officially
as a kind of national hero, it is quite possible that he may have
been familiar with it. In any case, the passage in which the
sergeant tells Grock about the freeing of Petrowski might have
been written by any Polish romantic author:

'Haven't they buried him yet?' asked the Marshal, still staring
down and in some abstraction.
'If they have,' said Schwartz, 'he has rolled the stone away and
risen from the dead.'[147]

Thus the story succeeds in different ways. Most superficially
it succeeds as a kind of detective story: like one of the stories
described in the note to the Beaconsfield edition, as 'a well-told
tale, [providing] some characteristic light entertainment'.[148]
It also succeeds as an effective sort of Polish propaganda, which
teaches a particular view of Germany, while at the same time
attempting to do something like justice to the German romantic
tradition. More importantly, it succeeds in achieving its effects
by strictly literary means, so that an imaginary incident from
Polish history becomes an allegory on the meaning of
Prussian materialism and the ultimate victory of Polish
nationalism.

The political side of 'When Doctors Agree' can be discussed
more briefly, for it is a comparatively simple story. The interminable argument between Dr Campbell, the saintly philanthropist, and Angus, the student doctor, is a debate about
Christianity and Atheism, which is not altogether unlike the
arguments between Turnbull and MacIan, the two other
argumentative Scots of Chesterton's fiction. The murder of
James Haggis is chiefly interesting as an illustration of
Chesterton's belief in the seriousness of ideas: the humanitarian
kills the radical, because he sees him as an obstacle to his
plans for slum clearance in Glasgow. For although Haggis's
belief in 'Retrenchment and Reform'[149] is sincerely held, in
Campbell's view it threatens a large and helpless part of the
community. But Haggis's obscurantism and Campbell's

humanitarianism are equally genuine: the doctor kills with the same conviction with which the Glasgow Baillie obstructs his reforms. Similarly Angus kills Dr Campbell for entirely logical reasons, and the antagonism between them follows the severely logical pattern of Chesterton's other stories. The humanitarian who loves the group but detests the individual is opposed first by a Christian radical who is kind to individuals, but has no sense of the common good, and then by a Christian fundamentalist, who hates the Doctor, because he believes him to be as cruel and as inhuman to individuals as his radical antagonist was to the group. And when Dr Campbell finally converts Angus to Atheism, Angus is free to kill him.

But the most interesting point is the way in which it seems to imply a sharp distinction between Christianity and social good works. There is after all no suggestion that Campbell's slum relief is anything but admirable or that what is called 'the whole lifetime of charity and good works'[150] is anything but genuine. One must therefore suppose that Haggis's opposition to Campbell does result in a great deal of harm, and that Campbell's moral philosophy, which he describes as a kind of social surgery, does in its way make perfect sense: 'As we sacrifice a finger to save the body, so we maun sacrifice a man to save the body politic. I killed him because he was doing evil, and inhumanly preventing what was guid for humanity: the scheme for the slums and the lave.'[151]

The sociology and politics do not however provide the central focus of this unusual parable. Campbell is finally killed, because he persuades someone who detests him to accept his own moral philosophy; Angus's conversion to scepticism enables him to treat 'the silver-haired saint of sociology'[152] as he had treated Haggis. Although he comes to believe that his religious faith was a dream, he hates the man who has awakened him: 'I still think you were doing evil; even though you were serving truth. You have convinced me that my beliefs were dreams; but not that dreaming is worse than waking up.'[153] Campbell is identified with an eighteenth-century sceptic and philanthropist, but it is his scepticism which is questioned and not his philanthropy:

'What a disguise there is in snowy hair and the paternal stoop of age! . . . In some odd way, indeed, I seemed suddenly to see old age itself as a masquerade. The white hair had turned into a white wig, the powder of the eighteenth century; and the smiling face underneath it was the face of Voltaire.'[154]

But although the identification of Campbell with Voltaire does not in itself cast doubt on his role as a humanitarian, the suggestion remains that without Christianity, his humanitarian plans are, in Angus's words, 'cruel and inhuman'.[155] Campbell loves mankind, but not individual men; '. . . he cared less about the individual than about the public or the race'.[156]

For in spite of its protestations that humanitarianism is good, the story really does question the value of social reforms which are not inspired by Christianity. The theology which Chesterton outlined in *The Everlasting Man* is therefore brought to its logical conclusion. Human good is a preparation for grace, but without grace, human good becomes corrupt; the best accomplishments of nature are indeed good, but without grace they cannot remain so.[157]

The story might therefore be read as a grim and prophetic commentary on the fate of scepticism in a post-Christian society. In a Christian society, Campbell is free to continue his destructive sceptical work and free also to accomplish a great deal of genuine social good, but his freedom exists only so long as the society in which he lives remains in some sense Christian. He is free to do good works only so long as the Christian order he opposes continues to exist. The moment when scepticism will find itself in greatest danger is the moment when Christians become sceptics. The suggestion is not only that Christianity provides the moral restraint which protects scepticism from the people it vilifies ('Day after day, you have been battering down the scruples which alone defended you from death'),[158] but that it will be destroyed by those who will blame it for having deprived their world of its significance. Its bitterest enemies will be its final converts.

It is interesting that during the twenties and thirties Chesterton consistently refused to look upon the Left as a political danger. His position on this question does not change in his final novel. Socialism and Communism are dismissed as false but not dangerous philosophies, except to the extent that they are distractions from the real danger of the Servile State which they unconsciously help to introduce. In *The Paradoxes of Mr Pond*, as in all Chesterton's fiction, the serious political danger is seen as the danger from the Right. In *The Return of Don Quixote*, Braintree's Syndicalism receives real if qualified approval and Herne's medievalism is revealed as the final trick of a Capitalist ruling class: one does not look forward to the success of the League of the Lion, which after Herne's abdication and Archer's accession to power becomes frankly Fascist. In *Four Faultless Felons*, the novel begins with the story of a plot which is carried out by a reactionary extremist and ends with the story of the opposition of financial interests to true reform. In *The Paradoxes of Mr Pond*, the story 'Pond the Pantaloon' presents a situation which is essentially the same.

The conspiracy in England, 'aiming at a *coup d'état*',[159] is never described in detail. Sir Hubert Wotton tells the story to Gahagan, who in turn tells it to the narrator. The vagueness about the conspiracy may therefore be explained partly as a matter of diplomatic reticence. But the fact that it is supposed to have happened many years before and that it 'was backed by a Continental Power of similar leanings'[160] would seem to suggest that these political leanings were Rightist rather than of the Communist variety. The references to 'gun-running' and 'secret drilling',[161] and the emphasis given to Dyer's impatience with constitutional checks and to his love of military efficiency also suggests an outlook which is usually associated with Fascism rather than Communism. Wotton's claim that Pond 'saved England'[162] may not be altogether convincing, but the way in which he is supposed to have done so provides an interesting illustration of a recurrent Chestertonian theme. His plan for defeating the conspiracy consists in hiding the document as an ordinary parcel among thousands of other ordinary parcels. In this way, he makes use of the common-place democratic institution of the post in order to defend democracy. The document is protected by being lost as it were in the crowd; it is saved, because it travels in the ordinary way.

Fortunately, perhaps, very little attempt is made to allegorize in this rather simple story. One is grateful, for example, that the change of the colour of the box from white to the black associated with reaction seems to have as little political significance as Dyer's Hitler-like moustache. The only obviously allegorical point which is made is that the conspirators are defeated by their own thoroughness. The efficiency by which Dyer tries to impress his superiors with his loyalty eventually puts him into a position where there is no-one left to suspect but himself.

There may also be some significance in the part played by Hankin, who is the clown in the story. As Gahagan remarks, he is relevant because of his irrelevancy:

'He is like the Clown in Shakespeare . . . he [seems] to be there by accident unconnected with the story and yet he is the chorus of the tragedy. The Fool is like a fantastic dancing flame lighting up the features and furniture of the dark house of death.'[163]

Practically speaking he does do two valuable things: he proves that it is impossible to enter the station without being heard, and he helps Wotton to disarm Dyer. Dressed in the circus costume of a clown from 'the old-fashioned pantomime',[164] and holding the red-hot poker which Pond has given him, he startles Dyer into the action which amounts to a confession. More significantly, however, he stands as a representative of the real poor in England which the revolution is supposed to help. The point seems to be that Hankin, like all Chesterton's common men, is essentially apolitical, and the revolutionary movement which has his betterment as its ostensible aim understands him as little as he does it. When Sir Hubert sees Hankin for the first time, he believes that he has 'his first real glimpse of those depths in which despair manufactures the many revolutionary movements which it had been his duty to combat'.[165] The irony of the story is that the Common Man, with 'a face and figure so symbolic of desolation and dreary tragedy',[166] helps to support the social authority which has oppressed him. For although Hankin fails to understand the meaning of the adventure into which he has stumbled, he nonetheless finds himself in conflict with Dyer: the bewildered representative of the English people is an unconscious enemy of the revolution which is supposed to improve his lot.

'The Unmentionable Man', the fifth chapter in *The Paradoxes of Mr Pond*, presents another version of the political problem dealt with in 'The Loyal Traitor' in *Four Faultless Felons*. The political crisis which threatens the anonymous republic is not of course the same as that which threatens Pavonia. The government is indeed also under the influence of a financier about whom we learn little, except that he is 'a millionaire named Kramp',[167] and there is a sense in which the same revolution which is averted in Pavonia is about to take place in the republic with the outbreak of a transport strike. Kramp, who is supposed to control both the government and the transport lines paralysed by the strike, is an obvious equivalent to Lobb who controls Pavonia. But there is no exact equivalent to the earlier revolutionary council or the ruling junta, unless one considers the somewhat preposterous Tarnowski, 'The Tiger of Tartary',[168] as another version of John Conrad. In fact the real parallel with the earlier story is provided by M. Louis, who is a more interesting version of King Clovis.

The story is after all another study of the meaning of kingship in a modern State. M. Louis, the man—who cannot be deported—represents both a political force which is outside ordinary political calculations, and the monarchy which has disappeared amid the wars and revolutions which have introduced the republic. For although the republic is a theoretically egalitarian society, it is undermined by economic injustice: 'Like many such [republics], it did not find all its troubles were over with the establishment of political equality; in face of a world deeply disturbed about economic equality.'[169] We see nothing of the members of the government, apart from the brief glimpse of Dr Koch, the Minister of the Interior who interviews the king. But a picture of the republic gradually emerges from what the defenders and the enemies of the regime say about it. The importance of the king is that he is able to reconcile these conflicting views. Although Tarnowski, the Communist revolutionary, pretends to be a bourgeois bookseller, and Marcus, the minor government official who believes in the individualistic theory of free contract, pretends to be a Socialist, their real roles as enemy and defender of the republic are obvious from the first. Also from the first their political thought is defined in relation to that of the king, who represents a synthesis of what is best in both their positions. The weakness of the revolutionary's analysis is implied by the glibness of the Marxist jargon with which he attempts to hide his identity and his real view of the social problem:

'Myself of the *bourgeoisie*, I have yet remained apart from politics. I have taken no part in any class-war proceeding under present conditions. I have no reason to identify myself either with the protest of the proletariat or with the present phase of capitalism.'[170]

The king is everything which the Marxist is supposed to be. As Pond somewhat unnecessarily points out, he might easily be mistaken for a Communist agitator, since he is genuinely popular with the strikers and his passionate concern for social justice is evident to everyone. Although he expresses this concern in language which pre-dates Marxism, his view expresses everything that is positive in the Marxist social theory. Similarly his belief in the older and more traditional concept of distributive justice expresses everything that is positive in Marcus's Liberal theory of free contracts and the ultimate Social Contract on which free contracts are based. In a word, the king is presented as the embodiment of all that is best in Socialism and Republicanism; he is at once the real revolutionary leader and the real republican.

Tarnowski's *Realpolitik* and his belief in scientific Socialism fail to appeal to the poetry of the strikers, and Marcus's embarrassed attempts to defend the republic reveal how badly it is in need of defence. For the Communist, the king appears to be usurping the role of a revolutionary; for the Liberal, he appears to be blackmailing a discredited government. Both the Liberal and the Socialist claim to be following respectively the scientific politics of the eighteenth and nineteenth centuries, but it becomes clear that the king's romantic politics transcend historical epochs and are in fact more practical than either of their alternatives.

The social circumstances of the Communist and the Liberal are also inconsistent. Tarnowski is theoretically on the side of the strikers and opposed to the status quo, but he lives in not altogether unpleasant middle-class comfort. Marcus is a fanatical individualist, who is theoretically opposed to the strike and on the side of the government, but he lives the life of the poorest worker. Once again the king reconciles these social inconsistencies. He is at home in every social class. In his conversations in the café, he receives with equal ease and urbanity students, children from the slums, a farmer and a lady. The love of justice and the passion for social equality, which take such antagonistic forms in the Liberal's almost anarchical devotion to freedom and the Communist's single-minded devotion to the proletariat, find their balance in kingship, which reconciles all the divergent elements of class and social interest.

In *The Resurrection of Rome*, Chesterton argues that the idea of monarchy is opposed to neither radical Liberalism nor to social equality.[171] In his final novel, he provides a parable which makes the same point with equal force. The republic based upon 'the idea of equality and justice'[172] to which Marcus remains loyal, and the revolution to which Tarnowski devotes his life are balanced and brought into equilibrium by the king. Significantly the only political group which are excluded from this synthesis are the politicians themselves. It might therefore be said that 'The Unmentionable Man' marks the final stage in Chesterton's personal political development, and represents the synthesis in Chesterton's own political views, in which he finally reconciles both his early interest in Socialism and Liberalism with his later detachment from party politics.

The view of monarchy which the story presents might also be described as a synthesis of Chesterton's fiction. The romantic dream of the return of the king, which inspires MacIan's Jacobitism and Herne's medievalism, finds in this story its most simplified but most hopeful realization. In *The Ball and the Cross*, monarchy means the sacrifice of justice to order; in *The Return of Don Quixote*, the realities of industrial society turn the king into a Don Quixote figure who can remedy social evils only by dealing with them one by one and leaving the national problem of social justice as the subject for Braintree's cheerless Syndicalism. In both cases, monarchy proves unworkable. But in 'The Unmentionable Man', the king returns not as the reactionary tyrant implied by MacIan's dream or as the short-sighted puppet of the ruling-class as in *The Return of Don Quixote*, but as a practical politician, who, like Shaw's King Magnus, belongs to no political party, and has a greater popularity than any republican or Socialist popular leader.[173]

It is also tempting to see M. Louis as occupying the kind of central and harmonizing position in Chesterton's imaginary republic which Chesterton tried to occupy in the little world of Distributist politics.[174] Like M. Louis, Chesterton claimed to be the leader of both the political Left and the Right, and the moderating influence which he tried to exercise on the warring factions of his own movement was similar to the kind of political influence which the King exercises in the last of his novels. The historian of Distributism concludes his account of the movement with the pathetic complaint that the Distributist

G*

paper was captured by the right wing of the movement
immediately after Chesterton's death.[175] This may perhaps be
true. But it is of course impossible to guess whether Robbins is
right in saying that Chesterton would have supported the
Republicans in the Spanish Civil War or whether the new
editor of *G. K.'s Weekly* was right in claiming Chesterton's
authority for the support the paper gave to the Loyalists.[176] But
what is significant is that both groups could so plausibly claim
the dead Chesterton as their leader.

Maisie Ward records with something like distaste the story of
the interminable wrangles between the Distributist factions, and
she argues that the movement, in addition to being a financial
and emotional strain on Chesterton, was a distraction from his
true career as a writer. The financial and emotional strain
certainly existed, as even Titterton and Robbins admit. But to
argue that politics kept Chesterton from literature is to mis-
conceive his view of both literature and politics. The literary
works which Distributism is supposed to have prevented him
writing, if they were to be anything like the literary studies on
Browning and Stevenson which he actually wrote, would have
been political manifestos with a political or social idea at the
heart of every one of them.[177] The distinction between Chesterton's literary and political writings is in fact illusory, because it
is a distinction which Chesterton never accepted. For him
literature was itself an important political force, and whether it
took the form of an essay for the *Illustrated London News* or a
satiric poem, or a novel, he regarded it always as an expression
of the political concern which he called his 'legitimate liking for
direct democratic appeal'. And indeed this is particularly true
of his novels, and that is why it is fitting that in the last of them
he should describe a political synthesis which escapes political
categories and transcends, as Distributism was supposed to
transcend, the bitter divisions between Left and Right.

6 Conclusion

There are two general conclusions which may be drawn from a study of Chesterton's novels. The first concerns the somewhat unexpected political view which an analysis of them reveals, and the second the correlation between their political meaning and their literary value.

It is of course true that the fiction does reflect fairly accurately the political thought which one finds in the other writing. Early novels such as *The Napoleon of Notting Hill* and *The Ball and the Cross* and pre-World War One novels such as *Manalive* and *The Flying Inn* again and again echo essays written at the same time. The preoccupation with Distributism which characterizes the post-War essays is also characteristic of the post-War novels and short stories. In 'The Resurrection of Father Brown', for example, the priest-detective makes a somewhat improbable appearance as a kind of Distributist reformer in South America. And in one of the last and most melodramatic of the stories, 'The Crime of the Communist', the action is almost entirely concerned with the familiar Distributist argument that revolutionary Socialism and modern Capitalism are essentially the same phenomenon. Ronald Knox, in making a selection of the stories, found that the didactic purpose sometimes crowded out the detective interest: '. . . have we not good reason to complain of an author,' he asks, 'who smuggles into our minds, under the disguise of a police mystery, the very solicitude he was under contract to banish?'[1] It is also true that in a number of the stories one finds evidence of the same allegorical imagination which gives the best novels their remarkable power. A story such as 'The Chief Mourner of Marne' is perhaps more successful as a sermon on the sacrament of penance than as a story about an unusual duel, and a story such as 'The Dagger with Wings' probably fails equally as a detective story and as a political tract. But there remains a considerable group of stories in which the didactic purpose is brilliantly fulfilled by purely literary means. And although the imperceptive reader may miss the social or political point which is at the centre of stories such as 'The Invisible Man' and 'The Queer Feet', they are stories which nonetheless deserve Frank Swinnerton's description as fables that mesmerize. Often the very settings have a symbolic value. Thus the Dantesque imagery of bitter cold which pervades 'The Sign of the Broken Sword' is altogether relevant to a story which deals with the theme of treason.

But the most interesting and important feature which a study of the fiction reveals is the treatment of medievalism in the novels. The common view of Chesterton's social philosophy is that it expresses a longing for a literal return to medieval times. A careful study of the novels indicates the falsity of such a view. The shortest summary of what they have to say about the restoration of a medieval social order is that it is a dangerous political dream. In *The Napoleon of Notting Hill*, Adam Wayne's neo-medievalism brings back poetry and pageantry to modern life, but it also creates a neo-Imperialism which is as oppressive as the Imperialism it was supposed to replace. In *The Ball and the Cross*, MacIan's dream of a medieval theocracy turns out to be a nightmare of authoritarian terror and oppression. Even in a later novel such as *Tales of the Long Bow*, which corresponds most closely to the popular view of his medievalism, surprisingly little is said about a return to a medieval past: what is achieved by the successful Distributist revolution is the protection of a newly created and broadly based agrarian society.

But the most subtle and ironic treatment of medievalism is found in the novel which was serialized in *G. K.'s Weekly*, at a time when Chesterton was simultaneously director of the Distributist League and editor of the paper which was its organ. *The Return of Don Quixote* is perhaps the best example of the way in which the best fiction is at once sophisticated and well-balanced propaganda for a political philosophy and extraordinarily effective literature. The medieval experiment which the hero introduces does little to alter the political realities of modern life, except to the extent that it distracts the people from the existence of the real social problems which it leaves unaltered. The restoration of pageantry and colour to political life which delights Herne and his followers is also a means of deceiving them. It might be argued that the Distributist criticism of State Socialism and Capitalism is now turned against Distributism itself. Certainly nothing that Chesterton's critics have written about the folly of romantic medievalism in politics hits as shrewdly as his own criticism of it in what is ostensibly his most flamboyantly medieval novel.

The novels also associate the illusion which medievalism represents with the unreality of the medieval world which is actually restored. The medievalism of Notting Hill depends ultimately on the frivolous improvisations of Auberon, who not only claims no special knowledge of history but in fact regards the entire project as a joke. The medievalism of *The Ball and the Cross* and that of *The Return of Don Quixote* are equally bogus and egotistical and invite the same kind of doubts. There is, for example, no reason to believe that Herne's few days of antiquarian research have really qualified him as the medieval specialist he is supposed to be, and the result of this hastily conducted research shares something of the theatrical quality of the amateur play-acting with which it begins.

At the same time the ironical treatment of medievalism does not imply the rejection of 'medieval' values. The dream of restoring a medieval social order may be a dangerous illusion, but there is a sense in which the illusion is necessary. It has in fact the qualities of a myth. Those who mistake it for a reality destroy the society they are trying to reform, but those who recognize it as an ideal possess a valuable means of understanding and judging the modern world. Perhaps the best example of the way in which medievalism becomes a way of understanding modern political life is found in *The Man Who Knew Too Much*. The medieval pageant in which Horne Fisher takes part provides him with the historical perspective he needs in order to understand the squalid charade of modern politics in which he is also involved. Sometimes those who misunderstand the function of the medieval myth and those who understand it are the same people. Adam Wayne and Evan MacIan learn eventually from the romanticism which at first deludes them. And in *The Return of Don Quixote*, Herne's superficial studies finally provide him with the principles which enable him to condemn his own medieval political experiment.

Another way in which the novels reveal an unexpected side of Chesterton's political and social philosophy is more directly

related to their allegorical quality. This has to do with the use
of opposed but complementary characters who help to define a
complete and balanced political point of view. The success with
which this method is used varies greatly from novel to novel,
and indeed it is fully used only in the early novels and in a certain
number of the novels which were published in the early and
mid twenties. The elements involved in the balance remain
remarkably constant. The main conflict is always between a
kind of idealism on the one hand and a kind of irony on the
other, and the resolution of the conflict always involves a
reconciliation of the political forces which have been previously
opposed. In *The Napoleon of Notting Hill*, Auberon's irony and
Adam's fanaticism are finally revealed as the two essentials of
political sanity which achieve their equilibrium in the Chestertonian common man. In *The Ball and the Cross*, the quarrel
between MacIan and Turnbull dramatizes the conflict between
romantic Christianity and revolutionary Socialism, and is
finally resolved by an affirmation of the values which each of
them represents. In the other pre-War novels little attempt is
made to create a political synthesis in this way. Nonetheless in
Manalive, Innocent Smith derives a kind of cumulative wisdom
from the various political types whom he meets on his journey
around the world, and in *The Flying Inn*, Humphrey Pump
represents a complete expression of what Chesterton meant by
the common man.

It is in the early post-War Distributist novels that the use of
political and social typology achieves its most interesting form.
In *The Man Who Knew Too Much*, Horne Fisher makes a far
more detailed case against the corruptions of parliamentary
government than one finds in *The Flying Inn*. Admittedly the
emphasis is generally negative, but in a story of almost unrelieved political disaster, some attempt is made to understand
the motives of those who bring the disaster about. In *Tales of
the Long Bow*, a series of marriages between different political
and social types illustrates the pastoral side of Distributism. But
the most successful use of typology is found in *The Return of Don
Quixote*. Themes that were treated individually in the earlier
novels are now brought together as the first complete expression
of the Distributist political and social viewpoint. The political
forces which are reconciled in the final synthesis are various and
unexpected. Instead of the familiar opposition between

characters representing idealism and irony, the novel introduces three central characters, each of whom possesses valuable political insights and dangerous political limitations. Herne, a romantic idealist in the tradition of Wayne and MacIan, is ostensibly the directing force of the novel's action. Braintree, who has affinities with Turnbull and Lord Ivywood, is at once the embodiment of the revolutionary spirit which demands social justice and the doctrinaire spirit which ignores the variety and complexity of real life. Murrell, who recalls the ironic detachment of Auberon, also represents a kind of Tory scepticism about the possibility of political improvement, which was characteristic of Horne Fisher.

The kinds of women these men fall in love with and the part played by women add a further complexity to the novel. Herne's impersonal idealism turns into a kind of neo-Fascism under the influence of the strong-minded Rosamund Severne; whereas Braintree's Syndicalism is eventually humanized under the influence of Olive Ashley's romantic idealism. Murrell undergoes a rather different transformation. His attempt to find the lost illumination colour becomes a romantic quest during which he falls in love and discovers an instance of the social injustice which is the real subject of the book. There is little in Chesterton's other writing which prepares one for the surprising resolution of this many-sided conflict. The resolution involves first of all a sharp distinction between religion and politics. The idealism which leads to political disaster also leads to religious conversion. But the movement of disillusioned romantics towards medieval religion involves a corresponding affirmation of the Syndicalist solution of worker-control for the social problem which romantic medievalism was unable to solve.

It is also important to note that this grouping and re-grouping of political types is achieved not by the mechanical manipulation of characters, but by purely literary means. The action is controlled by a developing pattern of imagery which changes as the story proceeds. The pageant which becomes a real-life drama and the quest for colour which brings the pageant to an end are symbolic as well as literal events. The broken monument in the park represents the vague romanticism which inspires much of the action of the novel, but it also represents the tragic separation of religion and idealism, which is one of the novel's central themes. In a novel which Chesterton called a parable for social reformers,[2] the monument of the dragon standing alone without the angel that destroys it is an emblem of the need for a balance between the ideal and the practical sides of life. And the crimson illumination-paint which Olive Ashley seeks is at once the colour of the stained-glass window, which represents the religious values that are absent from modern life, and the colour of Braintree's revolutionary red tie, which represents the political solution to modern problems.

The way in which the novels sometimes fail to use imaginative means successfully is best illustrated perhaps by the final group of novels. The chapters which make up *The Poet and the Lunatics* are never more than random illustrations of a central theme, and they are illustrations that do remarkably little to advance the main action, which remains curiously static. The order of events is entirely haphazard, and the chapters seem merely to mark time until the somewhat predictable conclusion is reached. Even the elaborate and ingenious attempt to unify *Four Faultless Felons* does not quite disguise the essential dissimilarity of the stories that are supposed to be unified. And in *The Paradoxes of Mr Pond* the breakdown in unity is so complete that instead of a novel one is left with a series of loosely related short stories. The defects of the earlier novels are also present and present in an exaggerated form. The intrusive symbolism which occasionally mars some of the earlier novels is also found in the later fiction where the heavy-handed symbolic details have little relevance to the action they are supposed to clarify: every garden is an ironic Eden and every sunrise and sunset the symbolic background for a trivial event or a minor climax.

More significantly the literary decline is a political decline as well. The definition of social sanity in *The Poet and the Lunatics* is as vague and confused as the manner in which the story is narrated. It is also difficult to say what coherent political meaning emerges from the bewildering mixture of political and social themes which one finds in *Four Faultless Felons*. It is perhaps significant that most of the themes which are treated in the later novels have received their successful and definitive treatment in the early fiction. Indeed much of the repetitiousness and sense of fatigue which characterize the literary decline in the late novels can be explained in terms of their almost parasitic dependence on the political concerns of the earlier fiction. This apparent need to rely on reworking old material may explain why so much of the action of the later novels is set in an indeterminate period of the past and why so much of the political background is concerned with the politics of Edwardian rather than contemporary times.

It would not be difficult to multiply examples of the new vagueness of outlook and the new lack of imaginative grip. The effect is not always an unhappy one. The rather confused tolerance which is now expressed for Imperialism is balanced by the new tolerance which is extended towards the Jews, who for the first time are represented in something like a favourable light. The old hostility towards Germany is also modified, and in *The Paradoxes of Mr Pond*, the very effective Polish propaganda of 'The Three Horsemen of Apocalypse' includes a defence of German romanticism; and 'A Tall Story', the final chapter of the book, may be read as a kind of apology for Chesterton's contribution to anti-German hysteria during World War One. But the most important example of what the new blandness and loss of imaginative power involve is provided by the treatment of the theme of kingship in the final novels.

It is of course true that the exploration of this theme provides a partial exception to the general absence of contemporary politics in the late novels. To some extent at least the treatment of this theme represents Chesterton's last attempt to come to terms with a political force which he recognized as genuinely modern. But the treatment of the theme owes as much to the earlier fiction as it does to any new awareness of what was happening in contemporary politics. The king, who makes his appearance in *Four Faultless Felons* as Clovis the Third of Pavonia, and in Mr Pond's imaginary republic as the Unmentionable Man, derives his real interest from being a member of the group of monarchs which begins with Auberon Quin in *The Napoleon of Notting Hill* and ends with Michael Herne in *The Return of Don Quixote*. In relation to these figures from the earlier fiction, the king of the later fiction is a new and somewhat disquieting version of a very familiar Chestertonian type. At first the change in his role seems to be entirely an improvement. Instead of the ineffectual romantic who releases political forces he can neither understand nor control, he is now the practical statesman standing above party politics, but ready to intervene in them when the interests of the nation require. Saving the people from a corrupt parliament seems to be his favourite occupation. In Pavonia, he prevents a revolution by championing the policy of reform that the politicians have neglected, and in Mr Pond's anonymous republic he succeeds in reconciling the conflicting values of revolutionary Socialism and Liberal idealism. In a word, he represents an easy solution to the difficult problems of modern politics.

But these un-Chestertonian virtues of efficiency and success are the very qualities which make him a rather ominous figure. In one of the late essays, Chesterton calls monarchy the mood of the hour.[3] What is disturbing about the expression he gives to this mood in the final novels is the apparent lack of awareness of how dangerous it could be. The political role he imagines for the king is perhaps harmless enough. And since he is supposed to represent genuine authority, it is probably unfair to call him a Fascist figure. But the way in which he combines contempt for parliamentary government with a fondness for authoritarian action does suggest the kind of Fascist solution which some of Chesterton's followers were accused of advocating shortly after his death.

Thus what at first seems to be the one important imaginative development in the late novels is in fact a final indication of the way in which they represent a failure in political imagination. The greatness of the failure can be measured only by a comparison between what the king had been with what he has now become. The comic subtlety that gave an unexpected meaning to medievalism, and the delicate balance between a multitude of political types that gave an extraordinary power to the best of his fiction have disappeared, and one is left instead with the grim and humourless figure of a king whose negative qualities make him an Auberon who has lost his wit and a Herne who has learned nothing from experience.

Notes

PREFACE

1   *The Ball and the Cross* (Beaconsfield: Darwen Finlayson, 1963), p. 8.
2   Professor W. W. Robson, 'Father Brown and Others', *G. K. Chesterton: A Centenary Appraisal*, edited by John Sullivan (London: Elek, 1974), p. 58.

1. INTRODUCTION

1   See, for example, Maisie Ward, *Gilbert Keith Chesterton* (London: Sheed and Ward, 1944), p. 413.
2   C. S. Lewis, 'Notes on the Way', *Time and Tide*, 9 November 1946, pp. 1070–1.
3   Hugh Kenner, *Paradox in Chesterton* (London: Sheed and Ward, 1948).
4   Letter to Rev. Kevin Scannell, 7 January 1966 (private collection).
5   T. S. Eliot, 'Obituary Note', *The Tablet*, 20 June 1936, p. 785.
6   ibid., p. 785.
7   Two writers who illustrate this attitude are D. B. Wyndham Lewis and Emile Cammaerts. See Lewis's introduction to *G. K. Chesterton: An Anthology* (London: Oxford University Press, 1957), pp. i–xxi, and Emile Cammaerts's, *The Laughing Prophet: The Seven Virtues and G. K. Chesterton* (London: Methuen, 1937). For a personal account of the possessive attitude towards him found among English Catholics and the hostile feelings this sometimes provoked, see George Bull, 'In Praise of Chesterton', *The Tablet*, 3 May 1969, p. 442.
8   Bernard Bergonzi, 'Chesterton and/or Belloc', *Critical Quarterly*, I, 1959, pp. 64–71.
9   'Notes on Nationalism', *The Collected Essays, Journalism and Letters*, edited by Sonia Orwell and Ian Angus, volume III (London: Secker and Warburg, 1968), pp. 365–6.
10 Evelyn Waugh, 'Chesterton', the *National Review* [New York], 22 April 1961, p. 251.
11 ibid., p. 252.
12 Graham Greene, 'G. K. Chesterton', *Collected Essays* (London: The Bodley Head, 1969), pp. 136–7.
13 Chesterton, *Culture and the Coming Peril* (London: University of London Press, 1927), p. 18.
14 *Autobiography* (London: Hutchinson, 1937), pp. 288–9.
15 ibid., p. 289.
16 Chesterton, 'Old Curiosity Stop', *Appreciations and Criticisms of the Works of Charles Dickens* (London: J. M. Dent, 1911), pp. 519–60.
17 Chesterton, 'Portrait of a Friend', *Autobiography*, Chapter XIV, pp. 288–306.

18   ibid., p. 289.
19   Quoted by Anthony Everett Herbold in *Chesterton and G. K.'s Weekly*
      (Unpublished doctoral dissertation, University of Michigan, 1963),
      pp. 41–2.
20   M. H. Abrams, *A Glossary of Literary Terms* (New York: Holt, Rinehart,
      and Winston, 1965), p. 2.
21   ibid., p. 3.
22   Chesterton, *William Blake* (London: Duckworth, 1910), p. 141.
23   ibid., p. 141.
24   ibid., p. 142.
25   Chesterton, *G. F. Watts* (London: Duckworth, 1904), p. 65.
26   *The Poet and the Lunatics: Episodes in the Life of Gabriel Gale* (London:
      Darwen Finlayson, 1962), p. 92. For full bibliographical details see
      Chapter IV, note 1.
27   John Holloway, *The Victorian Sage: Studies in Argument* (New York:
      W. W. Norton, 1965), pp. 10–11.

2. THE EARLY NOVELS

1   *The Napoleon of Notting Hill* (Beaconsfield: Darwen Finlayson, 1964),
     p. 8. The novel was first published by John Lane, 22 March 1904. See
     John Sullivan, *G. K. Chesterton: A Bibliography* (London: University of
     London Press, 1958), p. 25. Subsequent references to the novel will be
     abbreviated to *N.N.H.*
2   *Autobiography* (London: Hutchinson, 1937), p. 112.
3   Chesterton, *Orthodoxy* (London: John Lane, The Bodley Head, 1908),
     p. 113.
4   ibid.
5   ibid., p. 109.
6   ibid., p. 108.
7   ibid., p. 143.
8   ibid., p. 144.
9   Cecil Palmer, *The Collected Poems of G. K. Chesterton* (London: Cecil
     Palmer, 1927), p. 104.
10   *Autobiography*, p. 342.
11   ibid., p. 113.
12   *N.N.H.*, p. 14.
13   This phrase is somewhat misleading. The 'greyness', in the sense of
     dullness and the absence of romance, is real enough, but it is not the
     result of any lack of colour. The bright colours which Auberon
     restores to London have in fact always been there; what was lacking
     was a pattern which would give them meaning. An emblem of what
     Auberon accomplishes is suggested by Juan del Fuego's action at the
     beginning of the novel. By using part of the Colman's mustard poster
     for his improvised flag, he gives the colour yellow, which has always
     been present and always been ignored, a dignity and a significance
     which it never had as part of an advertisement. (*N.N.H.*, p. 23.)
        Chesterton develops the same idea in a later book: 'We hear the
     realists (those sentimental fellows) talking about the grey streets and
     the grey lives of the poor. But whatever the poor streets are they are
     not grey; but motley, striped, spotted, piebald and patched like a
     quilt, . . . a London gutter-boy walks unscathed among furnaces of
     colour. Watch him walk along a line of hoardings, and you will see
     him now against glowing green, like a traveller in a tropic forest; now

black, like a bird against the burning blue of the Midi, now *passant* across a field gules, like the golden leopards of England ... There is no blue much bluer than Reckitt's Blue and no blacking blacker than Day and Martin's; no more emphatic yellow than that of Colman's Mustard. If, despite this chaos of colour, like a shattered rainbow, the spirit of the small boy is not exactly intoxicated with art and culture, the cause certainly does not lie in universal greyness or the mere starving of his senses. It lies in the fact that the colours are presented in the wrong connection, on the wrong scale, and, above all, from the wrong motive. It is not colours he lacks, but a philosophy of colours.' Chesterton, *What's Wrong With the World* (London: Cassell, 1910), pp. 214–5.

14 This quotation is part of a passage which is worth quoting at some length. In it, Chesterton argues that the spirit in which one states one's political aims is more important than the details with which they are elaborated: 'When a great revolution is made, it is seldom the fulfilment of its exact formula; but it is almost always in the image of its own impulse and feeling for life. Men talk of unfulfilled ideals. But the ideals are fulfilled; because spiritual life is renewed. What is not fulfilled, as a rule, is the business prospectus. Thus the Revolution has not established in France any of the strict constitutions it planned out; but it has established in France the spirit of eighteenth century democracy, with its cool reason, its bourgeois dignity, its well-distributed but very private wealth, its universal minimum of good manners. Just so, if Socialism is established, you may not fulfil your practical proposal. But you will certainly fulfil your ideal vision. And I confess that if you have forgotten these important human matters in the telling of a leisurely tale, I think it very likely that you will forget them in the scurry of a social revolution.' Chesterton, 'Why I am not a Socialist', the *New Age*, 4 January 1908, p. 190.

15 *N.N.H.*, p. 30.

16 ibid., p. 16.

17 ibid.

18 As special correspondent for the *Court Journal*, the King narrates the story in styles which are parodies of Edwardian journalism. See *N.N.H.*, pp. 144–59.

19 *N.N.H.*, p. 175.

20 ibid., p. 182.

21 ibid.

22 ibid., p. 26.

23 Even the fact that Adam Wayne's hair is red may have the same significance. For in *G. F. Watts*, Chesterton comments on the quality of the colours found in Watts's paintings: 'Then there is that tremendous autochthonous red, which was the colour of Adam, whose name was Red Earth.' (London: Duckworth, 1904), p. 129.

24 See Maisie Ward's account of the matter:
His Auberon's little elfish face and figure was recognized by old Paulines as suggested by a form master of their youth; but by the entire reviewing world as Max Beerbohm. The illustrations by Graham Robertson were held to be unmistakably Max. Frances notes in her diary: 'A delightful dinner party at the Lanes. ... The talk was mostly about *Napoleon*. Max took me into dinner and was really nice. He is a good fellow. ... He seems only pleased at the way he has been identified with King Auberon. "All right, my dear chap," he said to G., who was trying to apologize. "Mr Lane and I settled it all at a

lunch." ' *Gilbert Keith Chesterton* (London: Sheed and Ward, 1944), p. 153.

Chesterton's own comments on the identification explain its significance: 'No person is, in the most serious sense, so wise and understanding as Mr Max Beerbohm. And I grieve to say that, in describing the effect of streets in altering his moods he wrote: "In Notting Hill High Street I become frankly common." Which is absurd; and impossible; and therefore quite uncommon. The fairies punished him by putting parts of him into my unfortunate story; along with an admirable portrait of him in Mr Graham Robertson's illustrations. But I confess that the original idea, in the conscious intellectual sense, was concerned with places of that kind in general; and my book might have been "The Washington of Walham Green", or "The Kosciuszko of Kensington Oval", or "The Garibaldi of Gunnersbury", or "The Charlemagne of Chiswick", instead of "The Napoleon of Notting Hill". For I have never been able to conceal entirely from a derisive world the fact that I was driving at something; though I had then got no further than asking in rather a wild way "Is there nothing that will save Notting Hill from being frankly common?" ' 'A Note on Notting Hill', *The Week-end Review*, 20 December 1930, p. 915.

25   Chesterton, *Heretics* (London: The Bodley Head, 1905), pp. 220–1.
26   *N.N.H.*, p. 192.
27   ibid., p. 192. It is worth noting that the common man is also described as a universal type: an abstraction rather than a particular human being: 'I know of something that will alter that antagonism, something that is outside us, something that you and I have all our lives perhaps taken too little account of. The equal and eternal human being will alter that antagonism, for the human being sees no real antagonism between laughter and respect, the human being, the common man, whom mere geniuses like you and me can only worship like a god.'

28   *The Ball and the Cross* (Beaconsfield: Darwen Finlayson, 1963), pp. 186–7. The first English edition was published in London, by Wells Gardner and Darton, 24 February 1910, but the novel had been serialized in part in the *Commonwealth*, 1905–1906. See John Sullivan, op. cit., pp. 32–3. The *Commonwealth* was the organ of the Christian Social Union.

29   *The Ball and the Cross*, p. 187. Subsequent references to the novel will be abbreviated to *B.C.*
30   ibid.
31   ibid., p. 188.
32   ibid., p. 187.
33   ibid.
34   ibid.
35   ibid., p. 188.
36   ibid.
37   ibid., p. 189.
38   ibid.
39   ibid., pp. 188–9.
40   ibid., p. 191.
41   ibid., p. 190.
42   ibid.
43   ibid., p. 192.
44   ibid., p. 190.
45   ibid.

46 ibid., p. 191.
47 ibid., p. 192.
48 ibid., p. 191.
49 Jacques Maritain, *The Peasant of the Garonne* (London: Chapman, 1968), pp. 21–2. It is interesting to note that François Mauriac discusses the same question with reference to Maurice Barrès and Paul Bourget, who are two of the writers MacIan names as heroes in what he calls 'the conquering march of Catholicism'. *B.C.*, p. 132. For Mauriac, the distinction between Left and Right corresponds to two views of human nature: 'Nous nous interrogeons souvent sur ce qui sépare essentiellement la droite de la gauche. Je vois d'abord cette ligne de partage: il y a ceux qui font follement confiance à l'homme, la postérité de Rousseau; et les sages qui s'en méfient, mais dont la méfiance a vite fait de tourner au mépris. . . . En 1897, ce mépris va aller, chez certains, jusqu'à considérer que l'innocence présumée d'un condamné pour trahison doit peser moins lourd que les intérêts supérieurs qui exigent que sa condamnation soit maintenue.' François Mauriac, *Mémoires Intérieures* (Paris: Flammarion, 1959), p. 189.
50 *B.C.*, p. 192.
51 See, for example, James Stephens, 'The Period Talent of G. K. Chesterton', the *Listener*, 17 October 1945, pp. 513–4; and George Orwell, *The Collected Essays, Journalism, and Letters of George Orwell*, Vol. I, p. 189. See also Orwell, Vol. III, p. 366 and Vol. IV, pp. 96–7.
52 Robert Hugh Benson, *The Dawn of All* (Leipzig: Tauchnitz edition, 1911). This is the second of two novels in which Benson tried to present a picture of the world of the future. In the first, *Lord of the World*, Catholicism is described as almost completely destroyed; in *The Dawn of All*, Catholicism is described as finally triumphant.
53 The crisis in Benson's second novel occurs when Dom Adrian Benett, a Benedictine monk, is executed, because he is unable to believe that a miraculous cure has taken place. Although the hero, Monsignor John Masterman, is at first upset by the incident, he is finally persuaded by the monk himself that the execution is required for the common good.
   In the novel, some of the events recorded with approval are the reintroduction of heresy trials, the domination of the world by a group of Catholic monarchs, and the involvement of the pope in a plan to defeat the Socialist stronghold of Berlin.
54 *B.C.*, pp. 194–5.
55 ibid., p. 201.
56 ibid., p. 198.
57 ibid., p. 199.
58 ibid.
59 ibid.
60 ibid., p. 203.
61 ibid., p. 200.
62 ibid., p. 204.
63 It is interesting that the quality of the early romances of both authors should be misrepresented in a similar way. The pessimism of their work has been largely ignored, and 'Wellsian' and 'Chestertonian' are terms which are used to denote a superficial and rather cheap optimism. For a recent study of Wells's fiction, see Mark R. Hillegas, *The Future as Nightmare: H. G. Wells and the Anti-Utopians* (New York: Oxford University Press, 1967).
64 *B.C.*, p. 200.

65 ibid., p. 202.
66 ibid., p. 197.
67 ibid., p. 202.
68 ibid.
69 ibid.
70 ibid., p. 203.
71 *A Lodge in the Wilderness* (London: Thomas Nelson, [1916]). The book was published anonymously in November, 1906, and a second edition with the author's name was published early the following year.
72 ibid., p. 61. 'Next, there is the school of which we may take Mr. Chatterton as a representative. In theory they are full-blooded and masculine enough, though their heroics smack of Peckham. They love to rhapsodize about "Old England" and the Elizabethans, and beer and cricket, and heaven knows what. Their complaint is that a special extension means a weakening in intensity of the national life, and they also will throw Rome and Athens at your head. They are all for the virility of England, they say, as against the neurotic restlessness of the Imperialist. With them, again, I have a certain sympathy, though the taunt of "neurotic" comes ill from gentlemen whose style is so explosive and delirious. The answer to their arguments depends upon the question of the value of space and of the whole material basis in any spiritual development . . .'
73 ibid., pp. 209 and 245.
74 Alan Sandison, *The Wheel of Empire* (London: Macmillan 1967), p. 188.
75 *A Lodge in the Wilderness*, p. 71.
76 ibid., p. 70.
77 Thus we are told that Carey's country estates are meant 'to show the world a more excellent way'. (ibid., p. 12). Miss Haystonum, in referring to the spirit of the empire, says, 'it is the spirit which giveth life.' ibid., p. 29.
78 ibid., p. 156.
79 *B.C.*, p. 202.
80 ibid., pp. 237–8.
81 ibid., p. 173. See also, Book of Job, Chapters 38–42.
82 ibid., pp. 173–4.
83 ibid., pp. 175–6.
84 ibid., p. 174.
85 ibid., p. 239.
86 ibid., pp. 239–40.
87 An earlier remark prepares them for this discovery: ' ". . . You two were the only people he ever was afraid of." Then he added in a low but not inaudible voice: "except one—whom he feared worse, and has buried deeper." ' *B.C.*, p. 224.
88 *B.C.*, p. 238.
89 ibid., p. 247. In one of his essays, Orwell refers to a prophetic quality which he finds in the writings of both Belloc and Chesterton: 'Many earlier writers have foreseen the emergence of a new kind of society, neither capitalist nor Socialist, and probably based upon Slavery . . . A good example is Hilaire Belloc's book, *The Servile State*, published in 1911 [sic] . . . The remedy it suggests, [a return to small-scale peasant ownership] is for many reasons impossible; still it does foretell with remarkable insight the kind of things that have been happening from about 1930 onwards. Chesterton, in a less methodical way,

predicted the disappearance of democracy and private property, and
the rise of a slave society which might be called either capitalist or
Communist.' George Orwell, 'James Burnham and the Managerial
Revolution', op. cit., vol. IV, pp. 162–3.

90 *B.C.*, p. 252.
91 ibid.
92 Beatrice, like Turnbull, had been an unbeliever. See *B.C.*, pp. 120–21.
93 ibid., p. 254.
94 ibid., p. 245.
95 ibid., p. 248.
96 Chesterton, 'The Harp of Alfred', *The Ballad of the White Horse*
    (London: Methuen, 1911), p. 66.

3. THE PRE-WAR NOVELS

1 A note in the Penguin edition of *The Man Who Was Thursday* (1967),
   p. 186. The note was originally published in the *Illustrated London
   News*, 13 June 1936.
2 'Foreword', *The Man Who Was Thursday: A Play in Three Acts*. Adapted
   from the novel of G. K. Chesterton by Mrs Cecil Chesterton and
   Ralph Neale (London: Ernest Benn, 1926), p. 5.
3 *The Man Who Was Thursday: A Nightmare* (Beaconsfield: Darwen
   Finlayson, 1963), p. 9. The first edition was published by J. W.
   Arrowsmith at Bristol in February, 1908. See John Sullivan, *G. K.
   Chesterton: A Bibliography* (London: University of London Press,
   1958), pp. 27–8. Subsequent references to this novel will be
   abbreviated to *M.W.W.T.*
4 *M.W.W.T.*, p. 18.
5 ibid., p. 69.
6 ibid., p. 18.
7 Ronald Knox, 'Introduction', *Father Brown: Selected Stories*, by G. K.
   Chesterton: (London: Oxford University Press, 1966), pp. xi–xii.
8 *M.W.W.T.*, p. 192.
9 ibid., p. 13.
10 ibid.
11 ibid.
12 ibid., p. 192.
13 ibid., p. 13.
14 ibid., p. 177.
15 ibid., pp. 132–3. Compare this passage with Chesterton's description
   of the art of Aubrey Beardsley: '. . . there is a certain brief mood, a
   certain narrow aspect of life, which he renders to the imagination
   rightly. It is mostly felt under white, deathly lights in Piccadilly, with
   the black hollow of heaven behind shiny hats or painted faces: a
   horrible impression that all mankind are masks.' Chesterton, *The
   Victorian Age in Literature* (London: Williams and Norgate, 1913),
   pp. 225–6.
16 C. S. Lewis, 'Notes on the Way', *Time and Tide*, 9 November 1946,
   p. 1071. It is interesting that Bernard Bergonzi makes use of the same
   comparison to come to a very different conclusion: 'His
   [Chesterton's] novels are perhaps even more neglected than they
   deserve, for one of them at least—*The Man Who Was Thursday*, which
   is not a novel at all but a symbolic romance—deals with a potentially
   major theme; the whole problem of personal identity, so intriguing

to our own age. But we need only compare it with, say Kafka's symbolic fables on comparable themes, to see that Chesterton's story never rises above the level of a charade, or at least a prolonged and ingenious joke.' B. Bergonzi, 'Chesterton and/or Belloc', *Critical Quarterly*, I, 1959, p. 65.

17 *M.W.W.T.*, p. 45.
18 ibid., p. 190.
19 ibid., pp. 190–91.
20 Thus the meaning of Gregory's role as accuser is made explicit in the following passage: ' "Now there was a day," murmured Bull, who seemed really to have fallen asleep, "when the sons of God came to present themselves before the Lord, and Satan came also among them." ' ibid., p. 190.
21 *M.W.W.T.*, p. 46.
22 ibid., p. 134.
23 ibid., pp. 128–9.
24 See John Buchan, *The Courts of the Morning* (London: Hodder and Stoughton, 1929).
25 *M.W.W.T.*, p. 141.
26 ibid., p. 150.
27 ibid., p. 134.
28 ibid., p. 39.
29 ibid., p. 49.
30 See Christopher Dawson, 'The Nature and Destiny of Man', *Enquiries into Religion and Culture* (London and New York: Sheed and Ward, 1933), pp. 324–5.
31 *M.W.W.T.*, pp. 49–50.
32 See Christopher Dawson, 'Nihilism and Apocalypticism', *Progress and Religion* (London: Sheed and Ward, 1931), pp. 230–1.
33 R. A. Knox, 'Chesterton in his Early Romances', *The Dublin Review*, October, 1936, p. 361.
34 ibid., p. 361.
35 See, for example, Moon's conversation with Inglewood: ' " Have you noticed this about him," asked Moon, with unshaken persistency, "that he has done so much and said so very little? When first he came he talked, but in a gasping, irregular sort of way, as if he wasn't used to it. All he really did was actions . . .

    ' "I see why the mummers were mum. They *meant* something; and Smith means something too. All other jokes have to be noisy . . . The only silent jokes are the practical jokes. Poor Smith, properly considered, is an allegorical practical joker." '

    Manalive (Beaconsfield: Darwen Finlayson, 1964), pp. 83–4. The novel was first published in London in February 1912, in 'Nelson's New Two-shilling Novels'. See John Sullivan, op. cit., pp. 40–1.
36 *Manalive*, p. 40.
37 ibid.
38 ibid., p. 74.
39 On one occasion this typology is used as a partial explanation and excuse for anti-Semitism: 'Moses Gould was as good a fellow in his way as ever lived . . . But wherever there is conflict, crises come in which any soul, personal or racial, unconsciously turns on the world the most hateful of its hundred faces. English reverence, Irish mysticism, American idealism, looked up and saw on the face of

Moses a certain smile. It was that smile of the Cynic Triumphant, which has been the tocsin for many a cruel riot in Russian villages or medieval towns.' *Manalive*, p. 143.

40 *Manalive*, p. 75.
41 ibid., p. 72.
42 ibid., p. 189.
43 ibid., p. 129.
44 ibid., p. 133.
45 ibid., p. 137.
46 ibid., pp. 140–1.
47 See Julius West, *G. K. Chesterton: A Critical Study* (London: Martin Secker, 1915), p. 48.
48 Garry Wills, *Chesterton: Man and Mask* (New York: Sheed and Ward, 1961), pp. 123–4.
49 *Manalive*, p. 150.
50 ibid.
51 ibid., pp. 150–1.
52 ibid., p. 151.
53 Chesterton's criticism of Russian Liberalism is very similar to the view expressed by Maurice Baring in his article: 'The Causes of the Failure of the Russian Revolution,' the *Dublin Review*, July and October 1910, pp. 239–60.
54 *Manalive*, pp. 155–6.
55 ibid., p. 156.
56 ibid., pp. 157–8.
57 ibid., p. 158.
58 ibid.
59 ibid.
60 ibid., p. 163.
61 ibid., p. 148.
62 ibid., p. 156.
63 ibid.
64 ibid., p. 163.
65 ibid., p. 12.
66 ibid., p. 30.
67 Atkins in commenting on Orwell writes: 'But he did not see himself in the role of Innocent or Fool as he once called it. The Fool was a Chestertonian figure who really held out no hope for the world of decency.' See John Atkins, *George Orwell: A Literary Study* (London: John Calder, 1954), p. 2.
68 The converse is also true. Evil results in a kind of intellectual blindness which amounts to stupidity. Professor Lucifer is finally destroyed by his failure to understand the monk he imprisons. And Dr Warner, who is ostensibly the most brilliant person taking part in the Beacon House trial, is unable to see anything more in it than 'pointless and incompetent tomfoolery.' *Manalive*, p. 184.
69 *The Flying Inn* (London: Methuen, 1914), p. 83. The novel was first published by Methuen, 22 January 1914. See John Sullivan, op. cit., pp. 43–4. Subsequent references to this novel will be abbreviated to *F.I.*
70 C. S. Lewis, op. cit., p. 1071.
71 *F.I.*, p. 11.
72 It is perhaps significant that Hilaire Belloc's and Cecil Chesterton's discussion of this question has strong anti-Semitic overtones: 'The country not only by an overwhelming majority, but with an over-

whelming intensity, gave the mandate that the Chinese should go, and
that they should go at once. It [the results of the 1906 election] was a
mandate based upon a mixture of popular emotions, not the least of
which was the desire to chastize those South African Jews who had
compelled our politicians as their servants to exploit for financial
ends the popular enthusiasm in the matter of the South African war.
It was, again, a demand for the signal punishment of the first attempt
made since modern industrialism began, to move labour in large
batches from place to place upon a scheme arranged by capital for the
interests of capital alone. Popular instinct seized at once upon the
enormous danger of that initial experiment, and perceived with
sound sense that if it were not made an example of, and if the South
African Jews were not taught a sharp lesson, the whole outlook and
theory upon which this vile experiment had been based would become
the permanent theory and outlook of international capitalism.'
Hilaire Belloc and Cecil Chesterton, *The Party System* (London:
Stephen Swift, 1911), p. 74.

73 \ *F.I.*, p. 151.
74   ibid., p. 201.
75   ibid., p. 202.
76   See, for example, the passage which describes him walking towards
      Joan Brett through a long vista of brilliantly decorated rooms,
      carrying a tropical bird and talking to himself. His short-sightedness
      and his eloquent but empty rhetoric, and the peculiar oriental
      environment he has created for himself, all contribute to the picture
      of an imperceptive, isolated, and ruthless politician. It is also
      interesting that the same details which give Ivywood typical meaning
      also help to humanize him. And in scenes such as this, he acquires
      something of the pathos of a Casaubon: 'She could now see that the
      long lane ended in rooms that from afar off looked like the end of a
      kaleidoscope, rooms like nests made only from humming-birds or
      palaces built of fixed fireworks. Out of this furnace of fragmentary
      colours, she saw Ivywood advancing towards her, with his black
      suit and his white face accented by the contrast. His lips were moving;
      for he was talking to himself, as many orators do. He did not seem to
      see her; and she had to strangle a subconscious and utterly senseless
      cry, "He is blind!"' *F.I.*, pp. 98–99.
77   *F.I.*, p. 96.
78   ibid., p. 269.
79   See, for example, this passage from a debate with Bernard Shaw and
      Cecil Chesterton: 'Imagine to yourself the first Socialist Parliament.
      Imagine they are discussing—well, anything; I don't care what it is.
      One thing I am quite certain of is that there will be an eloquent
      speech by Mr Vincent Churchill on one side, replied to magnificently
      by Mr Churchill Vincent on the other; that Lord Robert Cecil—
      who will by a quaint custom retain his title—will be replied to by the
      Democrat, Archibald Primrose; and that, in short, the whole of the
      set of people who now have the power, will keep it in their
      hands. . . . I should ask what ground have you for actually believing
      that the Socialist system—that is to say, collective ownership of
      property and capital—will make it under immediate conditions in
      England any more difficult for a certain class in possession of the
      original machinery to bamboozle the rest of the nation into the
      belief that they are really appointed by political evolution?' 'A Debate
      on Socialism', the *New Age*, 18 March 1909, p. 420.

80 For discussion of Chesterton's views on this question, see A. J. Maycock, 'Introduction', *The Man Who Was Orthodox: A Selection from the Uncollected Writings of G. K. Chesterton* (London: Dennis Dobson, 1963), pp. 37-9. Chesterton's views provoked this exasperated complaint from Shaw: 'Have I survived the cry of Art for Art's sake and of War for War's sake, for which Mr Chesterton rebukes Whistler and Mr Rudyard Kipling, to fall a victim to this maddest of all cries: the cry of Beer for Beer's sake?' *The Nation*, 28 August 1909, quoted by Maycock, p. 37.

81 C. S. Lewis, op. cit., p. 1071.

82 *F.I.*, p. 123.

83 ibid., pp. 59-60.

84 ibid., p. 278.

85 ibid., p. 270.

86 ibid., p. 256.

87 ibid.

88 ibid.

89 'G. K. Chesterton: Child and Man, the Making of an Optimist', *The Times Literary Supplement*, 7 November 1936, p. 894.

90 See the poem by this name, in *The Collected Poems of G. K. Chesterton*, (London: Cecil Palmer, 1927), pp. 157-60.

91 *F.I.*, p. 253.

92 See the following passage: 'A voice called out to him quietly from the other end of the tunnel. There was something touching and yet terrible about a voice so human coming out of that inhuman darkness. If Philip Ivywood had been really a poet, and not rather its opposite, an aesthete, he would have known that all the past and people of England were uttering their oracle out of the cavern.' *F.I.*, p. 147.

93 ibid.

94 See Chesterton, *Utopia of Usurers and Other Essays* (New York: Boni Liverright, 1917).

95 Julius West, *G. K. Chesterton: A Critical Study*, p. 166.

4. THE DISTRIBUTIST NOVELS

1 The *New Witness*, which was published from 7 November 1912 until 4 May 1923, was edited first by Cecil Chesterton and after he joined the army, by Gilbert from 19 October 1916. It succeeded the *Eye-Witness*, which was published from 22 June 1911 until 31 October 1912, and was edited first by Belloc and then, from 20 June 1912, by Cecil Chesterton. Harold Robbins, who was involved in Distributist politics from the beginning, and has written the most complete account of the movement, believes that the principles and philosophy of Distributism were first stated explicitly in the *New Witness*. He also argues that Distributism and what he calls the Campaign for Clean Government were distinct but related Movements, although he admits that not everyone understood the relationship: 'In a sense, it was a weakness of the *Eye-Witness* and the earlier *New Witness* [a period which he says ended about 1916] that they attracted so many men who were interested in the matter of clean government, but were not prepared to be interested in the rest of the philosophy.' *The Last of the Realists: G. K. Chesterton and his Work*, *The Cross and the Plough* vol. 15, no. 1, 1948, p. 16.

After Belloc resigned the editorship of the *Eye-Witness* in June 1912, he made a statement on the paper's policy which Desmond Mac-Carthy summarized in these words: 'Belloc explained that the value of the *Eye-Witness* lay in providing a place where certain truths of advantage or necessity to the public could be told, and that it aimed particularly in narrowing the difference between the comments on public affairs that were spoken and those which were printed.' '*Eye-Witness*', *G.K.'s Weekly*, 25 September 1926, p. 23.

2   *G.K.'s Weekly* did not begin publication until 21 March 1925, although a specimen issue was published 8 November 1924, and the office and senior staff of the *New Witness* were kept in existence throughout the interim period. There was therefore a real continuity between the two papers, and *G.K.'s Weekly* could rightly claim to incorporate the *New Witness*. The Distributist League was founded 17 September 1926, with an inaugural meeting in Essex Hall, Strand, and the following week Chesterton was elected president. The League played an important part in supporting *G.K.'s Weekly*, which continued to be its official organ until the *Distributist* began publishing in 1932. Within two weeks of the League's first meeting, sales of *G.K.'s Weekly* had risen from 4650 to 7000. By 27 November they were more than 8000. See Maisie Ward, *Gilbert Keith Chesterton* (London: Sheed and Ward, 1944), p. 435.

3   ibid., pp. 374–5.

4   ibid., p. 375.

5   G. K. Chesterton, *The Man Who Knew Too Much* (Beaconsfield: Darwen Finlayson, 1964), p. 139. The novel was first published by Cassell in November 1922, and included four other stories: 'The Trees of Pride', 'The Garden of Smoke', 'The Fire of Swords', and 'The Tower of Treason'. The novel had been serialized in *Cassell's Magazine* and the four stories in the *Storyteller*. The English edition was published by Cassell and the American edition by Harpers. See John Sullivan, *G.K. Chesterton: A Bibliography* (London: University of London Press, 1958), pp. 56–7. Subsequent references to the novel will be abbreviated as *M.W.K.*

6   Maisie Ward, op. cit., p. 375.

7   See Maurice Baring, *The Puppet Show of Memory* (London: Heinemann, 1922), pp. 77–8, [*C*(London: Heinemann, 1924), p. 6, and *M.W.K.*, p. 141] and Robert Speaight, *Maurice Baring* in *D.N.B.* (London: Oxford University Press, 1959), pp. 58–9.

8   This is a painting of Baring, Chesterton, and Belloc (1932) which belongs to Mrs George Balfour, but is on loan to the National Portrait Gallery. See Robert Speaight, 'Maurice Baring', p. 59.

9   Maisie Ward, op. cit., p. 375.

10 Chesterton, *Appreciations and Criticisms of the Works of Charles Dickens* (London: J. M. Dent, 1911) pp. 180–1.

11 ibid., p. 180.

12 ibid., p. 183.

13 Gabriel Marcel, 'Maurice Baring,' *La Nouvelle Revue Française*, July 1927, p. 458.

14 See C. F. G. Masterman, *The Condition of England* (London: Methuen, 1960). Masterman's curious description of Chesterton's political disillusionment is worth noting: '. . . The music of his rustic flute has kept not for long its happy country tone, and has taken a stormier note from the tempest-tossed children of mankind. So the sunlight fades in the vision of a people which has abandoned Liberty, Equality

and Fraternity, of political parties bought for ignoble ends, a nation which has turned its back upon the clean ways of progress, and lies deferential and prostrate before an oligarchy of rich men; who only cannot be bought because they have sold themselves already.' ibid., pp. 186–7.

15   See C. Creighton Mandell and Edward Shanks, *Hilaire Belloc: The Man and His Work* (London: Methuen, 1916), p. 124. The authors see Belloc's own satire as 'an illustration of the passage in *The Party System*, where Mr Belloc advocates the annulling of political evils by laughing at them.' ibid.

16   In her biography, Maisie Ward has described how closely they collaborated: 'Shaw's name for Gilbert and Belloc—the Chesterbelloc—had come by the public to be used for the novels in which they collaborated. Belloc wrote the story, Chesterton drew the pictures, and the resulting product was known as a Chesterbelloc. A number of letters from Mr Belloc beg Gilbert to do the drawings early in order to help the story, "I have already written a number of *situations* which you might care to sketch. I append a list. Your *drawing* makes all the difference to my *thinking*: I see the people in action more clearly."' Maisie Ward, op. cit., p. 466.
    Chesterton illustrated the following Belloc novels: *Emmanuel Burden* (London: Methuen, 1904); *The Mercy of Allah* (London: Chatto and Windus, 1922); *Mr Petre* (London: J. W. Arrowsmith, 1925); *The Emerald* (London: J. W. Arrowsmith, 1926); *The Haunted House* (London: J. W. Arrowsmith, 1927); *The Missing Masterpiece* (London: J. W. Arrowsmith, 1929); *The Man Who Made Gold* (London: J. W. Arrowsmith, 1930); *The Postmaster-General* (London: Cassell, 1936). See John Sullivan, op. cit., pp. 156–9.

17   The situations are not of course identical, but Mr Clutterbuck trusts Charles Fitzgerald at least as much as Horne Fisher trusts his brother. See Hilaire Belloc, *Mr Clutterbuck's Election* (London: Eveleigh Nash, 1908), pp. 303–9.

18   See, for example, Hilaire Belloc, *A Change in the Cabinet* (London: Methuen, 1909), p. 255. In a letter to *G.K.'s Weekly*, a reader suggests that Bailey might be a portrait of Chesterton: 'Whom is Belloc talking about? Himself or you? You say you do not hate the Jews, yet you take every possible opportunity to vilify them.' 18 July 1925, p. 399. In his answer, Chesterton comments on what he calls the letter-writer's 'highly innocent reading of Mr Belloc's satire,' (ibid., p. 400) and outlines a theory of Zionism, in which he makes it clear that he considers the Jewish population as permanently alien: 'They produced a friction in the world by being alien to the moral tradition around them'. ibid., p. 399. For a more complete account of Chesterton's views on the same subject, see 'The Problems of Zionism', *The New Jerusalem* (London: Hodder and Stoughton, 1920), pp. 264–301. The book was published after his trip to the Holy Land in 1919 and was first serialized in the *Daily Telegraph*, except for the last part of the chapter on Zionism, which the paper refused to print.

19   See Hilaire Belloc, *Mr Clutterbuck's Election*, p. 301.
20   See Hilaire Belloc, *A Change in the Cabinet*, p. 255.
21   See Hilaire Belloc, *Mr Clutterbuck's Election*, p. 264.
22   C. S. Lewis, 'Notes on the Way', *Time and Tide*, 9 November 1946, p. 1070.
23   *On the Place of Gilbert Chesterton in English Letters* (London: Sheed and Ward, 1940), p. 81. Quoted by Maisie Ward, op. cit. p. 517.

24   Hilaire Belloc, *But Soft: We Are Observed* (London: J. W. Arrow-
     smith, 1928). p. 7 and pp. 63–4.
25   For a discussion of Chesterton's conversion to Catholicism, see
     Maisie Ward, 'Rome via Jerusalem', *Chesterton*, pp. 374–98.
26   *M.W.K.*, pp. 189–90.
27   Ronald Knox, 'Chesterton in his Early Romances', the *Dublin
     Review*, p. 363.
28   *M.W.K.*, p. 9.
29   ibid., p. 170.
30   At the end of chapter two, Fisher tells March, 'I was certainly never
     born to set it right.' *M.W.K.*, p. 54.
31   ibid., pp. 54 and 137.
32   ibid., p. 52. Compare this chapter with the police case which Chester-
     ton discusses in *Irish Impressions*, pp. 182–5.
33   *M.W.K.*, p. 54.
34   ibid., pp. 30–31.
35   ibid., p. 170.
36   ibid., p. 146.
37   Harold Robbins, op. cit., p. 16.
38   Belloc was elected to Parliament in 1906 as a Liberal candidate, and
     in the first election of 1910 as an Independent Liberal. The Liberal
     Party's decision to run a candidate against him in the second
     election of 1910 convinced him that he could not win. The speech was
     given in November, 1910. See Robert Speaight, *The Life of Hilaire
     Belloc* (London: Hollis and Carter, 1957), pp. 294–5.
39   *M.W.K.*, p. 167.
40   ibid., pp. 152–67.
41   ibid., p. 153.
42   See G. K. Chesterton, 'Dukes', *Alarms and Discursions*, (London:
     Methuen, 1910), p. 69. This essay provides one of the most
     complete discussions of Chesterton's view of the English aristocracy.
43   *M.W.K.*, p. 166.
44   ibid., p. 167.
45   ibid., p. 52.
46   ibid., p. 54.
47   ibid., pp. 72–3.
48   ibid., p. 89.
49   ibid., p. 73.
50   ibid., pp. 74–5.
51   'The Sentimentalist', *Alarms and Discursions*, p. 218.
52   ibid., p. 215.
53   ibid., p. 214.
54   *M.W.K.*, p. 89.
55   ibid., p. 77.
56   ibid., p. 88.
57   ibid., p. 89.
58   ibid., p. 107.
59   ibid., p. 108.
60   Chesterton makes this point in his study of Cobbett: 'He was simply
     a man who had discovered a crime: ancient like many crimes; con-
     cealed like all crimes . . . He knew now that England had been
     secretly slain.' See Maisie Ward, op. cit., p. 412.
61   *M.W.K.*, p. 189.
62   ibid., pp. 115–6.
63   ibid., p. 170.

64 François Mauriac, *Mémoires Intérieures* (Paris: Flammarion, 1959), p. 175.
65 ibid., p. 176.
66 *M.W.K.*, p. 173.
67 ibid., p. 176.
68 ibid., p. 186.
69 *Romans*, VIII: 28.
70 *M.W.K.*, p. 189.
71 ibid.
72 ibid.
73 ibid., p. 168.
74 *M.W.K.*, p. 189. Although Chesterton seems to have dreamed about the good society, he refused to call it a Utopia. See the reply to Shaw in which he explains the political position that he and Belloc share: 'We do not "plank down" a Utopia, because Utopia is a thing uninteresting to a thinking man; it assumes that all evils come from outside the citizen and none from inside him.' Chesterton, 'The Last of the Rationalists (A Reply to Mr Bernard Shaw)', *The New Age*, 29 February 1908, p. 349.
75 *M.W.K.*, p. 189.
76 David Lodge, 'Tono-Bungay and the Condition of England', *The Language of Fiction: Essays in Criticism and Verbal Analysis of the English Novel* (London: Routledge and Kegan Paul, 1966), p. 242.
77 If the novel had not been written before the formation of the Distributist League, one would be tempted to interpret the League of the Long Bow as a guarded reference to it. In any case, one cannot help wondering whether the League of the Long Bow in this novel and the League of the Lion in *The Return of Don Quixote* may have suggested the name which the Distributist association finally took. There are indications that they were at first uncertain about what they would call themselves: 'We think we may say that the League, Society, Club, Fellowship, Guild, or Army of Distributists is already in being.' *G. K.'s Weekly*, 21 August 1926, p. 398.
78 Kathleen Tillotson, in her eloquent defence of the author as narrator, makes an important distinction, which should be noted: 'The "narrator", here as elsewhere, is a method rather than a person; indeed the "narrator" never is the author as man; much confusion has arisen from this identification and much conscious art has been overlooked.' 'The Tale and the Teller', *Mid-Victorian Studies* (London: University of London, The Athlone Press, 1965), p. 15.
79 Chesterton, *Tales of the Long Bow* (Beaconsfield: Darwen Finlayson, 1968), p. 78. The novel was first published by Cassell and Co., London, June 1925. See John Sullivan, *G. K. Chesterton: A Bibliography* (London, University of London Press, 1958), p. 60. Subsequent references to the novel will be abbreviated to *T.L.B.*
80 ibid., p. 168.
81 See Maisie Ward, 'The Living Voice', op. cit., pp. 531–47.
82 *T.L.B.*, p. 145.
83 ibid., pp. 30 and 122.
84 ibid., p. 190.
85 ibid.
86 ibid., pp. 190–1.
87 ibid., p. 191.
88 ibid.
89 ibid., p. 135.

H

90 ibid.
91 ibid., p. 33.
92 *The Poet and the Lunatics* (London: Darwen Finlayson, 1962), pp. 170–2. Subsequent references to this novel will be abbreviated as *P.L.* For full bibliographical details see Chapter 5, note 1.
93 *T.L.B.*, p. 29.
94 ibid., pp. 170–85.
95 ibid., p. 170.
96 ibid., p. 169.
97 ibid., p. 170.
98 G. K. Chesterton, 'Why I am not a Socialist', the *New Age*, 4 January 1908, pp. 189–90.
99 H. G. Wells, 'About Chesterton and Belloc', the *New Age*, 11 January 1908, pp. 209–10.
100 G. K. Chesterton, 'Why I am not a Socialist', pp. 189–90.
101 *T.L.B.*, p. 165.
102 ibid., p. 167.
103 ibid., p. 76.
104 ibid., pp. 60–1.
105 ibid., p. 98.
106 ibid., pp. 169–70.
107 ibid., p. 59.
108 ibid., p. 131.
109 ibid.
110 ibid., p. 127.
111 ibid., p. 137.
112 ibid., p. 68.
113 ibid., p. 146.
114 ibid.
115 ibid., p. 124.
116 ibid.
117 ibid.
118 John Ruskin, 'The Veins of Wealth', *Unto This Last*, vol. XVII, *The Works of John Ruskin*, edited by E. T. Cook and Alexander Wedderburn (London: George Allen, 1905), p. 53. The theme of 'poisoned wealth' is also treated in many of Bernard Shaw's plays.
119 G. K. Chesterton, *What I Saw in America* (New York: Dodd and Mead, 1922).
120 See especially, 'The American Business Man', ibid., pp. 97–120.
121 *What I Saw in America*, pp. 139–41.
122 *T.L.B.*, p. 186.
123 'The question which I always ask Socialists, and which they never answer, is simply this: "As the English trust everything to the Churchills and call that Democracy, why should they not trust everything to the Churchills and call that Socialism?" ' 'A Shriek of Warning, Part I', the *New Age*, 15 April 1909, p. 500.
    And again: 'This is the simple and staring mistake of my brother and all the Socialists. They look eagerly and untiringly to the political oligarchy to oppose Socialism; but it will never oppose Socialism. It will achieve Socialism, as it achieved the Reformation. And when it is achieved we shall find it a splendid failure, as all thinking people have found the Reformation. Puritanism was a failure, because it left out the human hunger for symbol; it was a failure, but the class which built on it was a success. Manchester anarchy was a failure, because it left out the instinct of brotherly responsibility; it was a failure, but the

class that built on it was a success. Collectivism will be a failure because it will leave out the human instinct of possession, it will be a failure, but the class that builds on it will be a success.' Chesterton, 'A Shriek of Warning, Part II', the *New Age*, 29 April 1909, pp. 9–10.

124 *T.L.B.*, p. 151.
125 ibid., p. 153.
126 G. K. Chesterton, *The Return of Don Quixote* (London: Darwen Finlayson, 1963). The first English edition was published 6 May 1927, by Chatto and Windus. See John Sullivan, op. cit., p. 64.
127 *T.L.B.*, p. 168.
128 Maurice Baring, *C* (London: Heinemann, 1924); *Cat's Cradle* (London: Heinemann, 1925); and *Daphne Adeane* (London: Heinemann, 1926).
129 *T.L.B.*, p. 187.
130 *Napoleon of Notting Hill* (Beaconsfield: Darwen Finlayson, 1964), p. 188.
131 ibid., pp. 187–8.
132 G. B. Shaw, 'Chesterton on Eugenics and Shaw on Chesterton', *The Nation and the Athenaeum*, 11 March 1922, p. 862.
133 The serialization ended in the middle of the chapter entitled 'The Parting of the Ways': chapter XV in the novel (end of second paragraph, p. 179), chapter XIV in *G. K.'s Weekly*.
134 This seems to have been one of the reasons for discontinuing its serial publication. In Chesterton's explanation of the decision to the readers of *G. K.'s Weekly*, he speaks of the difficulty of publishing an elaborately planned novel in very brief episodes: 'It was started at another stage of our career on the advice of those who specially asked for a serial; but it is obviously quite unfitted for a short paper that is like a pamphlet. It is unfortunately planned on a larger scale than most of the same writer's stories; and the climax of its various issues is yet to come.' 'An Explanation: You Can End This Story Here', *G. K.'s Weekly*, 30 November 1926, p. 135.

It should also be noted, however, that the novel, although planned earlier, was at least partly written during publication. Titterton speaks of it being dictated at the printer's office: 'I have heard other things dictated in that little room; *Tops and Tails*, and instalments of "Don Quixote", and poems.' 'The outline of G.K.C.', *G. K.'s Weekly*, 8 January 1927, p. 190.
135 Maisie Ward, op. cit., p. 465.
136 Chesterton was on the Continent when the strike began, but Titterton, the Managing Editor, decided to support the workers and the 'type-written strike-issue' of *G. K.'s Weekly* for 15 May 1925, carried the head-line, 'Stand by the Strikers'. In spite of the anger of many readers, Chesterton later endorsed this decision in an article which defended the Trade-Union movement: '. . . And while we ourselves have always preferred the policy of small property, we have never hesitated to defend the proletarian organization as the only actual defence of the classes without property.' 'The Pride of England', *G. K.'s Weekly*, 22 May 1926, p. 160. For readers' reaction to the paper's decision, see *G. K.'s Weekly*, 22 May 1926, p. 162; 5 June 1926; and 19 June 1926, p. 237.
137 My own reading of the novel in this regard would seem to be supported by Chesterton's description of Herne's coronation in *G. K.'s Weekly*, as 'his enthronement as a Dictator, in the Mussolini manner'. 'An Explanation: You Can End This Story Here', p. 135.
138 It is interesting that this sentence is omitted from the Penguin edition of the biography. See Penguin edition, 1958, p. 348.

139   *The Return of Don Quixote* (London: Darwen Finlayson, 1963), pp. 206–7. The first edition was published in London by Chatto and Windus, 1927. Subsequent references to this novel will be abbreviated as *R.D.Q.*

140   *R.D.Q.*, p. 218.

141   ibid., p. 69.

142   ibid., p. 62.

143   ibid., p. 67.

144   ibid., pp. 69–70.

145   'The Man With the Golden Key', *Autobiography* (London: Hutchinson, 1936), pp. 31–56.

146   See Lucy Masterman, 'The Private Chesterton: Poems for Every Occasion', *Manchester Evening News*, 8 May 1936. Also see Michael Asquith, 'G. K. Chesterton: Prophet and Jester', the *Listener*, 6 March 1952, p. 391. Admittedly he is speaking on an elaborate children's game Chesterton spent a day in preparing, and this was not at Beaconsfield.

147   *R.D.Q.*, p. 119. The lines are repeated with a somewhat different punctuation on p. 204, when 'protection' then reads 'perfection'.

148   G. K. Chesterton, *The Surprise* (London: Sheed and Ward, 1952). According to Dorothy Collins the play was written 'some six years before Chesterton's death' [i.e. *c.* 1930] 'Preface', ibid., p. 9. Dorothy Collins speaks of the play as having been incomplete and refers to changes that she made in getting it ready for publication, although she does not say what these are. Private conversation.

149   *R.D.Q.*, p. 148.

150   ibid., pp. 133–4.

151   ibid., p. 147.

152   ibid., p. 156.

153   The conclusion of the judgment scene also provides a brief but very effective glimpse of Eden's unexpected sensibility which, interestingly enough, is expressed in the language of the theatre: 'A spasm of something indescribable, like a twitch of involuntary humiliation, crossed the crabbed face of old Eden, and he said testily, "I wish this scene would end." ' *R.D.Q.*, p. 204.

154   ibid., p. 75.

155   ibid., p. 157.

156   ibid., p. 169.

157   ibid., p. 121.

158   'But of all those who were shocked at the judgment which had condemned them, perhaps not one had been more amazed than the man whom the judgment had justified.' ibid., p. 208.

159   See Braintree's words to Murrell at the end of chapter five: 'Douglas,' he said, 'you needn't act your allegory any more. . . . You haven't said it with your own tongue, but you've said it with ten thousand other tongues to-night. You've said, "Yes, John Braintree, you can get on all right with the nobs. It's the mobs you can't get on with. You've spent an hour in the drawing-room and told them all about Shakespeare and the musical glasses. Now that you've spent a night in the poor streets, tell me—which of us knows the people best?" ' *R.D.Q.*, pp. 54–5.

160   ibid., p. 187.

161   See *G. K.'s Weekly*, 19 June 1926, p. 227; 26 June 1926, p. 246; and especially 10 July 1926, pp. 285, and 288.

162   *R.D.Q.*, p. 189.

163   ibid., p. 200.
164   ibid., p. 182.
165   *The Ball and the Cross* (Beaconsfield: Darwen Finlayson, 1963), p. 188.
166   *R.D.Q.*, p. 192.
167   ibid., p. 178.
168   ibid., p. 179.
169   ibid.
170   ibid., p. 181.
171   ibid., p. 201.
172   See chapters VIII–X.
173   *R.D.Q.*, p. 65. See the Book of Revelation, XIII: 1–10.
174   *R.D.Q.*, p. 64.
175   ibid. pp. 81–2. When Murrell gives her the jar of paints, there is a
      passage which is linked to the description of her childhood. 'There is
      no explaining how the mere shape and detail of things lost in child-
      hood can startle and stab the emotions; but when she saw the shape of
      that obsolete pot of paint, with its large stopper and the faded trade
      mark of decorative fishes upon it, her eyes were stung with tears so
      that she herself was startled by them. It was as if she had suddenly
      heard the voice of her father.' *R.D.Q.*, p. 161.
176   ibid., p. 86.
177   ibid., pp. 97–8.
178   ibid., p. 213.
179   ibid., p. 222.
180   ibid., p. 214.
181   ibid., p. 211.
182   ibid., p. 222.
183   ibid. In his study of G. F. Watts (London: Duckworth, 1904),
      Chesterton discusses what he calls 'the spiritual and symbolic history
      of colours' (p. 126), and he makes a distinction very similar to the
      distinction which Dr Hendry makes between the opaque illumination
      colour and the transparent stained glass: 'And I think a broad
      distinction between the finest pagan and the finest Christian point of
      view may be found in such an approximate phrase as this, that
      paganism deals always with a light shining on things, Christianity
      with a light shining through them. That is why the whole Renascence
      colouring is opaque, the whole pre-Raphaelite colouring transparent.
      The very sky of Rubens is more solid than the rocks of Giotto: it is like
      a noble cliff of immemorial blue marble. The artists of the devout age
      seemed to regret that they could not make the light shine through
      everything, as it shone through the little wood in the wonderful
      Nativity of Botticelli. And that is why, again, Christianity, which has
      been attacked so strangely as dull and austere, invented the thing
      which is more intoxicating than all the wines in the world, stained
      glass windows.' *G. F. Watts*, p. 130. Admittedly the terms of the
      contrast have changed between 1904 and 1926. In *The Return of Don
      Quixote*, the pre-Raphaelite colouring has changed from transparent to
      opaque, and the contrast is now between the transparency of
      Medievalism which has received a theological basis, and the opaque-
      ness of a Medievalism which has not.
184   '. . . In case there should be concealed somewhere a fanatic who has
      actually read the story up to this point, it may be well for his benefit to
      indicate the point.' 'An Explanation: You Can End This Story Here',
      p. 135.
185   ibid.

186   See the essay in which he discusses the question of Catholicism and intellectual independence: 'I myself have advanced several economic and political suggestions, for which I never dreamed of claiming anything more than that a loyal Catholic can offer them. . . . In any case, my own experience of the modern world tells me that Catholics are much more and not less individualistic than other men in their general opinions. Mr Michael Williams, the spirited propagandist of Catholicism in America, gave this as a very cogent reason for refusing to found or join anything like a Catholic party in politics. He said that Catholics will combine for Catholicism, but it is quite abnormally difficult to get them to combine for anything else. This is confirmed by my own impressions and is contrasted very sharply with my recollections about most other religious groups.' 'On Courage and Independence', *The Thing* (London: Sheed and Ward, 1929), p. 167.

187   *R.D.Q.*, p. 134.
188   ibid., p. 167.
189   ibid., p. 99.
190   ibid., p. 98.
191   ibid., p. 155.
192   ibid., p. 156.
193   ibid., p. 65.
194   ibid., p. 151.
195   ibid., p. 27.
196   ibid., p. 183.
197   ibid., pp. 139–40.
198   ibid., p. 158.
199   ibid., p. 129.
200   ibid., p. 215.
201   ibid., p. 223.

5. THE LATE NOVELS

1   *The Poet and the Lunatics: Episodes in the Life of Gabriel Gale* (London: Darwen Finlayson, 1962), pp. 46–7. The first edition was published by Cassell in July 1929. The stories were collected from *Nash's Magazine* and *The Storyteller*. See John Sullivan, *G. K. Chesterton: A Bibliography* (London: University of London Press, 1958), pp. 71–2. Subsequent references to this novel will be abbreviated as *P.L.*

2   *P.L.*, p. 76. Compare this passage with Father Brown's explanation of his method of detection: ' "I had planned out each of the crimes very carefully," went on Father Brown, "I had thought out exactly how a thing like that could be done, and in what style or state of mind a man could really do it. And when I felt quite sure that I felt exactly like the murderer myself, of course I knew who he was . . . I mean that I really did see myself, and my real self, committing the murders. I didn't actually kill the men by material means; but that's not the point. Any brick or bit of machinery might have killed them by material means. I mean that I thought and thought about how a man might come to be like that, until I realized that I really *was* like that, in everything except final consent to action. It was once suggested to me by a friend of mine, as a sort of religious exercise." ' Chesterton, 'The Secret of Father Brown', *The Father Brown Stories* (London: Cassell, 1966), pp. 464–5.

3   From this point of view, the comparison which Chesterton makes between Shakespeare and Chaucer has its own unintentional irony:

'When all is said, there is something a little sinister in the number of mad people there are in Shakespeare. We say that he uses his fools to brighten the dark background of tragedy; I think he sometimes uses them to darken it. . . . Chaucer describes a whole crowd of many-coloured personalities, of all possible types and tendencies. But I do not remember that, in the whole five volumes of Chaucer, there is such a thing as a madman.' *Chaucer* (London: Faber and Faber, 1932), p. 237.

4 Chesterton discusses this mental crisis, which occurred during his Slade schooldays, in his *Autobiography*: 'At this time I did not very clearly distinguish between dreaming and waking; not only as a mood, but as a metaphysical doubt, I felt as if everything might be a dream. It was as if I had myself projected the universe from within, with all its trees and stars; and that is so near to the notion of being God that it is manifestly even nearer to going mad. Yet I was not mad, in any medical or physical sense; I was simply carrying the scepticism of my time as far as it would go.' *Autobiography* (London: Hutchinson, 1937), p. 92. Maisie Ward speaks of this period as a mental extreme of danger and refers to the fears of Chesterton's friends that he was going mad. See Maisie Ward, *Chesterton* (London: Sheed and Ward, 1944), p. 44.

5 This scene takes place at the end of chapter four, when the setting of the Saunders story causes Gale to remember Diana and his own unhappiness. It is an effective scene, because in it he becomes a person with feelings and a memory. See *P.L.*, p. 92.

6 *P.L.*, p. 70.
7 ibid., p. 28.
8 ibid., p. 41.
9 ibid., p. 46.
10 ibid., pp. 48–9.
11 Like Ivanhov, Bakunin was an Anarchist who made a dramatic escape from a Russian prison and fled to Western Europe.
12 Prince Kropotkin helped make his version of Anarchism respectable in Edwardian England. See, for example, the *New Age*, 9 May 1908, in which a study of Anarchy by Peter Latouche is reviewed: 'In the end we have no doubt whatever that it is Kropotkin and not Karl Marx who will prevail.' p. 37.
13 *Autobiography*, pp. 252–4.
14 *P.L.*, p. 39.
15 ibid., p. 36.
16 ibid., p. 35.
17 ibid., p. 39.
18 ibid.
19 ibid.
20 ibid.
21 ibid., p. 43.
22 ibid., p. 44.
23 ibid., p. 49.
24 ibid.
25 ibid.
26 ibid., pp. 48–9.
27 ibid., p. 36.
28 ibid., p. 142.
29 ibid., p. 164.
30 ibid., p. 165. Compare this with Gale's comment on Ivanhov in the

earlier story: 'What exactly is liberty? First and foremost, surely, it is
the power of a thing to be itself. In some ways the yellow bird was free
in the cage. It was free to be alone. It was free to sing. In the forest its
feathers would be torn to pieces and its voice choked for ever. Then I
began to think that being oneself, which is liberty, is itself limitation.
We are limited by our brains and bodies; and if we break out, we
cease to be ourselves, and, perhaps, to be anything.' *P.L.*, p. 48.

31 *P.L.*, p. 166.
32 'The Paradise of Thieves', *The Father Brown Stories*, p. 184.
33 These are the words of Miles Consterdine's Russian mentor, Alyosha,
who introduces him to the Russian view of life which Baring expresses
in the novel. *Tinker's Leave* (London: Heinemann, 1927), p. 148. It is
interesting that this attitude towards wealth should be associated with
the Russian folk theme of Ivan the Fool: 'It is the failure who by us is
the greatest success. Ivan the Fool, who gains the kingdom—which is
not always of this world. That is what we all of us want to grasp.'
ibid., p. 148.
34 *P.L.*, p. 28.
35 ibid., pp. 14–15.
36 ibid., p. 26.
37 ibid., p. 11.
38 ibid., p. 20.
39 ibid., pp. 23–4.
40 *The Faerie Queene*, I, ix, 34 and 41.
41 *P.L.*, p. 28.
42 ibid., p. 18.
43 ibid., p. 92.
44 ibid.
45 ibid., p. 184.
46 ibid., p. 178.
47 ibid., p. 170.
48 ibid., p. 28.
49 ibid., p. 182.
50 ibid.
51 ibid.
52 ibid., p. 184.
53 *M.W.W.T.*, p. 44.
54 See, for example, Eric Hobsbawm's comments on British detective
stories: '. . . as the immense vogue of the British detective novel—a
purely middle-class creation—shows, the forces of established order
are haunted by its instability. This is perhaps why they have to
exorcise the threat over and over again by the imagined apprehension
and punishment of relays of incredibly subtle and dangerous male-
factors. And perhaps also why it must be shown that the breakdown of
the official machinery of order—the ever-baffled police—is not such a
terrible disaster. For the private detective, the clubman hero or
bourgeois terrorist (Hannay, James Bond or Bulldog Drummond) is in
the last analysis powerful enough to redress the balance between order
and anarchy. But how terrible and ubiquitous that threat is! . . . The
murderer, however ostensibly sympathetic, becomes a monster who
murders time and again, as he does in every detective novel, for
purposes not entirely explicable by the technicalities of maintaining
suspense. The British detective novel, in fact, is not only reassurance
but a call to conformity and solidarity to those who personify the
social order in times when all conspires to undermine it.' Hobsbawm,

'The Criminal as Hero and Myth', *Times Literary Supplement*, 23 June 1961, p. vi.

55 *The Return of Don Quixote* (London: Darwen Finlayson, 1963), pp. 216–7.

56 Perhaps this point is expressed most tellingly in one of the last of the Father Brown stories, in which Father Brown comments on the murder of Raggley, who is described as a Tory Radical: '. . . Do you suppose if he [the Prime Minister] and the other public men were shot dead to-morrow, there wouldn't be other people to stand up and say that every avenue was being explored, or that the Government had the matter under the greatest consideration? The masters of the modern world don't matter. Even the real masters don't matter much. Hardly anybody you ever read about in a newspaper matters at all. . . . But Raggley did matter. He was one of a great line of some half a dozen men who might have saved England. They stand up stark and dark like disregarded sign-posts, down all that smooth descending road which has ended in this swamp of merely commercial collapse. Dean Swift and Dr Johnson and old William Cobbett; they had all without exception the name of being surly or savage, and they were all loved by their friends, and they all deserved to be. . . . And when there is a foul and secret murder of a man like that—then I do think it matters, matters so much that even the modern machinery of police will be a thing that any respectable person may make use of . . .' 'The Quick One', *The Father Brown Stories*, pp. 613–4.

57 Perhaps the best example of this is his well-known poem 'The Secret People'. See for example the concluding stanza:

> We hear men speaking for us of new laws strong
> and sweet,
> Yet is there no man speaketh as we speak in the
> street.
> It may be we shall rise the last as Frenchmen rose
> the first,
> Our wrath come after Russia's wrath and our wrath
> be the worst.
> It may be we are meant to mark with our riot and
> our rest
> God's scorn for all men governing. It may be beer
> is best.
> But we are the people of England; and we have
> not spoken yet.
> Smile at us, pay us, pass us. But do not quite forget.

The Collected Poems of G. K. Chesterton (London: Cecil Palmer, 1927), p. 160.

58 Charles Williams, 'Gilbert Keith Chesterton', *Poetry at Present* (Oxford: Clarendon Press, 1930), p. 99. This is the quality in Chesterton which Orwell singles out for admiration. In his criticism of D. B. Wyndham Lewis ('Timothy Shy' in the *News Chronicle*) and J. B. Morton ('Beachcomber' in the *Daily Express*) for their writing of Catholic propaganda, he contrasts them with Chesterton, whose work, he believes, they are continuing: 'From either a literary or a political point of view these two are simply the leavings on Chesterton's plate. Chesterton's vision of life was false in some ways, and he was hampered by enormous ignorance, but at least he had courage. He was ready to attack the rich and powerful, and he damaged his career by doing so.

H*

But it is the peculiarity of both "Beachcomber" and "Timothy Shy" that they take no risks with their own popularity.' *The Collected Essays, Journalism and Letters*, ed. Sonia Orwell and Ian Angus (London: Secker and Warburg, 1968), vol. III, p. 175.

59 *P.L.*, p. 190.
60 The idea for Pinion seems to be based on Chesterton's experience during his first visit to America: 'Then again there is a curious convention by which American interviewing makes itself out much worse than it is. The reports are far more rowdy and insolent than the conversations. . . . An interesting essay might be written upon points upon which nations affect more vices than they possess; and it might deal more fully with the American pressman, who is a harmless clubman in private, and becomes a sort of highway-robber in print.' *What I Saw In America* (New York: Dodd and Mead, 1922), pp. 60–1.
61 *Four Faultless Felons* (Beaconsfield: Darwen Finlayson, 1964), pp. 63–4. The first edition was published in August 1930, by Cassell. And the stories were collected from *Cassell's Magazine* and *The Storyteller*. See John Sullivan, op. cit., p. 75. Subsequent references to the novel will be abbreviated as *F.F.F.*
62 *F.F.F.*, p. 18.
63 ibid., p. 37.
64 ibid., pp. 37, 54, 63.
65 ibid., p. 36.
66 ibid.
67 ibid. Compare this with an excerpt from *Tales of the Long Bow* (Beaconsfield: Darwen Finlayson, 1968): 'Vote for the League of the Long Bow. They Are The Only Men Who Don't Tell Lies.', p. 161.
68 *F.F.F.*, p. 21.
69 ibid., p. 22.
70 ibid., p. 31.
71 ibid., p. 28.
72 ibid., p. 19. John Hume describes Dr Snow as a silly old man who has 'only fallen in love with his own prophecies of disaster'. ibid., p. 52.
73 *F.F.F.*, p. 64.
74 ibid., p. 76.
75 ibid.
76 ibid., p. 77.
77 *P.L.*, p. 76.
78 See *R.D.Q.*, chapters VIII–X.
79 *F.F.F.*, p. 77.
80 ibid., pp. 112–3.
81 ibid., p. 79.
82 ibid., p. 115.
83 ibid., p. 131.
84 ibid., p. 164.
85 ibid.
86 J. Conrad, *Nostromo: A Tale of the Seaboard* (London: Gresham Publishing Co., 1925), p. 5.
87 M. Baring, *Cat's Cradle* (London: Heinemann, 1925).
88 M. Baring, *C* (London: Heinemann, 1924).
89 M. Baring, *Daphne Adeane* (London: Heinemann, 1934).
90 M. Baring, *The Coat Without Seam* (London: Heinemann, 1934).
91 See Gabriel Marcel, 'La Princesse Blanche', *La Nouvelle Revue Française*, 1 March 1931, p. 457. See also Robert Speaight, 'An Appreciation', the *Tablet*, 29 December 1945, p. 316.

92 *F.F.F.*, p. 165.
93 Alan Nadoway comes to the same conclusion that Rosamund and
    Olive Ashley come to in *The Return of Don Quixote*, when they decide
    that Seawood Abbey should become a monastery again: '. . . and I
    understand something in human life and history I never understood
    before. Why the people who do have those wild visions and vows, who
    want to expiate and to pray for this wicked world, can't really do it
    anyhow and all over the place. They have to live by rule. They have
    to go into monasteries and places; it's only fair on the rest of the
    world.' *F.F.F.*, p. 167.
94 ibid., p. 161.
95 ibid., p. 126.
96 ibid., p. 127.
97 ibid., pp. 167–8.
98 ibid., p. 169.
99 The name means presumably 'Peacock-Land', from the Latin word,
    pavo, pavonem. This would explain why Lobb lives in 'a small but
    comfortable house in Peacock Crescent' (*F.F.F.*, p. 179) and why
    Sebastian wears a 'peacock-coloured scarf' (ibid., pp. 172 and 193)
    and why we are told that in Pavonian history, peacock fans were
    carried into battle (ibid., pp. 193 and 207). Generally in Chesterton's
    writing, the peacock is a symbol not only of pride, but more specifi-
    cally a symbol of the pride of Imperialism. See, for example, 'The
    House of the Peacock', in *The Poet and the Lunatics*, where Gale speaks
    of peacock feathers as an emblem of 'the wrong imperialism': '. . . St
    Michael is handing out spears to the good angels; while Satan is
    elaborately arming the rebel angels with peacock's feathers . . . The
    right side was arming for a real and therefore doubtful battle, while
    the wrong side was already, so to speak, handing out the palms of
    victory. You cannot fight anybody with the palms of victory.' *P.L.*,
    p. 128.
        In one of his early essays, Chesterton explains the origin of his use of
    the symbol, which he applies to an incident during the Boer War:
    '. . . In a very old ninth-century illumination which I have seen,
    depicting the war of the rebel angels in heaven, Satan is represented as
    distributing to his followers peacock feathers—the symbols of an evil
    pride. Satan also distributed peacock feathers to his followers on
    Mafeking Night.' 'The Red Town', *Alarms and Discursions*, p. 41.
100 *F.F.F.*, p. 170.
101 ibid., p. 177.
102 ibid., p. 176.
103 In the *Autobiography*, in defending himself against the charge of anti-
    Semitism, Chesterton discusses theories about the origin of anti-
    Semitism which he regards as false and offers his own alternative
    explanation: 'I am not at all ashamed of having asked Aryans to have
    more patience with Jews or for having asked Anglo-Saxons to have
    more patience with Jew-baiters. The whole problem of the two
    entangled cultures and traditions is much too deep and difficult, on
    both sides, to be decided impatiently. . . . I have seen a whole book
    full of alternative theories of the particular historic cause of such a
    delusion about a difference; . . . that it was revolutionary envy of the
    few Jews who happened to be the big bankers of Capitalism; that it
    was Capitalist resistance to the few Jews who happened to be the chief
    founders of Communism. All these separate theories are false in
    separate ways; as in forgetting . . . that Capitalism and Communism

are so very nearly the same thing, in ethical essence, that it would not
be strange if they did take leaders from the same ethnological elements.' ibid., p. 76.

104 *F.F.F.*, p. 178.
105 See the passage in which he discusses the reasons for the defeat of
Carthage in the Second Punic War: 'It may sound fanciful to say that
men we meet at tea-tables or talk to at garden-parties are secretly
worshippers of Baal or Moloch. But this sort of commercial mind has
its own cosmic vision and it is the vision of Carthage. It has in it the
brutal blunder that was the ruin of Carthage. The Punic power fell,
because there is in this materialism a mad indifference to real thought.
By disbelieving in the soul, it comes to disbelieving in the mind. Being
too practical to be moral, it denies what every practical soldier calls
the moral of an army. It fancies that money will fight when men will
no longer fight.' Chesterton, *The Everlasting Man* (London: Hodder
and Stoughton, undated), p. 168. See John Sullivan, *G. K. Chesterton:
A Bibliography* (London: University of London Press, 1958), p. 60.
106 *Scoop: A Novel about Journalists* (London: Chapman and Hall, 1964),
p. 80.
107 ibid., pp. 80–1.
108 *F.F.F.*, p. 175.
109 ibid., p. 219.
110 ibid., p. 175.
111 See Chesterton's speech at the Canadian Literary Fund luncheon for
Rudyard Kipling, 12 July 1933, in which he argues that two important elements for a literature are a national legend and a spectacular
landscape. B.B.C. Sound Archives.
112 *F.F.F.*, pp. 207–8.
113 For example, the only cartoon by Thomas Derrick which he refused to
publish in *G. K.'s Weekly* was one which showed Queen Victoria
floating upon a cloud, and giving her approval to an alliance between
England and Nazi Germany. See Maisie Ward, *Return to Chesterton*
(London: Sheed and Ward, 1952), pp. 54–5.
114 See, for example, Maisie Ward, *Chesterton*, p. 235, and 'An Alphabet',
the *New Age*, 29 October 1908, p. 11. See also *The Ball and the Cross*
(London: Darwen Finlayson, 1963), pp. 174–5.
115 *Autobiography*, pp. 259–60.
116 23 January 1936, p. 277. For the identification of the authorship of the
article, see John Sullivan, *Chesterton Continued: A Bibliographical
Supplement* (London: University of London Press, 1968), p. 55.
117 Cecil expressed this view in his 'Open Letter to Edward VII', the
New Age, 11 February 1909, pp. 317–8. In this article, he suggests an
alliance between the monarchy and the English people against what
he calls the plutocracy, and he pays special tribute to the theory of
Bolingbroke, 'the greatest speculative Englishman of the dark ages
which intervened between the Reformation and the French Revolution.' ibid., p. 318. Compare this with Chesterton's tribute to Bolingbroke in his *Short History of England* (London: Chatto and Windus,
1917), pp. 187–91.
118 Chesterton, *A Short History of England* (London: Chatto and Windus,
1917), p. 125. For a scathingly hostile review of Chesterton's *History*,
see A. F. Pollard, 'Mr Chesterton's Latter-day Pamphlet', in the
T.L.S., 22 November 1917, p. 564. For the identification of the
authorship of the article, see *T.L.S.*, 23 November 1967, p. 1113.
Pollard's comments on Chesterton's interpretation are worth quoting

at some length: 'To Mr Chesterton the supreme moment in English history occurred in 1381, when Richard II, after Wat Tyler's murder (by a Mayor of London) put himself for the moment at the head of a mob. The mob is Mr Chesterton's hero, and he outdoes Carlyle in his hero-worship. Consequently, he forgets to mention on this occasion that it slew an Archbishop of Canterbury. He also states that Parliament compelled Richard to revoke the charters he granted the villeins, though Richard revoked his charters in July and Parliament did not meet till November.' ibid., p. 564.

119   *A Short History of England*, pp. 125–6.

120   *F.F.F.*, p. 170.

121   'The Wrong Incendiary', *A Miscellany of Men* (London: Methuen, 1912), pp. 75–6.

122   Chesterton, *What's Wrong With the World* (London: Cassell, 1912), pp. 292–3.

123   ibid., p. 292.

124   See, for example, the text of the B.B.C. talk in which he reviews W. H. Chamberlin's *Russia's Iron Age*: 'I have read a score of very able defences of Bolshevism. All agree, especially the Bolshevists, that Bolshevism is what I call a tyranny. It does the good work a tyranny can do. Mr Chamberlin admires its efficiency in education, perhaps more than I should; many more people are taught to read and write. I always wonder whether many people, or any people, are taught to see and hear. You could not persuade Ukrainian peasants that there was no famine; but you could persuade newspaper readers in the North that there is not much unemployment. But most will agree that the tribute to education is a great tribute. On the other side, they must recognize the testimony of the same witness that the whole country is full of fear. You know by now I have no illusions about our own country, where everybody is in fear of the sack. But the sack is not the same as being shot or jailed at any minute without any trial; and, as to starvation, Mr Chamberlin, a very sober writer, does not hesitate to say definitely that Moscow forced on the famine to break the independence of the peasantry.' 'Attitudes to Poverty', the *Listener*, 6 March 1935, p. 423.

Maurice B. Reckitt, who was one of the directors of *G. K.'s Weekly*, and a founding member of the Distributist League, has commented on the effect of the Russian revolution on the Christian Socialist group, to which he also belonged: '. . . the catastrophic achievements of a militant Marxism in eastern Europe were suggesting that the word "revolutionary", which Church socialists had been accustomed to employ with a somewhat light-hearted vagueness, would require in future to be used more circumspectly.' *Maurice to Temple: A Century of the Social Movement in the Church of England*. Scott Holland Memorial Lectures, 1946 (London: Faber and Faber, 1946), p. 167.

125   *The Paradoxes of Mr Pond* (London: Darwen Finlayson, 1963), p. 107. The novel was published by Cassell in March 1937. And the stories were collected from *The Storyteller*. See John Sullivan, *G. K. Chesterton: A Bibliography*, p. 86. Subsequent references to the novel will be abbreviated as *P.M.P.*

126   The sympathy which Mr Pond expresses for Carl Schiller, the Jewish shop-keeper, might suggest that the story represents an attempt to do something like justice to the Jews at a time when their persecution in Germany was just beginning (*P.M.P.*, p. 171). This is indeed partly true. But the story is also a kind of apology to those who suffered from

the hysterical anti-German feeling, to which Chesterton himself contributed during the First World War. And the pity expressed for the Carl Schillers is exceeded by the contempt expressed for the mindless bigotry of the Mrs Hartog-Haggards.

127 The visit took place in 1927, and Chesterton was received with immense enthusiasm. See Maisie Ward, *Chesterton*, pp. 488–9. An indication of how pleased he was with the official recognition he received in Poland can be found in the essay in which he describes the trip and in which (uncharacteristically) he quotes a compliment from the welcoming speech: 'I will not say the chief friend of Poland, God is the chief friend of Poland.' 'On Poland', *Generally Speaking* (London: Methuen, 1930), pp. 42–3.

128 Chesterton was a candidate for the Lord Rectorship of Glasgow University in 1925 and very likely visited Professor Phillimore then. See Maisie Ward, *Chesterton*, pp. 468–9, and Mrs Cecil Chesterton, *The Chestertons* (London: Chapman and Hall, 1941), pp. 278–82.

129 *P.M.P.*, p. 12.

130 See, for example, the report of Chesterton's speech on Poland at Essex Hall in the Strand, 7 July 1927. The Polish Ambassador took the chair and Belloc moved the vote of thanks. Poland, Chesterton said, was a country known by the same name, 'by which our fathers knew her to exist in those days when she had disappeared from the map, yet continued to live as a nation'. Quoted in Cyril Clemens's *Chesterton as Seen by his Contemporaries*, with an introduction by E. C. Bentley (Webster Groves, Missouri: The International Mark Twain Society, 1939), p. 149.

131 See J. Conrad, 'Autocracy and War' (1905), *Notes on Life and Letters* (London: Gresham, 1925), pp. 83–114. See also 'The Crime of Partition' (1919), ibid., pp. 115–33.

132 Maisie Ward, *Chesterton*, p. 365. The article appeared in *The New Witness*.

133 *P.M.P.*, p. 12.

134 ibid., p. 13.

135 Bernard Shaw frequently complained about the tone of *The New Witness* during the war years, and he blamed Chesterton for his contribution to it: 'Not one chivalrous word escapes him when the Hun is his theme. We are to curse the Germans when they are up and kick them when they are down. . . . Mr Chesterton, by an extraordinary piece of luck, is really free to say what he likes about everything except music (which he does not want to say anything about); and this he would not be if the money behind the paper were political money or smart society money or commercial money. Therefore the diabolical element in Mr Chesterton's gospel of murderous hate on a basis of our heavenly nature as opposed to the hellish nature of the Prussian, is quite wanton: he is as free to be bravely magnanimous, chivalrous, Christian, fair and reasonable before Europe, and contrite before history and Heaven, as he is to be just the opposite. Otherwise he would chuck the *New Witness* as he chucked the *Daily News*. What makes his choice frightfully wicked to me is that it is not natural choice but artistic virtuosity.' 'How Free is the Press?', *The Nation*, 9 February 1918, pp. 599–600.

136 *P.M.P.*, p. 27.

137 ibid., p. 24.

138 ibid., pp. 24–5.

139 See, for example, his essays on Poland in *The End of the Armistice*

(London: Sheed and Ward, 1940), pp. 121–48. Also see Belloc's letter to Lady Phipps, 2 October 1933, in *Letters from Hilaire Belloc*, ed. Robert Speaight (London: Hollis and Carter, 1958), pp. 240–1.
140 *P.M.P.*, p. 23.
141 In his poem on Poland, the imagery is partly based on a contrast between the black double-headed eagle of Germany and the white eagle which is the emblem of Poland:

> Augurs that watched archaic birds
> Such plumèd prodigies might read,
> The eagles that were double-faced,
> The eagle that was black indeed;
> And when the battle-birds went down
> And in their track the vultures come,
> We know what pardon and what peace
> Will keep our little masters dumb.
>
> . . .
>
> But raised for ever for a sign
> Since God made anger glorious,
> Where eagles black and vultures grey
> Flocked back about the historic house,
> Where war is holier than peace,
> Where hate is holier than love,
> Shone terrible as the Holy Ghost
> An eagle whiter than a dove.

'Poland', *The Collected Poems of G. K. Chesterton* (London: Cecil Palmer, 1927), p. 74.
142 J. Conrad, op. cit., p. 113.
143 *P.M.P.*, p. 17.
144 ibid., p. 25.
145 Andrzej Towiański (1799–1878) taught that Poland represented in some mystical way 'the national incarnation of Christ' and was destined to become the 'Messiah' among the European nations. These ideas were taught by Mickiewicz to the Polish exiles in Paris in the 1840s. He also, like Towiański, taught that the martyred people of Poland, as part of the Mystical Body, were destined to rise 'on the third day': 'The first day had been the capture of Warsaw in 1794; the second day, the second capture of Warsaw in 1831. Mickiewicz did not live to see the third day, but many Poles looked forward to its realization in the 1863 uprising, which was the great political event for which Korzeniowski dreamed and wrote and planned.' See Eloise Knapp Hay, *The Political Novels of Joseph Conrad: A Critical Study* (Chicago and London: University of Chicago Press, 1963), pp. 36–7. She presents a précis of Cresław Milosz's article 'Apollo Nałecz Korzeniowski', which appeared in *Kultura* (Paris: February 1956).
146 See Desmond Gleeson's long account of the history of *G. K.'s Weekly* in *Return to Chesterton*. He points out that the editorial board of *G. K.'s Weekly* in its last phase included Gregory Macdonald, 'who had a knowledge of Poland and its problems unique in Fleet Street'. ibid., p. 222. Macdonald was afterwards the head of the Central European Service of the B.B.C. Also see 'On Poland', *Generally Speaking*, pp. 42–8.
147 *P.M.P.*, p. 25.
148 ibid., note on dust cover of Beaconsfield edition.
149 ibid., pp. 59–60.
150 ibid., p. 62.

151   ibid., p. 73.
152   ibid., p. 63.
153   ibid., p. 74.
154   ibid., p. 70.
155   ibid., p. 74.
156   ibid., p. 70.
157   *The Everlasting Man*, pp. 171–88.
158   *P.M.P.*, p. 74.
159   ibid., p. 83.
160   ibid.
161   ibid.
162   ibid., p. 82.
163   ibid., p. 102.
164   ibid., p. 96.
165   ibid., p. 94.
166   ibid.
167   ibid., p. 106.
168   ibid., p. 107.
169   ibid., p. 106.
170   ibid., pp. 113–4.
171   *The Resurrection of Rome* (London: Hodder and Stoughton, 1930), pp. 248–72.
172   *P.M.P.*, p. 119.
173   Chesterton knew and admired the Shavian play in which King Magnus appeared ('allowing for the very comparative truth in all such comparisons, I think *The Apple Cart* about the best play he ever wrote') and he praised Shaw's insight into the meaning of modern politics, and, particularly, his understanding that 'monarchy is now the mood of the hour everywhere'. 'Bernard Shaw and Breakages', *Sidelights on New London and Newer York, and other essays* (London: Sheed and Ward, 1932), p. 217.
174   See Maisie Ward, *Chesterton*, pp. 414–48; also see Mrs Cecil Chesterton, op. cit., pp. 276–8.
175   Thus Harold Robbins writes: '. . . the paper became almost at once an organ of the Right, and by that fact ceased to be the organ of Distributism, which rejects that idiotic division of mankind. I well remember the shock of going to the office of the paper in the Summer of 1938, and of seeing its windows plastered with advertisements of *The Right Book Club*.' 'The Great Deferment', *The Cross and the Plough*, vol. 15, no. 3, p. 7, 1948. Robbins called his book *The Last of the Realists: G. K. Chesterton and his Work*; it was published in four serial parts in *The Cross and the Plough*, which was the organ of the *Catholic Land Movement*. See vol. 15, nos. 1–4, 1948.
176   Belloc became editor of *G. K.'s Weekly* shortly after Chesterton's death from 1 October 1936 until 26 August 1937, when he was succeeded by Reginald Jebb, his son-in-law. As the *Weekly Review*, the paper continued from 17 March 1938 until 12 June 1947. From 18 February 1937 until 17 March 1938, the name of the paper was *G. K.'s Weekly and The Weekly Review*.
177   Ronald Knox, 'Introduction', *Father Brown: Selected Stories by G. K. Chesterton* (London: Oxford University Press, 1966), p. vii.

6. CONCLUSION

1 'Introduction', *Father Brown: Selected Stories by G. K. Chesterton* (London: Oxford University Press, 1966), p. xv.
2 See the dedication to W. R. Titterton in the first edition (London: Chatto and Windus, 1927), p. v.
3 'Bernard Shaw and Breakages', *Sidelights on New London and Newer York* (London: Sheed and Ward, 1932), p. 217.

Index

Abrams, M. H., *A Glossary of Literary Forms*, 7–8

Agrarianism:
  allegory on meaning of rural England, in 'Honest Quack', 162; restoration of rural England, in *The Poet and the Lunatics*, 150–1; restoration of rural England, theme of *The Long Bow*, 99; revolution, history of, in *The Long Bow*, 79; versus Progressive tradition, in *The Flying Inn*, 72

Allegory:
  as approach to characterization, 11–12,21; as clarification for fiction being a kind of propaganda, 9–10; as defined by Abrams, 7–8; as defined by G. K. Chesterton, 8–9; as related to 'parable', 8; astronomical allegory in *The Long Bow*, 100; double allegory in *The Man Who Was Thursday*, 40–1, 44–50; extended use, chided in *The Long Bow*, 100–1; in Chesterton's stories, 191; in *The Paradoxes of Mr Pond*, German romantic's death equated with Christian allegory, 181–2; to teach and persuade, ix

Anarchism:
  as a nihilistic hobby, 170–1; becomes respectable in Edwardian society via Kropotkin, 219 *n. 12*; in *The Ball and the Cross*, attitude anticipates that in *The Man Who Was Thursday*, 29; in *The Man Who Was Thursday*, 47–50; related to nihilism, through allegory of yellow hammer bird, in *The Poet and the Lunatics*, 144–6; treatment of anarchy in *The Man Who Was Thursday* anticipates themes in *The Poet and the Lunatics* and *The Paradoxes of Mr Pond*, 40

Anarchistic society, *see* Anarchism
Anarchy, *see* Anarchism

Anti-Semitism, 68; G. K. Chesterton outlines theory of Zionism, 211 *n. 18*; comment by Cecil Chesterton and Hilaire Belloc, 207–8 *n. 72*; discussed by Julius West, 75–6; Gould, Moses, character of, 53–4, 206–7 *n. 39*; in *Four Faultless Felons*, 158, 171; in *The Flying Inn*, 72; in *The Man Who Knew Too Much*, 83, 92; in *The Paradoxes of Mr Pond*, 178; Lewis, C. S., discusses effect Belloc's anti-Semitism had on G. K. Chesterton, 83; noted by Bernard Bergonzi, 3; tolerance for Jews shows up in later novels, 197

Apocalyptic sequences:
  as opposed to a dream, 32, 34; in *The Ball and the Cross*, 32, 35, 38; in *Four Faultless Felons*, 159; in *Manalive*, 64; in *The Man Who Knew Too Much*, 84, 96–7; in *The Man Who Was Thursday*, 44, 46–7; in *The Poet and the Lunatics*, 152

Art:
  dividing G. K. Chesterton's work into art and propaganda fails, 5–6; in *The Poet and the Lunatics*, realism in art, 141; painting and photography metaphors in *The Poet and the Lunatics*, 145; regarding use and value of art and poetry, 162; related to Christian notion of creation, 14–15; related to C. S. Lewis' *Abolition of Man* and acceptance of Nature, 162

Arthur [King of England], 24

Ashley, Olive (character in *The Return of Don Quixote*), 116; her play, "Blondel the Troubadour", controls novel's action, 118; provides element of allegory, 119; her search for lost illumination colours is novel's secondary plot, 118; provides images and symbols for allegory, 119

novels, 79; heroes of, in *The Man Who Knew Too Much*, 97; ideals of, compromised in Distributist marriages, 108; interpretation of Belloc's principles by A. J. Penty, 77–8; lack of social remedy unusual in *The Poet and the Lunatics*, 153–5; related to Catholicism only in *The Return of Don Quixote*, 84; Robbins, Harold, author of most complete account of, 209 *n. 1*; Robbins, Harold, view that demise of Chesterton brought demise of, 189–90; 'Song of Wheels', 78; *see also* 'Song'; subordination of political life to family virtues in, 103; *Tales of the Long Bow*, ends with a complete Distributist state, 99; *Tales of the Long Bow* and *The Return of Don Quixote* show complementary sides of Distributist politics, 113–14; tenet that Capitalism and Communism are the same, 171; tenet that Capitalism and revolutionary Socialism are the same, 191; turning point in Chesterton's fiction, 153–5

Distributist revolution, typical: damage to ideal of, by character of Enoch Oates, 108–11; defined by Durobin, in *Manalive*, 61; first complete definition, in *Tales of the Long Bow*, 99; not for export, 111; odd group of allegorical character types for, 105–7

Dives, King, 155

Dream sequences, *see* individual entries under Chesterton's works

Du Bos, Charles, 166

Durand (character in *The Ball and the Cross*): Chesterton's type character for the French middle class, 37; like Jules Durobin, in *Manalive*, 59

Eliot, George, 166

Eliot, T. S., 199 *n. 5*; comment on G. K. Chesterton as primarily a Catholic writer, 2–3

Expiation, as a theme: in *Four Faultless Felons*, 163–9; in *The Man Who Knew Too Much*, tied to revolution's moral meaning, 85, 88, 93; repentance always possible in life, 181; tied to apocalyptic vision of Horne Fisher, 96–7

Fabianism, *see* Socialism

Faerie Queene, The (Edmund Spenser), 151

Fascism, 26; Herne discovers that Syndicalism is equated with a Fascist state, 116; in medievalism, 126, 128; in *The Paradoxes of Mr Pond*, political danger lies to the Right, 184–5

Fisher, Horne (character in *The Man Who Knew Too Much*): an anti-Semite, 83; as expiatory victim of social revolution, 93; based on Maurice Baring, according to Maisie Ward, 80–2; man of action unable to act, 80, 87–8; version of the Chesterton detective, *only*, according to Knox, 85

Fool, the (Chestertonian): Chesterton on the Fool, as seen in Chaucer and Shakespeare, 218–19 *n. 3*; comparable roles of Innocent Smith and Father Michael, 64; in *The Paradoxes of Mr Pond*, Hankin equated with the Fool, a dancing flame, 186; version of, in title and hero *The Poet and The Lunatics*, 140

French Revolution, 37–8, 60–1

Garden settings, *see* individual entries under Chesterton's works

General Strike of 1926, 9, 116

Gilson, Etienne, 2, 199 *n. 4*

Goethe, Johann Wolfgang von, 26, 180

Grace: Chesterton's theology, as outlined in *The Everlasting Man*, reaches logical conclusion in *The Paradoxes of Mr Pond*, 184; death only escape, grace creates new life through repentance, 181; in *Four Faultless Felons*, allegory blends orders of grace and nature, 163; in harmony with Nature and symbolized in *The Return of Don Quixote*, 131–2; in *The Man Who Knew Too Much*, grace works through evil to achieve good, 95; makes acceptance of suffering possible, according to Maurice Baring, 166; theology of, in *The Ball and the Cross*, 38; theology of, in *Manalive*, 62–3

Greene, Graham, 4–5, 199 *n. 12*

Gunn, James, 'Conversation Piece' painter, 81, 210 *n. 8*